Science and Christianity in Pulpit and Pew

Science and

Christianity

in Pulpit and Pew

RONALD L. NUMBERS

OXFORD

UNIVERSITY PRESS

2007

OXFORD
UNIVERSITY PRESS

Oxford University Press, Inc., publishes works that further
Oxford University's objective of excellence
in research, scholarship, and education.

Oxford   New York
Auckland   Cape Town   Dar es Salaam   Hong Kong   Karachi
Kuala Lumpur   Madrid   Melbourne   Mexico City   Nairobi
New Delhi   Shanghai   Taipei   Toronto

With offices in
Argentina   Austria   Brazil   Chile   Czech Republic   France   Greece
Guatemala   Hungary   Italy   Japan   Poland   Portugal   Singapore
South Korea   Switzerland   Thailand   Turkey   Ukraine   Vietnam

Published by Oxford University Press, Inc.
198 Madison Avenue, New York, New York 10016

www.oup.com

Oxford is a registered trademark of Oxford University Press

Library of Congress Cataloging-in-Publication Data
Numbers, Ronald L.
Science and Christianity in pulpit and pew / Ronald L. Numbers.
   p. cm.
ISBN 978-0-19-532037-4; 978-0-19-532038-1 (pbk.)
1. Religion and science—History.   2. Church history—Modern
period, 1500–   I. Title.
BL245.N86 2007
261.5'5—dc22   2006030675

9 8 7 6 5 4 3 2 1

Printed in the United States of America
on acid-free paper

To the three teachers who influenced me the most:

Ray Hefferlin (Southern Missionary College)

Maurice M. Vance (Florida State University)

A. Hunter Dupree (University of California at Berkeley)

Contents

Science and Christianity
in Pulpit and Pew

Introduction

Once upon a time, not so long ago, the historical relationship between science and Christianity, indeed between science and religion generally, seemed simple. Prominent nineteenth-century scholars such as Andrew Dickson White (1832–1918) and John William Draper (1811–1882) assured their readers that science and religion existed in a state of perpetual opposition. White, in his earliest polemic on "The Battle-Fields of Science" (1869), depicted the religious struggle against science as "a war continued longer—with battles fiercer, with sieges more persistent, with strategy more vigorous than in any of the comparatively petty warfares of Alexander, or Cæsar, or Napoleon." In his *History of the Conflict between Religion and Science* (1874), Draper identified the primary aggressor as the Roman Catholic Church, whose "mortal animosity" toward science had left its hands "steeped in blood." Despite the efforts of less bellicose historians during the past quarter century or so to craft a more accurate and less prejudicial narrative, the notion of warfare between science and religion continues to thrive, particularly at both ends of the politicotheological spectrum. Secularists, ever fearful of religious encroachment, tend to see religion as the primary provoker of conflict; religious conservatives, dismayed by the allegedly corrosive effects of science on belief, identify hostile scientists as the assailants. It is truly, in the catchy phrase of the historian Jon H. Roberts, "The Idea That Wouldn't Die."[1]

In part, the warfare metaphor lives on because there have been so many actual conflicts over science and religion. Everyone knows about the trials of Galileo Galilei (1564–1642) in seventeenth-century Italy and of John Thomas Scopes (1900–1970) in twentieth-century Tennessee. And only a recluse would be unfamiliar with the current religiously charged controversies over intelligent design, stem cells, and global warming. Many of the bitterest conflicts over science have taken place *within* religious communities, where differences easily mutate into heresies. The historical problem is not so much the claim that science and religion have generated conflicts but the unwarranted generalizations made about the nature of the encounters. Proponents of the warfare thesis have typically failed to recognize that religious people and institutions have often cultivated the study of nature. During the Middle Ages, as David C. Lindberg and other medieval historians have convincingly shown, churchmen were the most ardent supporters of natural philosophy and natural history; during the early modern period, argues the Berkeley historian John L. Heilbron, "the Roman Catholic church gave more financial and social support to the study of astronomy for over six centuries, from the recovery of ancient learning during the late Middle Ages into the Enlightenment, than any other, and, probably, all other, institutions."[2]

Another popular "just-so" story about science and Christianity portrays the latter—or one of its subdivisions, such as Protestantism or Puritanism—as the fountainhead of modern science. This interpretation received a boost in 1925, when the theistic philosopher Alfred North Whitehead (1861–1947), in *Science and the Modern World*, argued that Christianity, by insisting that nature behaves in a regular and orderly fashion, allowed science to develop. Understandably, many Christians have found this self-congratulatory view more attractive than the narrative of conflict. Despite the manifest shortcomings of the claim that Christianity gave birth to science—most glaringly, it ignores or minimizes the contributions of ancient Greeks and medieval Muslims—it, too, refuses to succumb to the death it deserves. The sociologist Rodney Stark at Baylor University, a Southern Baptist institution, is only the latest in a long line of Christian apologists to insist that "*Christian theology was essential for the rise of science.*"[3]

Bereft of master narratives featuring conflict or a birthing role, historians of science and religion have turned increasingly to what has been called the complexity thesis, the notion that the record of the past is too chaotic to reveal a simple pattern. No one has advanced this view more successfully than John Hedley Brooke, who has identified a wide range of interactions between scientific and religious impulses. At times, religion has stimulated the investigation of nature; on other occasions it has inhibited it. To my knowledge, no reputable historian of science and religion now doubts the truth of this tangled view of the past. However, because this view tends to strip the subject of its polemical value, it has found comparatively little favor with present-day cultural warriors fighting one another in the trenches.[4]

Complicating matters further, even among historians who stress contingency, is the lack of consensus about the most important historical factors influencing the relationship between science and religion. Take, for instance, the debates over evolution, one of the most closely studied episodes in the history of the encounter, where various experts have highlighted the roles played not only by theology and geography but by birth order, class, race, and gender as well. In *The Post-Darwinian Controversies* (1979) a young James R. Moore underscored the importance of theology in determining individual responses to evolution in Great Britain and North America. He insisted that only "those whose theology was distinctly orthodox"—that is, Calvinist—could swallow Darwinism undiluted. (Contrast this with David L. Hull's equally hyperbolic claim "that almost all the early proponents of Darwinism were atheistic materialists—or their near relatives.")[5]

Subsequent studies by Jon H. Roberts, David N. Livingstone, and me have undermined Moore's sweeping claim about the uniqueness—or even the salience—of Calvinism, though none of us denies that distinctive theological convictions sometimes influenced how people viewed Darwin's theory. In a new introduction to his meticulously researched *Darwinism and the Divine in America* (1988), Roberts argues that "the great majority of American Protestant thinkers who remained committed to orthodox formulations of Christian doctrine actually rejected Darwinism; indeed, they denounced the theory of organic evolution in *any* guise that described speciation in terms of naturalistic agencies." The "crucial determinant," he maintains, "was their conviction that the theory of organic evolution could not be reconciled with their views of the origin, nature, and 'fall' of man, the nature and basis of moral judgment, and a number of other doctrines—all based on their interpretation of the Scriptures." My own research bears this out. I have also found that although mainstream Protestants often used interchangeable arguments in critiquing Darwinism, as one moves from the Protestant center to the periphery occupied by such groups as Pentecostals and Seventh-day Adventists, one finds unique theological teachings taking on greater significance.[6]

Given the theological heterogeneity of Protestantism, it is not surprising to find a range of responses to evolution. But even in the hierarchical Roman Catholic Church, where one might expect relative uniformity, we also find diversity. Catholics have agreed on little other than the belief that evolution, if it occurred, has been guided by God and has not included the origin of humans (especially the soul) by purely natural means. In an early essay on "varieties" of Catholic reactions to Darwinism, Harry W. Paul contrasted "the power Catholicism was able to exert against Darwinism in Spain" with its virtual impotence in Italy. Even more telling, however, are the revelations coming out of the recently opened Vatican archives of the Congregation for the Doctrine of the Faith, which hold the records of the old Congregations of the Holy Office and of the Index. In researching their book, *Negotiating Darwin: The Vatican Confronts Evolution, 1877–1902* (2006), Mariano Artigas, Thomas F. Glick, and Rafael A. Martinez discovered six instances in which the Vatican dealt with complaints about Catholic evolutionists, with two of the accused coming from Italy, two from England, and one each from France and the United States. These complaints resulted in no official condemnation of evolution, though some individual works were proscribed and placed on the *Index of Prohibited Books*. (In one case the pope vetoed a prohibition against evolution recommended by the cardinals.) The historians detected no common response, no "fixed agenda." The strongest opposition to Darwinism came not from the Vatican itself but from *La Civiltà Cattolica*, an unofficial but influential Catholic journal.[7]

After studying the reception of evolution in the predominantly Catholic cultures of Latin America, where the church hierarchy widely regarded Darwin as the "great enemy," Glick identified "centralization of power" rather than cultural isolation as the "crucial variable" in determining how various countries responded to evolution. In contrast to the largely Protestant United States, where church and state remained constitutionally separate and Protestant sects competed openly, the more centrally controlled Latin American countries presented an environment relatively inhospitable to new ideas. Nevertheless, Pietro Corsi has warned historians discussing Catholicism not to let the hierarchy's opposition to evolution lead to a view of Roman Catholic theology as "a monolithic structure of doctrines and beliefs, free from conflicts and tensions." In the Catholic countries of Italy and France, he argues, "the official voice of the Church—or its silence—did not prevent individual Catholics or groups of Catholic intellectuals from holding strong views that differed from those of the keepers of the dogma."[8]

In recent years the geographer and historian of science David Livingstone has also undermined assumptions of theological uniformity by pointing to significant local variations. In contrast to Moore, who insisted on the positive influence of Calvinism in the Darwinian debates, Livingstone has shown that, even among Calvinists, responses to evolution varied markedly from one locale to another. Irish Calvinists in Belfast, for instance, strongly resisted Darwinism, in large part, it seems, because of John Tyndall's (1820–1893) infamous 1874 presidential address to the British Association for the Advancement of

Science in that city, in which he arrogantly announced that all "religious theories, schemes and systems which embrace notions of cosmogony ... must ... submit to the control of science, and relinquish all thought of controlling it." In the Calvinist stronghold of Princeton, New Jersey, religious leaders responded much less defensively. James McCosh (1811–1894), longtime president of the College of New Jersey (as Princeton University was then called), embraced theistic evolution, as did Benjamin B. Warfield (1851–1921), a prominent professor at Princeton Theological Seminary and, surprisingly, a proponent of biblical inerrancy. Finding that Calvinists elsewhere had also been influenced by local circumstances, Livingstone began trumpeting the virtues of "putting science in its place," the title of one of his books. "I don't want to claim that everything about science is reducible to nothing but social space or physical location," he explained. "But I do want to say that issues like gender, or political empire, or whatever, always work themselves out through spatiality—in particular spaces, at particular times, in particular local cultures." Historians, he wisely urged, should quit speaking "of the encounter between science and religion in a generalized, decontextualized, delocalized way."[9]

For years—at least since the publication of Glick's *The Comparative Reception of Darwinism* (1974), which featured parallel essays on England, Germany, France, Russia, the Netherlands, Spain, the United States, Mexico, and the Islamic world—historians of evolution have been exploring the role of place at the national level. We now possess entire books on Darwinism in England, France, Germany, Italy, Spain, Russia, China, the United States, Mexico, Cuba, Chile, and Argentina. Edited collections explore the fate of evolution in a number of European countries, in several English-speaking nations, and in the Iberian world. Unfortunately, this plethora of national studies has obscured more localized differences and yielded fewer convincing generalizations than one might have wished. Thus David L. Hull's decades-old observation that no one had yet demonstrated a correlation "between the reception of Darwin's theory around the world and the larger characteristics of these societies," including their religious cultures, still largely holds.[10]

What these national studies have revealed is enormous complexity. Not only did Darwinism mean different things in different countries, but its meaning varied even within national settings. Suzanne Zeller, for example, has shown that the struggle of Canadians to survive in a harsh physical environment predisposed some to see a measure of plausibility in a Darwinian view of nature, but the divide between the largely English-speaking Protestants and the French-speaking Catholics makes it hazardous to speak of a *Canadian* response to evolution. Similarly, John Stenhouse has drawn attention to the way some New Zealanders drew on Darwinism to justify, in terms of "survival of the fittest," their harsh treatment of the native Maori. But rivalries among white Anglicans, Methodists, and Presbyterians undermine generalizations about New Zealanders as a whole.[11]

Some historians, particularly those under the sway of Karl Marx, have asserted the centrality of socioeconomic differences in the debates over evolution. Adrian Desmond, perhaps the most influential of this group, has noted that the godless "working classes" and the "lowlife in the medical schools," eager to create a new social and economic order, found Lamarckian evolution especially attractive.[12] James Secord, however, looking primarily at responses to one widely read evolutionary tract, *Vestiges of the Natural History of Creation* (1844), has argued that the ensuing debates "contributed to fracture lines *within* the middle class; they were intra- rather than interclass, with a crucially important religious dimension.... For working people themselves... the issues were very basic, involving food, housing, and fundamental political rights." Evolution, indeed science generally, rarely penetrated their consciousness.[13]

The historian of science Frank J. Sulloway has also downplayed class-based explanations. In a statistical analysis of the dynamics of intellectual revolutions, including the one associated with Darwin, he makes a strong case for paying more attention to psychosocial than to socioeconomic factors. Attitudes toward revolutionary theories such as Darwinism, he argues, reflected the participants' personalities, formed in large part by the order in which they were born into their families and by the ensuing competitive strategies they adopted in dealing with their siblings. For more than two hundred persons who debated Darwinism between 1859 and 1875, Sulloway found that later-borns were 4.6 times more likely to support evolution than firstborns. Social class had no bearing at all, though age and social attitudes did. Such findings led him to conclude that "the focus of the battle over the theory of evolution was *within* the family, not *between* families."[14]

Historians of evolution have rarely investigated the importance of race and gender, two analytical categories of great importance to social historians. And those who have looked at the role of race have minimized its predictive value. Even in the American South race rarely entered into the published discussions of Darwinism, and, as Eric D. Anderson has shown, African American intellectuals for decades regarded theories of plural human origins more threatening than Darwin's monogenetic theory. In two revealing studies of the 1920s Jeffrey P. Moran found African American elites much more willing than the conservative black clergy to embrace evolution.[15]

Because of Darwin's use of sexual selection and the implications that he drew about female inferiority, gender became integral to the evaluation of Darwinism—and problematic for some feminists. However, religious concerns tended to trump gendered ones. As Moran has shown, antievolutionists often spoke in the name of mothers concerned about the irreligious effects of evolution on their children. Among the mothers who spoke for themselves were Ellen G. White (1827–1915), the founding prophetess of Seventh-day Adventism and the godmother of creation science, who traced evolution back to its "satanic origin," and Aimee Semple McPherson (1890–1944), the flamboyant founder of the International Church of the Foursquare Gospel, who damned evolution in public debate in the early 1930s.[16]

The chapters that follow contribute to the ongoing complexification of the science-and-religion narrative, while at the same time addressing major themes and developments in the history of Christianity and science. In chapter 1, "Science and Christianity among the People: A Vulgar History," I focus on a class of people typically overlooked by historians of science and religion: the common folk or, as I refer to them in the title of this book, the ordinary people in the pews. In this sense the chapter contributes to the study of class differences, though the nonelites rarely expressed consciousness of their social standing.

Chapter 2, "Science without God: Natural Laws and Christian Beliefs," traces the history of what has come to be known as "methodological naturalism," the bane of intelligent design advocates, who see it as an agent of atheism. However, as I show, both Christians and skeptics, for different reasons, advocated this approach to studying nature. In fact, it was an evangelical theologian who coined the term—and endorsed the methods associated with it.

Although, for empirical reasons, I reject sweeping narratives of science and religion that place unwarranted emphasis on harmony or conflict, I readily acknowledge the existence of both types of experience. Chapter 3, "Reading the Book of Nature through American Lenses," vividly illustrates how the popular metaphor of God's two books, nature and the Bible, assisted many Christians in reconciling the findings of science with biblical accounts of the past. Chapter 4, in contrast, looks at possible conflict created by the idea of evolution. Although evolution provoked far fewer psychological crises than is sometimes assumed, "Experiencing Evolution: Psychological Responses to the Claims of Science and Religion" reveals that some Christians experienced real mental anguish—that is, conflict—when confronted with the claims of science.

Most histories of science and religion have portrayed science as the primary agent of change, constantly prodding the religious to modify their views of divine providence and their reading of Scripture. Indeed, in chapter 5, "Charles Hodge and the Beauties and Deformities of Science," I show how this leading Presbyterian theologian reacted to one scientific challenge after another, adopting some, rejecting others. As a result of geological and astronomical theories and discoveries, he came to see the "days" of Genesis 1 as cosmic ages, but he drew the line when it came to accepting anthropological claims of multiple human creations and biological evidence of evolution. However, theological and biblical scholarship was often changing independently of science. Chapter 6, " 'The Most Important Biblical Discovery of Our Time': William Henry Green and the Demise of Ussher's Chronology," shows how study of the Bible, not science, prompted an influential professor at Princeton Theological Seminary to expand the Old Testament genealogies, thus giving evangelical Christians more time in which to accommodate later anthropological findings.

In chapter 7, "Science, Secularization, and Privatization: A Concluding Note," I attempt to disentangle the threads of secularization and privatization. Some scholars have taken the disappearance of God-talk from scientific publications as evidence of the secularizing effects of science. But because so many scientists who adopted the increasingly neutral style of scientific writing remained devoutly religious, I see the fading of religious language as indicating a relocation of faith statements from the public (scientific) sphere to the private (religious) one, not as evidence of sweeping secularization. Science has markedly changed the world we live in, but it has not secularized it.

I

Science and Christianity among the People

A Vulgar History

The founders of modern science often treated the common people with contempt. The great German astronomer Johannes Kepler (1571–1630), in dedicating his *Mysterium Cosmographicum* (1596) to his noble patron, insisted that he wrote "for philosophers, not for pettifoggers, for kings, not shepherds." He dismissed "the majority of men" as too stupid and ignorant to appreciate his work. The English natural philosopher Isaac Newton (1642–1727) reportedly told an acquaintance that "he designedly made his *Principia* abstruse" to "avoid being baited by smatterers in Mathematicks." A spokesman for the newly founded Royal Society in England celebrated the fellows' lack of "ambition to be cry'd up by the common Herd."[1] Given the lack of interest that most people showed in the arcane worlds of natural philosophy and natural history, it may have been prudent of Kepler, Newton, and the founders of the Royal Society not to seek public approval. However, there is no excuse for historians of science and religion to adopt a similarly condescending attitude toward the common people.[2] Thanks to recent research on the history of popular science and popular Christianity, we are now in a good position to sketch out a new, populist narrative, one that features the views and attitudes of the common folk, commonly called the vulgar.

The Sacred and the Natural in Early Modern Times

In his classic study of *The Origins of Modern Science*, Herbert Butterfield famously claimed that "since the rise of Christianity . . . no landmark in history" has rivaled the scientific revolution in importance.[3] But for whom was the alleged revolution so important? Most Europeans could not read, and of those who could, only the most learned were fluent in Latin, the language of choice for natural philosophy. Even readers fluent in Latin could not always follow the reasoning of some of the leading philosophers of nature. When Francis Bacon (1561–1626) sent King James I of England a copy of his *Novum Organum* (1620), now regarded as one of the founding documents of modern science, the uncomprehending king likened it to "the peace of God, that passeth all understanding." Another acquaintance of Bacon's caustically noted "that a fool could not have written such a work, and a wise man would not." An editor of an early scientific journal complained that "every hard word," to say nothing of mathematical symbols, served as a barrier to reaching a broad reading public.[4]

What, then, did the "vulgar"—the farmers and merchants, the homemakers and artisans—think about the revolutionary scientific changes taking place around them? Unfortunately for us, they left little evidence of their thoughts, and much of what we have is filtered through the writings of those who observed them. The scant information we have suggests that the new astronomy, the traditional centerpiece of the scientific revolution, attracted little notice and even less assent. Despite all of the subsequent attention heaped on Nicholas Copernicus (1473–1543) for dislodging the earth from the center of the solar system and setting it in motion around the sun, he won few converts in the period between the publication of his *De Revolutionibus* (1543) and the end of the sixteenth century. A leading Copernican scholar has found only *ten* converts, though he may have missed one or two.[5] Even the intellectual elite of Europe virtually ignored the debate between geocentrists and heliocentrists before about 1615, the date Galileo Galilei (1564–1642) used to mark "the beginning of the uproar against Copernicus." The first popular exposition of Copernicanism did not appear until 1629. For Bible believers, the notion of the earth whirling around a fixed sun seemed to contradict passages in the Psalms that had the sun moving "out of his chamber" (19:4–5) and the earth abiding in its established place (119:90). Most astronomers and theologians seemed to have reached agreement by the beginning of the eighteenth century, but large numbers of laypersons remained unpersuaded that they were whipping around the sun at a ridiculously high speed. "Although we live in a very enlightened century, wherein all arts and sciences have been elevated nearly to their summit," wrote a Dutch Copernican in 1772, "one still finds many, even wise and prudent people, who cannot believe the motion of the earth.... They feel that it is contrary to Scripture."[6]

Even the notorious 1633 trial and condemnation of Galileo for teaching Copernicanism initially failed to arouse much popular interest. Although the Roman Inquisition took the unusual step of publicizing its condemnation of Galileo, and the papal nuncio to Cologne printed posters to notify the public, there was no popular outcry. After visiting Galileo in Italy in the late 1630s, the English poet John Milton (1608–1674) drew the attention of polite society to Galileo's so-called imprisonment (actually house arrest in his Tuscan villa) in the *Areopagitica* (1644). This, says Maurice A. Finocchiaro, "immortalized Galileo's image as a symbol of the struggle between individual freedom and institutional authority." But it was not until the middle of the nineteenth century that Galileo's trial became a cause célèbre in Western Europe and North America.[7]

Nevertheless, even away from the centers of urban culture, on remote farms and plantations, the new cosmology slowly transformed the ways many ordinary people viewed the world around them. They may have continued to talk about the sun's rising and setting, but they rarely resisted the growing conviction that, scientifically, if not experientially, the sun stood at the center of the solar system. "Astronomy, like the Christian religion," noted the Philadelphia astronomer David Rittenhouse (1732–1796) in 1775, "has a much greater influence on our knowledge in general, and perhaps on our manners too, than is commonly imagined. Though but few men are its particular votaries, yet the light it affords is universally diffused amongst us; and it is difficult for us to divest ourselves of its influence so far, as to frame any competent idea of which would be our situation without it."[8]

Although the vast majority of common people, lacking leisure and literacy, ignored the cosmological revolution—and remained indifferent to their alleged loss of status in the cosmos—we do know from Carlo Ginsburg's *The Cheese and the Worms* that at least one Italian villager read widely and thought deeply about the nature of the cosmos. The trial records of a late sixteenth-century miller known as Menocchio reveal that his shameless "preaching and dogmatizing" aroused the ire of the Inquisition and led to his arrest. Under oath, Menocchio shared his homespun cosmogony:

> I have said that, in my opinion, all was chaos, that is, earth, air, water, and fire were mixed together; and out of that bulk a mass formed—just as cheese is made out of milk—and worms appeared

in it, and these were the angels. The most holy majesty decreed that these should be God and the angels, and among that number of angels, there was also God, *he too having been created out of that mass at the same time.*

Not surprisingly, the Inquisition, unimpressed by Menocchio's creativity, found him guilty of heresy.[9]

Spinning cosmogonies may have excited few peasants and artisans, but considerable evidence shows widespread concern with astronomical phenomena seen by the naked eye: eclipses, meteors, and comets. No less than their socially superior neighbors, the common folk agonized over the meaning of such portents. Might the appearance of a heavenly messenger, they wondered, herald the onset of plague, famine, earthquake, or even the end of the world? Priests and pastors encouraged such questioning, hoping thereby to smite the hearts of their sinful parishioners. "For the eclipses, comets, and evil appearances of the outer planets bode ill," warned one Lutheran minister; "we should not ignore these signs as heathens might, but rather with that much more ardour call to God and pray that He may reduce the meaning of nature's omens, forgo punishment, or at least show some mercy."[10]

In contrast to such clergy, who fostered the view of comets as supernatural signs of God's wrath, astronomers increasingly stressed their natural periodicity. As almanacs, tracts, and news sheets flooded the market, they carried the scientific discussion of the meaning of astronomical anomalies to the masses. For those in the marketplace too busy (or too uneducated) to read for themselves, there would sometimes be public readings. In seventeenth-century England a team of pamphleteers promised that their chapbooks on comets came devoid of "any Cramp words or Quaint Language, but [appeared] in a homely and plain Stile." Ballads about current and foreboding events, writes Sara Schechner, "were sung on the commons and in the alehouses where they papered the walls." According to one contemporary account, the balladeer's "frequent'st Workes goe out in single sheets, and are chanted from market to market, to a vile tune, and a worse throat; whilst the poore Country wench melts like her butter to heare them. And these are the Stories of some men of Tyburne, or a strange Monster out of Germany: or . . . Gods Judgements." In contrast to Copernicanism, which left popular opinion unruffled, assurances of the periodicity of comets, suggests Schechner, may well have "depreciated their value as portents" and calmed worried minds.[11]

Popular interest in comets was not far removed from enthusiasm for astrology, which helped the bewildered cope with the vicissitudes of life by relieving them of personal responsibility—or scared them witless by predicting

Citizens of Prague observing the great comet of 1577. This engraving by Jiri
Daschlitzky appeared in Peter Codicillus, *Von einem Schrecklichen und Wunderbarlichen
Cometen* (Prague, 1577). Courtesy of Albert Van Helden and the Galileo Project (http://
galileo.rice.edu).

dire events. Despite frequent condemnations by religious leaders, the practice
of casting horoscopes thrived, engaging even Kepler and Galileo. "This wicked
art is everywhere practiced and run after by most men and women, but especially of some who would needs be taken to be professors of the Gospel of
the Lord Christ," fretted one Anglican critic in the mid-seventeenth century.
Christian astrologers, for the most part, remained impervious to such repri-
mands. As Keith Thomas has noted, "All claimed that their art was compati-
ble with their religion, and that the heavenly bodies were merely instruments
of God's will." Even pious physicians and their patients frequently found it
helpful to account for bodily humors in terms of celestial influences.[12]

Alchemy, especially its medicinal applications, also thrived in the shadow
of ecclesiastical suspicion. Because alchemists, in their effort to transmute
metals, tampered with the divine creation, some religious authorities accused
them of being "nothing but irreligious impostors who assume the power of

God and wage war on nature." Nonetheless, "respect for alchemical medicine was diffused through all ranks of society," claims Charles Webster. "Its devotees extended from the monarchs of England and Scotland, through court circles, the aristocracy, gentry, scholars, churchmen and religious nonconformists, to lawyers . . . surgeons, apothecaries, and distillers." Tracts addressed to "house fathers" and "house mothers" carried the religiochemical gospel into the homes of all classes. The high priest of alchemical medicine was a wildly eccentric sixteenth-century Swiss physician-prophet named Theophrastus von Hohenheim (1493–1541), better known as Paracelsus, whose vernacular writings attracted a large following. Poor practitioners and their patients seemed particularly fond of metallic and mineral remedies. As Neil Kamil has emphasized, the language of chemical medicine, the talk of distillation and fermentation, "was very familiar to rustic artisans, farmers, herdsmen, and midwives, mostly from practical experience, or just intuitive understanding of the process of transformation from the same basic set of sources."[13]

As the popularity of Paracelsian medicine suggests, religion and healing, the sacred and the natural, remained tightly intertwined in early modern Europe. During times of epidemics physicians might prescribe natural remedies and order quarantines, while the clergy encouraged the sick to gather together for fasting and prayer. In the words of one English cleric, "In the time of Pestilence, Penitencie and Confession are to be preferred before all other medicaments." When Catholic priests in Italy ordered public processions to seek divine relief from the plague, they occasionally clashed with public health authorities. When the plague struck the small Italian town of Monte Lupo in 1631, for example, the local priest defied the quarantine imposed by the public health magistracy and led his parishioners in a risky procession through the streets. Galileo's daughter, a nun, reported that on occasion the commissioners of health paid for intercessory prayers as well, as they did at her monastery in 1633: "For a period of 40 days we must, two nuns at a time, pray continuously day and night beseeching His Divine Majesty for freedom from this scourge."[14]

Whether out of morbid curiosity or a desire to acquire useful knowledge, the public did take advantage of opportunities to learn about human anatomy. In recycling some of Andreas Vesalius's famous drawings of the human body, a popular science writer in Germany invited readers to "come along and look at the Lord's work, for the Lord is wonderful and his work unfathomable." As he explained in one tract on healing, he intended his work for the "common man": "As I don't want to carry water to the Rhein, I do not write this little book for the educated people, for they already know this art. Nor do I write for those ignorant blockheads whose brains you could make into pig's troughs.

I write only for the simple, respectable, and devout little people who have until now, through God, asked for my advice and help."[15]

Even human dissections, sometimes performed in churches to accommodate the ticket-buying public, directed attention to God's handiwork and, when done on the bodies of hanged criminals, demonstrated the wages of sin. Persons who crowded into the anatomy theater in Amsterdam could scarcely avoid the dire message that appeared prominently on the wall:

> Evildoers who harm while still alive,
> Prove of use after their demise.
> Medicine seeks advantage, even from death.
> The carcass teaches without a breath.

At the University of Leiden the medical faculty invited the public to visit its anatomy theater, which, explains Lissa Roberts, functioned "as a museum of divinely sanctioned natural history and morality." Although people from all walks of life visited the exhibits, one medical student cheerfully noted that they appealed especially to country girls.[16]

The microscope, though invented about 1610, attracted little popular attention before the 1660s, when interest in examining objects invisible to the naked eye boomed among Europeans and Americans wealthy enough to purchase an instrument or fortunate enough to know someone who owned one. By the end of the century the English microscopist Robert Hooke was complaining that this valuable scientific instrument was being used mainly for "diversion and pastime." Among the religious the complexity of the observed objects, from tiny insects to human sperm, gave striking evidence of God's designing power. Before long, allusions to microscopic wonders had become a staple in the literature of natural theology.[17]

The early modern years in Europe also gave rise to what Katharine Park and Lorraine J. Daston have called a "culture of monsters and prodigies," embraced by "erudite humanist scholars...literate urban merchants and artisans...and by peasants, laborers, and others without direct access to the written word." From their examination of woodcuts, ballads, broadsides, and "prodigy books," Park and Daston have demonstrated a widespread fascination with the meaning of such marvels as grossly deformed humans, hermaphrodites, and conjoined twins, which raised a host of pressing theological questions. Did human monsters possess souls? Should *both* heads of Siamese twins be baptized? Were these marvels signs of divine wrath or "wonders of nature"? By the eighteenth century leading naturalists and theologians had largely lost interest in such questions, but among the unlettered they lingered for generations to come.[18]

The dissemination of scientific information exploded in the seventeenth century. Already in 1600 William Gilbert (1544–1603), author of a seminal work on magnetism, was complaining about the "ocean of books" inundating London, causing "the common herd and fellows without a spark of talent [to be] made intoxicated, crazy, puffed-up." The passage of time did nothing to stem the flood. But despite the growing interest in natural knowledge, the common people largely ignored the mechanical universe being constructed by René Descartes (1596–1650) and Isaac Newton. In fact, the gap between natural philosophers and the public may have been widening. "It is, because Philosophy has been spun out, to so fine a thread, that it could be known but only to those, who would throw away all their whole Lives upon it," explained an early historian of the Royal Society. "It was made too subtle, for the common, and gross conceptions of men of business."[19] Even Newton's magisterial *Philosophiae naturalis principia mathematica* (1687), which unified the physical laws of the heavens and earth, failed to attract more than an estimated hundred readers. One of Newton's colleagues claimed not to have "met one Man that puts an extraordinary value upon his Book."[20]

The Vulgar Enlightenment

The tide carrying Newton's ideas to the masses began to rise even during his lifetime, as men of science avidly sought public support for their ideas and activities. One of the earliest efforts to publicize Newton's achievement was a series of sermons funded by the pious chemist Robert Boyle (1627–1691) to demonstrate the truth of Christianity "against notorious Infidels, *viz.* Atheists, Theists, Pagans, Jews, and Mahometans." Begun in 1691, these lectures aimed at demonstrating "that the same God who created all things by the Word of his Power, and upholds and preserves them by his continual Concourse, does also by his All-wise Providence perpetually govern and direct the issues and events of things." As Larry Stewart has surmised, many parishioners no doubt "dozed in the middle of yet another denunciation of deism," but at least they had an opportunity to learn about the new science in nontechnical language they could understand. Sometimes, however, the Boyle lectures produced an unintended effect. When a fifteen-year-old printer's apprentice in the town of Boston, Benjamin Franklin (1706–1790), read one of these sermons, he found that "quite contrary to what was intended by them ... the Arguments of the Deists, which were quoted to be refuted, appeared ... much stronger than the Refutations." He promptly became a "thorough Deist."[21]

Newton's renown in France awaited the return in 1729 of the Anglophile philosophe Voltaire (1694–1778) from England, where he had been exiled a few years earlier and where he had become enamored of Newtonianism. His popularizations in the 1730s brought Newton's philosophy "within everybody's reach" and turned the now-deceased Englishman into an international celebrity. "Voltaire finally appeared," exclaimed one hyperbolic reviewer, "and at once Newton is understood or is in the process of being understood; all Paris resounds with Newton, all Paris stammers Newton, all Paris studies and learns Newton." By the second half of the eighteenth century, even children were learning about the immortal Newton and his divinely ordered universe. In one book for juvenile readers, *The Newtonian System of Philosophy, Adapted to the Capacities of Young Gentlemen and Ladies* (1761), the hero, Tom Telescope, helped children see "the Wonders of God in the Works of the Creation."[22]

During the eighteenth century, claims Stewart, "popular lectures and cheap pamphlets smashed the boundaries of public education." This occurred in rural as well as in urban areas. In France, for example, colporteurs hawked the inexpensive *Bibliothèque bleue* to country folk, and coffeehouses catered to the denizens of the rapidly expanding cities. On the continent as well as in the colonies newspapers and broadsides carried news of celestial novelties and terrestrial rumblings, of epidemics and fossils. They paid little attention, however, to the breakthroughs in celestial mechanics or to other scientific landmarks of the century. "Notwithstanding the great advances in learning and knowledge which have been made within the last two centuries," mourned the Anglican author of *The Inanity and Mischief of Vulgar Superstitions* (1795), "lamentable experience but too clearly proves how extremely deep these notions are still engraven upon the minds of thousands."[23]

While natural philosophers and learned parsons debated the possible physical causes of the horrendous earthquakes that struck repeatedly during the eighteenth century, the common people followed their hearts—and consciences. A notable quake in New England in 1727 prompted some women to lay "aside their Hoop Petticoats" in an act of repentance. In the wake of the earthquake New England ministers reported bumper crops of conversions and rebaptisms.[24] Similarly, Benjamin Franklin's instructions for erecting iron rods to protect buildings from lightning, announced in *Poor Richard's Almanack* for 1753, fostered discussions about understanding God's will. Because churches, with their high steeples, typically proved most vulnerable to lightning strikes, some clergy eagerly welcomed this innovative protection against the violence of nature. However, one French abbé, reflecting what Franklin described as "the superstitious prejudices of the populace," denounced the devices for presuming to guard "against the *Thunders of Heaven!*" Some of Franklin's friends in Philadelphia decried the "Superstition" that caused "the Ignorant...[to] imagine that it is the immediate Voice of the Almighty and the Streaming Lightening [*sic*] are Bolts launched from his Right Hand and commissioned to execute his Vengeance."[25]

Although eighteenth-century natural philosophers and their allies generally sought to still the fears of the public, on one subject they aroused widespread anxiety: masturbation. Before the early eighteenth century neither men of science nor men of the cloth had paid much attention to this common, if private, practice. That changed dramatically "in or around 1712" with the appearance of an anonymous tract titled *Onania; or, The Heinous Sin of Self Pollution, and all its Frightful Consequences, in both* SEXES *Considered, with Spiritual and Physical Advice to Those Who Have Already Injured Themselves by This Abominable Practice.* The enterprising author, probably an English surgeon who peddled "Prolific Powder" and "Strengthening Tincture" on the side, tied "willful self-abuse" to the crime of the biblical Onan, who had spilled his seed on the ground instead of inseminating his dead brother's widow. *Onania*, described by Thomas W. Laqueur as "one of the first books to be extensively advertised in the nascent country press," enjoyed immense popularity. The rise of masturbation "to prominence," writes Laqueur, "constitutes one of the most spectacular episodes of intellectual upward mobility in literary annals: in just over fifty years, it moved from Grub Street to the *Encyclopédie*, the greatest compendium of learning produced by the high Enlightenment." This newfound respectability derived less from *Onania* than from a book by the famous Swiss Calvinist physician S. A. D. Tissot (1728–1797), *L'Onanisme; ou, Dissertation physique sur les maladies produites par la masturbation* (Onanism; or, A Treatise upon the Disorders Produced by Masturbation, 1760), which became "an instant literary sensation throughout Europe." Tissot, a sworn enemy of "superstition," also authored a popular health manual, addressed primarily to country teachers and ministers but also to "the yeomen, several of whom, full of sense, judgment, and good will, shall read with pleasure this book and eagerly spread its maxims."[26]

In the English-speaking world one of the most successful eighteenth-century popularizers of science and medicine was the founder of Methodism, John Wesley (1703–1791), who wrote on subjects ranging from masturbation to electricity and natural history. Before departing for America in 1735, he spent several months studying medicine in hopes of being "of some service to those who had no regular physician among them." After a disappointing two years in Georgia, he returned to England, where he continued to take a special interest in the problems of the ill. Assisted by an apothecary and a surgeon, he opened his own dispensary in 1746. The next year he published a hugely successful medical guide, *Primitive Physick*, designed to provide the layperson with "a plain and easy way of curing most diseases." It recommended, as an adjunct to pills and potions, "that old-fashioned medicine—*prayer*." Such recommendations, as well as Wesley's well-known belief in witchcraft and satanic possession, prompted some Anglican clerics to charge him with fostering "superstition." As one of them complained in 1795, "The belief of these extravagancies was indeed gradually yielding to the powerful progress of science, but of late it has again been nourished and revivified, in no inconsiderable degree, by the many extraordinary relations, which the late venerable MR. WESLEY inserted in his *Arminian Magazine*."[27]

Many eighteenth-century clerics, like Wesley, combined physical healing and preaching in what the Puritan divine Cotton Mather (1663–1728) quaintly called the "Angelical Conjunction." In midcentury the Swedish physician-naturalist Carolus Linnaeus (1707–1778) met a country priest who had made "a considerable reputation for himself as a doctor amongst his parishioners." The encounter apparently inspired Linnaeus to propose giving every theology student an eight-day crash course in the fundamentals of medicine:

> The poor peasant shuns the pharmacy, where life is often sold at a high price, he dreads physicians and surgeons which he does not know how to choose. He puts his greatest trust in his own priest and likes to ask his advice in an emergency. It would be of very great benefit to the state if most rural clergymen would understand how to cure the most common diseases, which destroy so many thousands of country folk every year.

Although Linnaeus's proposal produced no immediate action, the Swedish Diet in 1810, over the protests of some clergy, voted to provide fifty scholarships for students at the Universities of Uppsala and Lund who wished to become priest-physicians. In both Europe and North America, clergy often led efforts to immunize the public against smallpox. Indeed, the Puritan theologian Jonathan Edwards (1703–1758) died from the disease after subjecting his entire family to inoculation.[28]

Popular Science and Religion

The first half of the nineteenth century witnessed major developments in one scientific discipline after another: from geology and chemistry to physics and pathology. These achievements coincided with a continuing revolution in publishing that, by the 1830s, was bringing scientific news to a huge reader-ship. As the Unitarian clergyman William Ellery Channing (1780–1842) ob-served, "Science has now left her retreats . . . her selected company of votaries, and with familiar tone begun the work of instructing the race. . . . Through the press, discoveries and theories, once the monopoly of philosophers, have be-come the property of the multitudes. . . . Science, once the greatest of distinc-tions, is becoming popular." Indeed, it was. The *Penny Magazine*, published by the British Society for the Diffusion of Useful Knowledge, was by this time reaching a million readers, by far the highest circulation of any periodical. The literary eruption continued into the second half of the century, which saw the appearance of science journalists, who translated the writings of scien-tists into popular language. "Never before," exclaimed one such popularizer, "was there such a profusion of books describing the various forms of life inhabiting the different countries of the globe, or the rivers, lakes and seas that diversify its scenery."[29]

By midcentury some members of the clergy were beginning to worry that the press threatened to drown out their messages from the pulpit. "Millions who listen, week after week, to the living voice of the preacher, are daily fed by the press; and millions more are only accessible by its instrumentality, and to them it is the great teacher," observed one concerned Scottish preacher. In-expensive books, he noted, were democratizing both reading and infidelity. "Speculations, decidedly hostile to true religion and to man's best interests, are no longer confined to the upper and more refined classes of society; but they have descended through the many channels opened up by the prolific press to the reading millions of the present time."[30]

The spread of "infidel" science in the middle third of the nineteenth century—facilitated not only by cheap books and magazines but also by itin-erant lecturers, traveling exhibits, and museums—provoked a religious back-lash, characterized by a torrent of popular literature on "science and religion," a novel phrase that began appearing with frequency in the period after about 1830. In the 1840s and 1850s in Britain the evangelical Religious Tract Society launched an extensive publishing program of inexpensive books and articles on science and religion, hoping thereby to teach the middle and working classes how the study of nature revealed the wisdom and goodness of God. One of the society's most successful authors, the disgraced minister turned schoolmaster and lecturer Thomas Dick (1774–1857), became widely known as "the Christian philosopher." A prolific writer, Dick aimed "particularly [at] the middle and lower ranks of the community." Espousing what was rapidly becoming an ob-solete view, he insisted that science, "from whatever motives it may be prose-cuted, is in effect and in reality, *an inquiry after God*. It is the study of angels and other superior intelligences." An American educator reported to Dick that his books "are read, Sir, daily, by thousands and tens of thousands in these United States. They are in all our schools, and libraries, and private families. Select Readings have been collated from them, and *Stereotyped* as a Class-book for our Primary Schools."[31]

Popular works on science and religion typically highlighted natural theology. Early in the century, for example, the English *Methodist Magazine* began running a section called "Physico- or Natural Theology," which provided readers with an "account of the gracious provisions of Providence, of the wisdom and design of the Creator." Dominating the discourse of design was the Anglican archdeacon William Paley (1743–1805), whose canonical *Natural Theology* (1802) featured "evidences of the existence and attributes of the Deity, collected from the appearances of nature." Arguably the most widely read and admired cleric in the English-speaking world of the early nineteenth century, Paley and his watchmaker God became synonymous with natural theology for decades to come. But despite its ubiquity in popular science writing, natural theology never rivaled revealed revelation in theological significance. As Aileen Fyfe has recently observed, natural theology "was always considered a devotional exercise, something that would illustrate and deepen . . . faith rather than provide a foundation for it." It might comfort but it rarely converted.[32]

Three decades after the appearance of Paley's book, the frequently reprinted set of *Bridgewater Treatises* (1833–1836) drew attention to "the Power, Wisdom and Goodness of God as Manifested in the Creation." Written mostly by well-known men of science, these testimonies, according to Jonathan Topham, ranked "among the scientific best-sellers of the early nineteenth century" and "attracted extraordinary contemporary interest and 'celebrity.'" A staple of mechanics' institute libraries, they were, suggests Topham, read more for their "safe science" than for their pious thoughts.[33]

The two mainline sciences that generated the most popular enthusiasm in the first half of the century were geology and astronomy. By the mid-1830s geology, with its stunning revelations of the history of life on earth, had become "the fashionable science of the day." The *American Journal of Science*, edited by the devout Benjamin Silliman (1779–1864), reported in 1841 that "lectures upon geology are demanded and given in all our larger towns; and the wonders of this science form the theme of discussion in the drawing-rooms of taste and fashion." The construction of the so-called geological column, based on the discovery of distinctive assemblages of fossils, prompted reinterpretations of the first chapter of Genesis that accommodated these findings. The Scottish divine Thomas Chalmers (1780–1847) led the way with his proposal that a vast, indefinite period of time had elapsed between an initial creation "in the beginning" and the relatively recent six-day creation associated with the Garden of Eden. During this gap in the biblical record the earth had experienced the series of catastrophes and creations revealed in the rocks. Another view, popularized in the early 1830s by Silliman and later by the Scot Hugh Miller (1802–1856), met the geological challenge to Genesis by interpreting the "days" of the first chapter as vast geological ages.[34]

We'll never know how many people wrestled with the implications of geology for understanding the Bible, though one Pennsylvania mill owner recorded his experience:

> The yet not fully understood science of geology may interfere with the literal sense of the first chapter of Genesis, but can never overthrow the Christian theory; and it is satisfactory to find eminent geologists—those who have adopted the opinion that the world has existed many thousand ages—fully and unequivocally believing in the truths of revelation.... Thus it was with me when geologists assumed the position that the world, instead of being the Almighty's work in six of our days, was clearly many thousands or millions of years in becoming what it now is. I felt confounded, but further reflection makes me think differently; and if geologists establish their position, and agree among themselves—which as yet they are far from doing—I shall find no difficulty in adopting the theory, without its interfering in the least with my religious sentiments.

In the early 1840s Silliman declared that "multitudes" had reached the same conclusion. A decade later another American estimated that only "half of the Christian public" remained wedded to the idea that the history of life on earth could be squeezed into a mere six thousand years.[35]

"Astronomy," proclaimed Silliman, "is, not without reason, regarded, by mankind, as the sublimest of the sciences," simultaneously inspiring awe and humility. The public devoured it. The Cincinnati astronomer Ormsby Mac-Knight Mitchel (1805–1862), one of the most popular lecturers in antebellum America, drew thousands of listeners a night to theaters and halls across the county, where he demonstrated the words of the Psalmist: "The heavens declare the glory of God." After listening enthralled as Mitchel described the wonders of the skies, one awestruck woman concluded that he was "doing more good by these lectures to draw men's minds toward God than many missionaries of the Gospel." Even Mitchel's espousal of the controversial nebular hypothesis did not dampen his hearers' enthusiasm—or tarnish his reputation as a man of God. In 1796 the French mathematical astronomer Pierre Simon Laplace (1749–1827) had proposed a way that the solar system could have developed naturally from the rapidly spinning atmosphere of the primitive sun, later identified as a nebula. Despite Laplace's notorious (and perhaps apocryphal) quip about not needing God as an explanation—"I have no need of that hypothesis"—his nebular theory gained a strong following among Christians, especially in America. Contemporaries marveled at its popularity. The nebular hypothesis "had scarcely been formed," observed one academic, "before it was seized as the Biblical cosmogony or doctrine of creation."[36]

No astronomical topic garnered more popular attention than the possibility of extraterrestrial life, or what was called "the plurality of worlds." Curiosity about this subject dated back to the seventeenth century, when telescopic revelations of the topography of nearby heavenly bodies raised questions about their possible habitability. Had God populated these remote regions of the universe with life forms similar to those on earth? Had he located hell on a comet? The first to popularize these issues and explore their theological implications was Bernard le Bovier de Fontenelle (1657–1757), whose *Entretiens sur la pluralité des mondes* (Conversations on the Plurality of Worlds, 1686) attracted such a wide readership that years later Voltaire complained that the book had "spoiled" the young women of his generation for more serious topics.[37]

A natural philosopher explains the plurality of worlds and the Copernican system to an inquisitive French noblewoman. From Bernard le Bovier de Fontenelle, *Entretiens sur la pluralité des mondes* (*Conversations on the Plurality of Worlds*), first published in Paris in 1686.

In 1815 Thomas Chalmers (the Genesis exegete) attracted throngs in Glasgow with his sermons on "the relation of Christianity to extraterrestrial life," which described the planets as "mansions of life and of intelligence." As one of his listeners later recalled,

> He had to wait nearly four hours before he could gain admission as one of a crowd in which he was nearly crushed to death. It was with no little effort that the great preacher could find his way to the pulpit. As soon as his fervid eloquence began to stream from it, the intense enthusiasm of the auditory became almost irrestrainable [sic]; and in that enthusiasm the writer, young as he was, fully participated. He has never since witnessed anything equal to the scene.

When Chalmers brought out his lectures in book form a couple of years later, it became an instant best seller, running, in the words of one astonished contemporary, "like wild-fire through the country." Speculation about extraterrestrial life—the scientific evidence, the theological implications—remained a hot topic of debate through the remainder of the century, often engaging the scientific elite as well as backyard philosophers. The theologically trained Richard A. Proctor (1837–1888), arguably the leading popularizer of science in the late nineteenth century, launched his career with *Other Worlds Than Ours* (1870). And down to the present, discussions of unidentified flying objects remain suffused with religious overtones.[38]

Although widespread, discussions of the possibility of life on other worlds caused far less public commotion during the first half of the nineteenth century than phrenology, the "science of mind" developed by two Germans, the anatomist Franz Joseph Gall (1758–1828), a deist, and his student Johann Spurzheim (1776–1832), who had abandoned theology for medicine. According to phrenological theory, the human brain comprised a number of distinct "organs"—some counted thirty-seven—each corresponding to an exotically named mental "faculty," such as amativeness (love of sex), acquisitiveness (love of money), and philoprogenitiveness (love of children). Because the relative strength of any propensity could be determined by measuring the size of its matching organ, it was not difficult for the initiated to "read" a person's character by carefully examining the skull. Plaster-of-Paris models of the skull, identifying each faculty, became ubiquitous in urban shops. Almost from the beginning the phrenologists encountered opposition from some theologians and clerics, who found such a naturalistic rendering of the human mind incompatible with the notion of free will and the sanctity of the soul. According to the American Unitarian Theodore Parker (1810–1860), phrenology

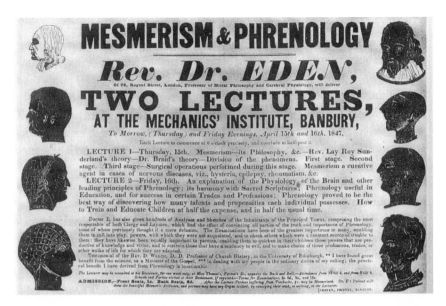

A handbill announcing lectures in mesmerism and phrenology, delivered in 1847 by the Rev. Dr. Eden in Banbury, England. Courtesy of Alison Winter.

weakened "the power of the old supernaturalism" by demonstrating "that man himself could be brought within the purview of science and that mental phenomena could be studied objectively and explained by natural causes."[39]

The great apostle of phrenology in Great Britain and North America was an apostate Calvinist from Scotland, George Combe (1788–1858), whose *Constitution of Man* (1828) during the middle third of the century probably outsold all other books, excepting only the Bible, *Pilgrim's Progress*, and *Robinson Crusoe*. By the time of the Civil War, Americans alone had purchased some two hundred thousand copies, eager to learn how to live longer, healthier, and happier lives. The "laws of nature," advised Combe, dictated how to live: what to eat and drink, where to live, when to marry. Violations would produce "formidable and appalling" results. According to one favorably impressed British writer, "If in a manufacturing district you meet with an artisan whose sagacious conversation and tidy appearance convince you that he is one of the more favourable specimens of his class, enter his house, and it is ten to one but you find COMBE'S *Constitution of Man* lying there." A London paper claimed in 1858:

> No book published within the memory of man, in the English or any other language, has effected so great a revolution in the previously received opinions of society [as *Constitution of Man*].... The influence of that unpretending treatise has extended to hundreds of

thousands of minds which know not whence they derived the new light that has broken in upon them, and percolated into thousands of circles that are scarcely conscious of knowing more about Mr. Combe than his name, and the fact that he was a phrenologist.[40]

Despite Combe's assurance that phrenology did not "directly embrace the interests of eternity" and that Christians had nothing to fear from phrenology, the materialistic implications of phrenology troubled many clerics and at least some lay readers. One schoolteacher recorded her torment that followed her reading of Combe's book:

> My mind was painfully exercised while I read, again and again, the 9th chapter, "On the Relation between Science and Scripture." Many of the views *seemed* to be at variance with Revelation. I could not disbelieve the evidence of my senses on the one hand, or relinquish my hold of scripture truth on the other. To recede appeared to be folly; to advance, madness.... "Perish the knowledge of the science," I thought, "if it can only be obtained by the abandonment of my hopes for eternity!"... But, after all, Mr. Combe's work had given me more light and assistance than I had obtained from any other source, and, after I had laid it aside, I found myself constantly acting upon the ideas I had received from its perusal.[41]

During the 1830s both Spurzheim and Combe visited the United States, electrifying large audiences up and down the East Coast. "When Spurzheim was in America," wrote one English observer, "the great mass of society became phrenologists in a day, wherever he appeared." In New Haven the venerable Professor Silliman served as his host. Over the next two decades their most fervent American converts, Orson Squire Fowler (1809–1887) and his bother Lorenzo (1811–1896), fomented a national craze. From their headquarters at Clinton Hall in New York City the Fowler brothers created a phrenological empire that reached into every segment of American society. Orson alone claimed to have examined "a *quarter of a million* [heads], of all ages and of both sexes." Each month twenty thousand families pored over the *American Phrenological Journal,* one of the nation's most successful magazines, and thousands of others went out and purchased the multitude of guides and manuals the Fowlers annually published on all aspects of mental and physical health. As part of their effort to improve the human race, they rapidly branched out from phrenology to embrace the whole gamut of health reforms then in vogue. Their "one great obstacle," they complained, was the conservative clergy. Thus in works titled *The Christian Phrenologist* (1843) and *Religion, Natural and Revealed*

(1844) Orson Fowler sought to reassure doubters, with only partial success, about the compatibility of "the religion of phrenology with the religion of the Bible."[42]

In 1844 an anonymous British author, later identified as the Edinburgh publisher Robert Chambers (1802–1871), wove together threads from the nebular hypothesis, historical geology, Lamarckian evolution, and phrenology into a sensational little book called *Vestiges of the Natural History of Creation*. As one contemporary journalist noted, it carried the debate over evolution "beyond the bounds of the study and lecture-room into the drawing-room and the public street." The historian James Secord credits *Vestiges* with bringing "an evolutionary vision of the universe into the heart of everyday life." For some time after its publication, recalled one Victorian reader, "the name of the book was in every mouth, and one would be accosted by facetious friends, 'Well, son of a cabbage, whither art thou progressing?'" Even decades after the appearance of Charles Darwin's monumental *Origin of Species*, *Vestiges* was outselling it. Chambers denied dispensing with the Creator, but critics thought otherwise. The teaching of *Vestiges*, fumed one irate Christian, is nothing but "atheism—blank atheism, cold, cheerless, heartless, atheism." An accused murderer blamed *Vestiges* and Voltaire for turning him into an infidel; the jury found him not guilty by reason of insanity. Though *Vestiges* circulated widely and sparked much debate, it failed, as Daniel Thurs has pointed out, to "inspire many itinerant lecturers or evolutionary societies," as phrenology had done.[43]

The heralded discovery of such invisible yet powerful forces as gravity, electricity, and magnetism led to much speculation about the material and spiritual implications of this unseen world. The reading public eagerly consumed news of "extraordinary experiments" and creative conjectures about the electrical nature of life. But it found most fascinating the notion of animal magnetism, an invisible fluid that coursed through the human body, discovered in the 1770s by Franz Anton Mesmer (1734–1814). According to the Jesuit-trained German doctor, obstructions to the free flow of this imponderable fluid caused disease, which could be cured by the magnetic emanations from another person's hands or eyes. Such treatment often put the subject in a deep trance, with unpredictable and sometimes entertaining results. When Mesmer moved to France in 1778, he touched off "an epidemic" of mesmeric enthusiasm. Despite the verdict of a royal commission that attributed the phenomena associated with mesmerism to imagination rather than magnetism, mesmeric healing flourished throughout late eighteenth-century Europe, where, despite Mesmer's own denial, it was often attributed to supernatural forces—or, alternatively, to satanic delusions.[44]

Mesmer's novel therapy attracted little American interest until 1836, when a French medical school dropout named Charles Poyen landed in Portland, Maine, and began lecturing, with striking success, on the topic. By the early 1840s itinerant mesmerists were traveling throughout New England; Boston alone claimed "two or three hundred skilful magnetizers." One successful practitioner, who hailed mesmerism as "a religious engine of great power," reportedly filled a Boston chapel with "more than two thousand for six nights running." Within a few years mesmerism had spread throughout the United States, enticing followers from all walks of life. One of Poyen's erstwhile disciples, Phineas P. Quimby (1802–1866), treated or taught an estimated twelve thousand people during a seven-year period in Portland; one of Quimby's patients, Mary Baker Eddy (1821–1910), went on to even greater heights as a healer. In the end, Quimby rejected traditional mesmerism for a modified version he called the "Science of Health." This "introduction of religion based on science," he announced optimistically, "is the commencement of the new world."[45]

During mesmeric trances hypnotized subjects (as we now call them) often gave and received messages they regarded as divinely inspired. Such supernatural communications closely paralleled those associated with spiritualism, which blossomed in midcentury America and, shortly thereafter, in Europe. Widely seen as a spiritual analogue of the telegraph, it became so popular for a time that the skeptical Theodore Parker predicted the likelihood of spiritualism's becoming "the religion of America." Because spiritualists, like scientists, placed so much stress on empirical evidence— hearing, seeing, and feeling— they laid claim to the mantle of science. One British believer argued that spiritualism stood "mid-way between the opposing schools" of faith and science; thus "it gives to the one a scientific basis for the divine things of old, whilst it restores to the other the much needed evidence of its expressed faith in the duality and continuity of life."[46]

On occasion mesmerism and spiritualism fused with phrenology, which in turn spawned interest in anatomy, physiology, and hygiene. Sporadic attempts at educating the American public in how to live gave way in the 1830s to a full-blown health crusade led by the egotistical and controversial Sylvester Graham (1794–1851), a sometime Presbyterian evangelist and temperance reformer, who sought to reform the eating, drinking, bathing, sleeping, and lovemaking habits of Americans. In 1839 he published his oft-repeated *Lectures on the Science of Human Life*. Graham and his fellow health reformers routinely linked physical and spiritual health. One Grahamite, Larkin B. Coles (1803–1856), whose books sold so well that a medical editor joked that it seemed "as though the friends of reform not only read, but eat the books," insisted that "it is as truly a sin against Heaven, to violate a law of life, as to break one of the ten commandments." A few years later Ellen G. White (1827–1915), founding prophet of the Seventh-day Adventists, adopted this slogan verbatim. During one of her own mesmericlike "visions," God stamped his imprimatur on her call for a vegetarian diet, dress reform, sexual purity, drugless medicine, and abstinence from stimulants.[47]

The quest for reliable information about the human frame led medical educators in the early nineteenth century to engage in what one disgustedly called "a traffic of dead bodies." To stem the illegal activities of grave-robbing "resurrectionists" and provide medical schools with needed cadavers, a number of state legislatures introduced bills to legalize the practice. This prompted one New York State legislator to remind his fellow lawmakers that "Holy Writ" declared that "God made man in is own image." "We may pass a bill to permit the immolation of this sacred image upon the altar of science," he argued, "yet . . . a higher law . . . will hold us responsible for granting so questionably a license to a class of men . . . who laugh at the jest and top off the bowl, while before them quivers the flesh of inanimate humanity." In response to some Christians' concerns about reassembling body parts at the time when Christ would resurrect the righteous, the British surgeon Thomas Wakley (1795–1862) replied with ridicule, "What an idea of omnipotence is conveyed in [the] supposition, that the miracle of the resurrection could be frustrated, or affected by the misdemeanour of a body-snatcher!" Public suspicion and hostility led to riots on both sides of the Atlantic. In Aberdeen, Scotland, an angry mob set the medical school on fire "amid the loud and continued cheers of not less than 20,000 individuals." As the demand for bodies grew to thousands a year, probably nothing brought "science to the poor man's door," as one critic memorably phrased it, more immediately than having his deceased loved ones serve as anatomical objects.[48]

In the medical sphere, epidemics continued to provoke the most intense public discussions of divine will, though as soon as diseases could be assigned to specific natural causes, religious explanations tended to give way to physical ones. Just as theological interpretations of smallpox had declined in the eighteenth century with the advent of inoculation, so, too, did religious explanations of cholera fade with the knowledge of its etiology. Charles E. Rosenberg has shown that, as long as the origin of cholera remained a mystery, religious persons felt free to regard it as a miracle, "a *scourge*, a *rod* in the hand of God." As a result of midcentury epidemiological investigations that traced the cause of cholera to contaminated water supplies, public health authorities learned how to keep the disease from spreading. Thus, when cholera threatened to strike the United States in 1866, community leaders (especially in New York

City) tended to devote their energies to improving sanitation rather than to discussing the theological meaning of the event. "Whereas ministers in 1832 urged morality upon their congregations as a guarantor of health," writes Rosenberg, "their forward-looking counterparts in 1866 endorsed sanitary reform as a necessary prerequisite to moral improvement." The extent to which parishioners absorbed this message from the pulpit remains unknown (and perhaps unknowable), but with the demise of cholera, other medical mysteries, especially ones associated with sexually transmitted diseases, became the focus of religiomedical speculation.[49]

Of Monkeys and Men

Before the publication of the landmark book *On the Origin of Species* (1859) by Charles Darwin (1809–1882), which substituted a natural explanation for a miraculous one, the issues that captured the people's imagination had seldom dovetailed with the breakthroughs that dominate the triumphalist history of science. Although it would be years before Darwin's volume would outsell *Vestiges*, it immediately acquired a notoriety unprecedented in the annals of mainstream science. As early as 1860 Darwin's disciple Thomas H. Huxley (1825–1895) hyperbolically described the phenomenon:

> Overflowing the narrow bounds of purely scientific circles, the "species question" divides with Italy and the Volunteers the attention of general society. Everybody has read Mr. Darwin's book, or, at least, has given an opinion on its merits or demerits; pietists, whether lay or ecclesiastic, decry it with the mild railing which sounds so charitable; bigots denounce it with ignorant invective; old ladies, of both sexes, consider it a decidedly dangerous book, and even savans, who have no better mud to throw, quote antiquated writers to show that its author is no better than an ape himself; while every philosophical thinker hails it as a veritable Whitworth gun in the armoury of liberalism, and all competent naturalists and physiologists, whatever their opinion as to the ultimate fate of the doctrines put forth, acknowledge that the work...is a solid contribution to knowledge which inaugurates a new epoch in natural history.

A year later an American Methodist proclaimed that "perhaps no scientific work has ever been at once so extensively read, not only by the scientific few, but by the reading masses generally; and certainly no one has ever produced such commotion." Darwin did not identify apes as the ancestors of humans until he published *The Descent of Man* (1871), but from the beginning the biggest buzz was about ape ancestors, not about natural selection or speciation. "The Darwinian theory would lose half its interest with the public," speculated one religious writer, "if it did not culminate in a doctrine on the origin of the human species." When *The Descent of Man* finally appeared, describing man as the descendent of "a hairy quadruped, furnished with a tail and pointed ears," it sealed the link between Darwinism and ape ancestors. "In the drawing-room it is competing with the last new novel," wrote a contributor to the *Edinburgh Review*, "and in the study it is troubling alike the man of science, the moralist, and the theologian."[50]

The disclosure of this pedigree did not sit well with many Christians. In contrast to the Bible, which "places a crown of honor and dominion on the brow of our common humanity," fumed one critic, "Darwinism casts us all down from this elevated platform, and herds us all with four-footed beasts and creeping things. It tears the crown from our heads; it treats us as bastards and not sons, and reveals the degrading fact that man in his best estate—even Mr. Darwin—is but a civilized, dressed up, educated monkey, who has lost his tail." Some Christian apologists adopted a more conciliatory position. Of these, perhaps the most influential was Henry Drummond (1851–1897), a Scottish associate of the American evangelist Dwight L. Moody (1837–1899) and the operator of an urban mission for the working classes of Glasgow. A charismatic speaker, he would on occasion draw an audience of twenty thousand to his center. Convinced that evolution followed a divine plan, he shared his insight in a book titled *Natural Law in the Spiritual World* (1883), which enjoyed phenomenal sales for decades. The intellectual elite never embraced Drummond, but "all the religious world," noted an admiring Matthew Arnold, "have accepted the book as a godsend, and are saying to themselves that here at last is safety and scientific shelter for the orthodox supernaturalism which seemed menaced with total defeat."[51]

As long as discussions of biological development remained confined mostly to scholarly circles, Christians who objected to evolution on biblical grounds saw little reason to rise up. However, as the debate spilled over into the public arena during the 1880s and 1890s, so-called creationists grew increasingly alarmed. "When these vague speculations, scattered to the four winds by the million-tongued press, are caught up by ignorant and untrained men," warned one alarmed premillennialist in 1889, "it is time for earnest Christian men to call a halt."[52]

In early twentieth-century America sporadic protests turned into an organized campaign against evolution, which culminated in the 1920s in the passage of several state laws banning the teaching of human evolution. The

populist politician William Jennings Bryan (1860–1925), resentful of the un-
democratic attempt of a "scientific soviet" to dictate to "the forty million
American Christians" what should be taught in their tax-supported schools,
appealed directly to the people. "Commit your case to the people," he advised
creationists. "Forget, if need be, the highbrows both in the political and college
world, and carry this cause to the people. They are the final and efficiently
corrective power." Ironically, at that very same time in Soviet Russia the Communist Party's Central Committee was indoctrinating workers, peasants, and
soldiers in biological evolution to wean them from relying on the Bible. Occasionally, this effort led to *real* conflict between science and religion when
communist agitators beat up protesting priests.[53]

The infamous Scopes trial in 1925 in Dayton, Tennessee, in which a young
high school teacher was convicted of violating the recently enacted law banning
the teaching of human evolution, pitted Bryan (for the prosecution) against the
agnostic lawyer Clarence Darrow (1857–1938). According to one Tennessee
newspaper, "In Constantinople and far Japan, in Paris and London and Bu-
dapest, here and there and everywhere, at home and abroad, in pagan and in
Christian lands, where controversialists gather, or men discuss their faith, to

A scientific lecturer from the Communist Party, circa 1920s, introducing Russian
soldiers to biological evolution in an effort to wean them from the biblical story of
creation. Courtesy of Alexei Kojevnikov.

The Reverend T. T. Martin, a Baptist evangelist from Blue Mountain, Mississippi, denouncing Darwinism in Dayton, Tennessee, during the Scopes trial in 1925. Two years earlier he had published a diatribe against evolution titled *Hell and the High Schools*. Courtesy of Elizabeth Dunham and the University of Tennessee Special Collections Library.

speak the name of Dayton is to drop a bomb, to hurl a hand grenade, to blow the air of peace to flinders." An American scholar calculated that the trial was discussed by "some 2310 daily newspapers in this country, some 13,267 weeklies, about 3613 monthlies, no less than 392 quarterlies, with perhaps another five hundred including bi-monthlies and semi-monthlies, tri-weeklies and odd types." His search had turned up "no periodical of any sort, agricultural or trade as well, which has ignored the subject." For the first time in history, radio transmitted a science-and-religion debate to the people. A new day in the popularization of science and religion had commenced.[54]

The headline-grabbing controversies about evolution may have eclipsed other popular debates over science and religion, but they did not exhaust the public's range of religiously inspired responses to scientific developments. The increasing use of animals for physiological and pharmacological investigations led to an ongoing battle over vivisection, which turned especially virulent in Protestant Great Britain and North America (but provoked little reaction in

Roman Catholic countries).[55] The germ theory of disease evoked a wide range of religious sentiment, from debates over government-sponsored campaigns to contain the syphilis germ (heatedly opposed by Catholics) to soul searching over the hygienic nature of the common communion cup.[56] Despite its name, Christian Science repudiated the very principles of scientific medicine—including the existence of germs—in favor of mesmeric-inspired mental healing. Christian Science, in turn, inspired various mind-healing alternatives, from the Episcopalian-sponsored Emmanuel Movement to the imitative Jewish Science.[57]

At the very time that scientific medicine was proving its worth in longer and healthier lives, growing numbers of Christians professed their faith in the healing power of prayer. Roman Catholics had never forsaken religious healing, but leading Protestants since the days of Martin Luther (1483–1546) and John Calvin (1509–1564) had adopted a skeptical attitude toward reports of modern healing miracles. In the late nineteenth and early twentieth centuries, however, the holiness revival that swept through Methodism spawned numerous independent ministries and Pentecostal sects, which embraced the healing power of prayer. During the twentieth century these groups captured the devotion of hundreds of millions of Christians around the world.[58] Scientific tests of the efficacy of intercessory prayer for healing, denounced in the late nineteenth century as sacrilegious, came to be hailed a century later as compelling testimony to the power of God.[59]

The turn-of-the-century rediscovery of the genetic basis of heredity handed biologists the intellectual tools they needed to guide evolution, for humans as well as corn and cows. The effort to breed better humans, called eugenics, found Catholics overwhelmingly opposed and Protestants divided.[60] The same was true for science-based sex education.[61] Christian ministers introduced many a parishioner to the principles and techniques of modern psychology, but both liberals and conservatives resisted the reductionist implications of Freudianism (which dismissed God as an illusion) and behaviorism (which viewed God as a scientifically irrelevant metaphor).[62]

Our vulgar history of science and Christianity has taken us far beyond the typical confines of the subject. It has shown that a focus on Copernicus, Galileo, Newton, and Darwin barely touches the issues troubling the greatest number of believers, most of whom remained oblivious to the alleged theological implications of elite science. In many instances the public reacted to popularized versions of science and theology, which trickled down from professional circles. In other cases—Christian Science, creation science, and Native American science come readily to mind—various publics constructed their own alternative "science."[63] While intellectuals wrestled with the theological ramifications of heliocentrism and the mechanical philosophy, the nature of force and matter, the manifestations of vitalism, the meaning of thermodynamics, relativity theory, and quantum physics, and the implications of positivism and scientific naturalism, the common people, to the extent that they paid any attention to science at all, concerned themselves largely with developments that impinged on their daily lives and self-understanding: diseases, disasters, and descent from apes.

2

Science without God

Natural Laws and Christian Beliefs

Nothing has come to characterize modern science more than its rejection of appeals to God in explaining the workings of nature. Numerous scientists, philosophers of science, and science educators have made this claim. In 1982 a U.S. federal judge, eager to distinguish science from other forms of knowledge, especially religion, spelled out "the essential characteristics of science." At the top of his list appeared the notion that science must be "guided by natural law." No statement, declared the judge, could count as science if it depended on "a supernatural intervention." Five years later the U.S. Supreme Court affirmed the judge's reasoning.[1]

Students of nature have not always shunned the supernatural. It took centuries, indeed millennia, for naturalism to dominate the study of nature, and even at the beginning of the twenty-first century, as we shall see, a tiny but vocal group of "theistic scientists" is challenging what they regard as the arbitrary exclusion of the supernatural from science. In exploring how naturalism came to control the practice of science, I hope to answer some basic questions about the identity and motives of those who advocated it. In particular I want to illuminate the reasons why naturalism, described by some scholars as the great engine driving the secularization of Western society, attracted so much support from devout Christians, who often eagerly embraced it as the method of choice for understanding nature. Naturalization, as we shall see, did not lead inevitably to secularization.

First, however, we need some clarification about terms. Historians have employed the word naturalism to designate a broad range of views, from a purely methodological commitment to explaining the workings of nature without recourse to the supernatural, largely devoid of metaphysical implications about God, to a philosophical embrace of materialism, tantamount to atheism. When Thomas H. Huxley (1825–1895) coined the term "scientific naturalism" in 1892, he used it to describe a philosophical outlook that shunned the supernatural and adopted empirical science as the only reliable basis of knowledge about the physical, social, and moral worlds. Although such metaphysical naturalism, rooted in the findings of science, has played an important role in the history of philosophy and religion, its significance in the history of scientific practice has remained small compared to what has recently come to be called methodological naturalism, the focus of this chapter.[2]

Naturalism and Natural Philosophy

Recorded efforts to explain naturally what had previously been attributed to the whimsy of gods date back to the Milesian philosophers of the ancient Greek world, who, six centuries before the birth of Christianity, declared such phenomena as earthquakes, lightning, and thunder to be the result of natural causes. A little later Hippocratic physicians expanded the realm of the natural to include most diseases, including epilepsy, "the sacred disease." As one Hippocratic writer insisted, "Each disease has a natural cause and nothing happens without a natural cause." The first-century Roman philosopher Lucius Annaeus Seneca, ever suspicious of supernatural causation, calmed the fears of fellow citizens by assuring them that "angry deities" had nothing to do with most meteorological or astronomical events: "Those phenomena have causes of their own."[3]

As these scattered examples show, belief in natural causes and the regularity of nature antedated the appearance of Christianity, with its Judaic notion of God as creator and sustainer of the universe. Although founded by a man regarded as divine and developed in a milieu of miracles, Christianity could, and sometimes did, encourage the quest for natural explanations. Long before the birth of modern science and the appearance of "scientists" in the nineteenth century, the study of nature in the West was carried out primarily by Christian scholars known as natural philosophers, who typically expressed a preference for natural explanations over divine mysteries. During the philosophical awakening of the twelfth century, for instance, Adelard of Bath (ca. 1080–ca. 1150), a much-traveled Englishman familiar with the views of

Seneca, instructed his nephew on the virtues of natural explanations: "I will take nothing away from God: for whatever exists is from Him and because of Him. But the natural order does not exist confusedly and without rational arrangement, and human reason should be listened to concerning those things it treats of. But when it completely fails, then the matter should be referred to God." A number of other medieval churchmen expressed similar views, on occasion extending the search for natural explanations to such biblical events as Noah's flood, previously regarded as a miracle.[4]

By the late Middle Ages the search for natural causes had come to typify the work of Christian natural philosophers. Although characteristically leaving the door open for the possibility of direct divine intervention, they frequently expressed contempt for soft-minded contemporaries who invoked miracles rather than searching for natural explanations. The University of Paris cleric Jean Buridan (ca. 1295–ca. 1358), described as "perhaps the most brilliant arts master of the Middle Ages," contrasted the philosopher's search for "appropriate natural causes" with the common folk's erroneous habit of attributing unusual astronomical phenomena to the supernatural. In the fourteenth century the natural philosopher Nicole Oresme (ca. 1320–1382), who went on to become a Roman Catholic bishop, admonished that, in discussing various marvels of nature, "there is no reason to take recourse to the heavens, the last refuge of the weak, or demons, or to our glorious God as if He would produce these effects directly, more so than those effects whose causes we believe are well known to us."[5]

Enthusiasm for the naturalistic study of nature picked up in the sixteenth and seventeenth centuries as more and more Christians turned their attention to discovering the so-called secondary causes that God employed in operating the world. The Italian Catholic Galileo Galilei (1564–1642), one of the foremost promoters of the new philosophy, insisted that nature "never violates the terms of the laws imposed upon her." In a widely circulated letter to the Grand Duchess Christina, written in 1615, Galileo, as a good Christian, acknowledged the divine inspiration of both Holy Scripture and the Book of Nature—but insisted that interpreters of the former should have no say in determining the meaning of the latter. Declaring the independence of natural philosophy from theology, he asserted "that in disputes about natural phenomena one must begin not with the authority of scriptural passages but with sensory experience and necessary demonstrations."[6]

Far to the west, in England, the Anglican philosopher and statesman Francis Bacon (1561–1626) was preaching a similar message of independence, warning of "the extreme prejudice which both religion and philosophy hath received and may receive by being commixed together; as that which undoubtedly will make an heretical religion, and an imaginary and fabulous philosophy." Christians, he advised, should welcome rather than fear the truth that God operates the world largely, though not exclusively, through natural laws discoverable by human effort. Although conceding that too great an emphasis on natural law might undermine belief in God, he remained confident that further reflection would "bring the mind back again to religion."[7]

The danger Bacon perceived did not take long to materialize. As natural philosophers came to view nature as "a law-bound system of matter in motion," a vast machine running with little or no divine intervention, they increasingly focused on the regularities of nature and the laws of motion rather than on God's intrusions. When the French Catholic natural philosopher René Descartes (1596–1650) boldly constructed a universe of whirling ethereal fluids and speculated how the solar system could have been formed by the action of these vortices operating according to the God-ordained laws of nature, he acquired considerable notoriety for nearly pushing God out of the cosmos altogether. His pious fellow countryman Blaise Pascal (1623–1662) accused Descartes, somewhat unfairly, of trying to dispense with God altogether, according Him only "a flip of the finger in order to set the world in motion." Fearing clerical retribution in the years after Galileo's trial, Descartes disingenuously declared his cosmogony to be "absolutely false."[8]

The English chemist Robert Boyle (1627–1691)—as ardent an advocate of the mechanical philosophy as Descartes yet as pious as Pascal—viewed the discovery of the divinely established laws of nature as a religious act. A devout Protestant with great reverence for the Bible, Boyle regarded revelation as "a foreign principle" to the study of the "laws or rules" of nature. He sought to explain natural phenomena in terms of matter in motion as a means of combating pagan notions that granted nature quasi-divine powers, not as a way to eliminate divine purpose from the world. According to the historians Edward B. Davis and Michael Hunter, viewing the cosmos as a "compounded machine" run according to natural laws struck Boyle as being "more consistent with biblical statements of divine sovereignty than older, non-mechanistic views" of an intelligent nature: "By denying 'Nature' any wisdom of its own, the mechanical conception of nature located purpose where Boyle believed it belonged: over and behind nature, in the mind of a personal God, rather than in an impersonal semi-deity immanent within the world." God's customary reliance on natural laws (or secondary causes) did not, in Boyle's opinion, rule out the possibility of occasional supernatural interventions, when God (the primary cause) might act "in special ways to achieve particular ends." This view became common among Christian men of science, as well as among clerics.[9]

No one contributed more to the popular image of the solar system as a giant mechanical device than the University of Cambridge professor of mathematics Isaac Newton (1642–1727), a man of deep, if unorthodox, religious conviction, who unblushingly attributed the perfections of the solar system to "the counsel and dominion of an intelligent and powerful Being." Widely recognized as the greatest natural philosopher of all time for his discovery of the role of gravity in the operation of the universe, he insisted that natural knowledge should be based on observations and experiments, not hypotheses. Although he chided Descartes for his attempt to explain the solar system by "mere Laws of Nature," he himself believed that God typically used them "as instruments in his works." In private correspondence he even speculated in Cartesian fashion about how God might have used natural laws to construct the solar system from a "common Chaos."[10]

Endorsed by such publicly religious natural philosophers as Boyle and Newton, the search for natural laws and mechanical explanations became a veritable Christian vocation, especially in Protestant countries, where miraculous signs and wonders were often associated with Catholic superstition. As one Anglican divine complained in 1635, some Protestants were even beginning to question of the efficacy of prayer, believing that God, working through second causes, "hath set a constant course in nature."[11]

For ordinary folk, as we have seen in chapter 1, the most compelling instances of supernaturalism giving way to naturalism occurred not in physics or chemistry but in such areas as meteorology and medicine, in explanations of epidemics, eclipses, and earthquakes. Already by the sixteenth century, supernatural explanations of disease had largely disappeared from medical literature except in discussions of epidemics and insanity, which remained etiological mysteries, and venereal diseases, the wages of sin. In writing about the common afflictions of humanity—fractures, tumors, endemic diseases, and such—physicians seldom mentioned God or the devil. Even when discussing the plague, the most dreaded disease of all, they tended merely to acknowledge its supernatural origin before passing quickly to its more mundane aspects. The great French surgeon Ambroise Paré (1510–1590), for example, explicitly confined himself to "the natural causes of the plague," saying that he would let divines deal with its ultimate causes. Priests and theologians may have placed greater emphasis on supernatural causes and cures, but in general they, too, easily accommodated new medical knowledge by maintaining that God usually effected His will through natural agencies rather than by direct intervention. Theological interests thus seldom precluded searching for natural causes or using natural therapies.[12]

The most dramatic, and in some ways revealing, episode in the naturali-zation of disease occurred in the British colonies of North America in the early 1720s. Christians had long regarded smallpox, a frighteningly deadly and disfiguring disease, as God's ultimate scourge to punish sinners and bring them to their knees in contrition. Thus when an epidemic threatened to strike New England in 1721, the governor of Massachusetts called for a day of fasting and repenting of the sins that had "stirred up the Anger of Heaven against us." However, the Puritan Cotton Mather (1663–1728), one of the town of Boston's leading ministerial lights, offered an alternative to repentance—inoculation with an attenuated but live form of smallpox—in hopes of pre-venting the disease by natural means. Having heard rumors of successful inoculations against smallpox in Africa and the Middle East, Mather, a fellow of the Royal Society of London and a natural philosopher in his own right, proposed that the untested, potentially lethal procedure be tried in Boston. The best trained physician in town, William Douglass (1691–1752), fearing that inoculation would spread rather than prevent the disease and resenting the meddling of ministers in medical matters, urged Mather to rely instead on "the *all-wise Providence* of God Almighty" and quit trying to thwart God's will. Mather and five other clerics countered that such reasoning would rule out all medical intervention. Cannot pious persons, they asked,

> give into the method or practice without having their devotion and subjection to the All-wise Providence of God Almighty call'd in question?...Do we not in the use of all means depend on GOD's blessing?...For, what hand or art of Man is there in this Operation more than in bleeding, blistering and a Score more things in Medi-cal Use? which are all consistent with a humble trust in our Great preserver, and a due Subjection to His All-wise Providence.

Besides, added Mather, Dr. Douglass risked violating the biblical commandment against killing by refusing to use inoculation to save lives. After postepidemic calculations demonstrated the efficacy of inoculation, smallpox, previously a divine judgment, became a preventable disease. Few Christians lamented the metamorphosis. And in generations to come their descendents would give thanks to God as medical science brought cholera, diphtheria, yellow fever, and even venereal diseases under natural control.[13]

The same process occurred in meteorology. Benjamin Franklin (1706–1790), who as a teenager in Boston had backed Douglass in his quarrel with Mather over smallpox inoculation, found himself on the opposite side of a similar debate a few decades later, after announcing the invention of a device to prevent another of God's judgments on erring humanity: lightning. When a French cleric denounced lightning rods as an inappropriate means of thwarting God's will, the American printer turned scientific celebrity scornfully replied, "He speaks as if he thought it presumption in man to propose guarding himself against the *Thunders of Heaven*! Surely the Thunder of Heaven is no more supernatural than the Rain, hail or Sunshine of heaven, against the Inconvenience of which we guard by Roofs & Shades without Scruple." Reflective Christians quickly accepted Franklin's logic, and before long lightning rods were adorning the steeples of churches throughout Europe and North America, protecting them not from God's wrath but from a dangerous and capricious natural occurrence.[14]

Reactions to the great earthquakes of 1727 and 1755 further illustrate the inroads of scientific naturalism on popular culture. On the night of October 29, 1727, a violent earthquake shook the northern colonies of America, producing widespread damage to property. Terrified residents, humbled by this apparent display of divine anger, set aside fast days and begged God to forgive them for such sins as Sabbath breaking, pride, and drunkenness. To promote repentance among his parishioners, Thomas Prince (1687–1758), the Puritan pastor of Boston's Old South Church, preached a sermon entitled *Earthquakes the Works of God and Tokens of His Just Displeasure*. In it he conceded that the ignition of gases in the earth's interior might have touched off the tremors—but then argued that such secondary explanations only demonstrated "how the mighty GOD works invisibly by sensible Causes, and even by those that are extremely little and weak, produces the greatest and most terrible Effects in the World." Cotton Mather similarly insisted on God's active role in producing such catastrophes. "Let the *Natural Causes of Earthquakes* be what the *Wise Men of Enquiry* please," he wrote. "*They* and their *Causes* are still under the government of HIM that is the GOD *of Nature*." Twenty-eight years later, on November 18, 1755, a second earthquake jolted New England. This time nearly two months passed before community leaders called for a public fast. When the aging Reverend Prince reissued his earlier sermon on earthquakes as tokens of God's displeasure, Professor John Winthrop IV (1714–1779) of Harvard College calmed the timorous with the assurance that, although God bore ultimate responsibility for the shaking, natural causes had produced the tremors. "I think Mr. Winthrop has laid Mr. Prince flat on [his] back, and seems to take some pleasure in his mortification," gloated one of the professor's admirers.[15]

Some people credited the mechanical philosophy with pushing God further and further into the distance, making him virtually irrelevant to daily life. The revelations of natural philosophy helped to convince the liberal Boston minister Charles Chauncy (1705–1787), for example, that "God does not communicate either being or happiness to his creatures, at least on this earth, by an immediate act of power, but by concurring with an established course of nature. What I mean is, he brings creatures into existence, and makes them happy, by the intervention of second causes, operating under his direction and influence, in a stated, regular uniform manner." But for every liberal such as Chauncy there were scores of Christians who continued to believe in miracles, prayer, and divine inspiration—while at the same time welcoming the evidence that epidemics, earthquakes, and lightning bolts derived from natural causes. And for every natural philosopher who lost his faith to science, many more found their beliefs untouched by the search for natural causes of physical events. For them, the search for natural laws led to a fuller understanding of God, not disbelief.[16]

The Decline of Natural Philosophy and the Beginnings of Modern Science

No single event marks the transition from godly natural philosophy to naturalistic modern science, but sometime between roughly the mid-eighteenth and mid-nineteenth centuries students of nature in one discipline after another reached the conclusion that, regardless of one's personal beliefs, supernatural explanations had no place in the practice of science. As we have seen, natural philosophers had often expressed a preference for natural causes, but few, if any, had ruled out appeals to God. In contrast, virtually all scientists (a term coined in the 1830s but not widely used until the late nineteenth century), whether Christians or non-Christians, came by the late nineteenth century to agree that God-talk lay beyond the boundaries of science.[17]

The roots of secular science can be traced most clearly to Enlightenment France, where the spirit of Descartes lingered. Although not a materialist—he believed in God and the existence of immaterial souls—Descartes had pushed naturalism to the point of regarding animals as mere machines. This extreme form of naturalism scarcely influenced the course of scientific investigation, especially outside of France, but it did spur some French Cartesians to go even further than Descartes. The French physician Julien Offray de La Mettrie (1709–1751), for example, suggested that humans are nothing but "perpendicularly crawling machines," a claim that even the French found sensational. While acknowledging God to be the author of the book of nature, La Mettrie insisted that "experience and observation," not revelation, should be "our only guides." Such methods might not lead to absolute truth about human nature, but they provided "the greatest degree of probability possible on this subject."

Like many men of science to follow, he was willing to trade theological certainty for such scientific probability.[18]

Much more influential on scientific practice was La Mettrie's countryman Georges-Louis Leclerc, comte de Buffon (1707–1788), an ardent admirer of Newton and one of the most prominent natural historians in the eighteenth century. Buffon called for an emphasis on the regularities of nature and a renunciation of all appeals to the supernatural. Those studying physical subjects, he argued, "ought as much as possible, to avoid having recourse to supernatural causes." Philosophers "ought not to be affected by causes which seldom act, and whose action is always sudden and violent. These have no place in the ordinary course of nature. But operations uniformly repeated, motions which succeed one another without interruption, are the causes which alone ought to be the foundation of our reasoning." Buffon professed not to care whether such explanations were true, so long as they appeared probable. A theist, though not a practicing Christian, Buffon acknowledged that the Creator had originally set the planets in motion, but considered the fact of no value to the natural philosopher. His methodological convictions inspired him to propose a natural history of the solar system, based on the notion that a passing comet, "falling obliquely on the sun," had detached the matter that later formed the planets and their satellites. Although his speculations never caught on, some Christian critics justifiably criticized him for trying "to exclude the agency of a divine Architect, and to represent a world begun and perfected merely by the operation of natural, undesigning causes."[19]

A far more successful account of the origin of the solar system came from the Frenchman Pierre Simon Laplace (1749–1827), who had abandoned training as a cleric for a career in mathematics and astronomy and eventually became one of the leading men of science in Europe. Finding Buffon's methodology attractive but his theory physically implausible, Laplace in 1796 proposed that the planets had been formed from the revolving atmosphere of the primitive sun, which, as it cooled and contracted, had abandoned a succession of Saturn-like rings, which had coalesced to form the planets. On the occasion of a visit in 1802 to the country estate of Napoleon Bonaparte, Laplace entertained his host with an account of his so-called nebular hypothesis. When the French leader asked why he had heard no mention of God, Laplace supposedly uttered the much-quoted words "Sire, I have no need of that hypothesis." The only first-hand account of the exchange simply reports Napoleon's disappointment with Laplace's explanation that "a chain of natural causes would account for the construction and preservation of the wonderful system." Either way, there was no mistaking the message.[20]

Choc de la Comète contre le Soleil

The primeval collision of a comet with the sun, according to Buffon. From George-Louis Leclerc de Buffon, *Histoire naturelle, générale et particulière* (Deux-Ponts: Sanson, 1785–1791), 1:153. Courtesy of William Ashworth and the Linda Hall Library of Science, Engineering, and Technology.

Laplace's thoroughly naturalistic hypothesis, authored by a notorious un-believer, represented the secularization of natural philosophy at its baldest. Not surprisingly, some Christians denounced Laplace for his transparently atheis-tic science. This was especially true in the English-speaking world, where the tradition of natural theology remained strong and where French science was widely viewed as tending toward godless materialism. It seemed clear to the Scottish divine Thomas Chalmers (1780–1847), for example, that if "all the beauties and benefits of the astronomical system [could] be referred to the sin-gle law of gravitation, it would greatly reduce the strength of the argument of a designing cause." One of the classic arguments for the existence of God rested on the observation that an object appearing to have been made for a particular purpose had been produced by an intelligent and purposeful designer. If the solar system looked as if it were not the result of necessity or of accident, if it appeared to have been made with a special end in mind, then it must have had a designer, namely God. But what happened to the argument if the arrangement had resulted simply from the laws of nature operating on inert matter?[21]

John Pringle Nichol (1804–1859), a minister-turned-astronomer at the University of Glasgow and an avid popularizer of the nebular hypothesis, of-fered one plausible answer. He dismissed Chalmers's argument that "we can demonstrate the existence of a Deity more emphatically from that portion of creation of which we remain ignorant, than from any portion whose processes we have explored" as downright dangerous to Christianity. Such fears, Nichol believed, stemmed from a misunderstanding of the term "law." To him, laws simply designated divine order: "LAW of itself is not substantive or indepen-dent power; no causal influence sprung of blind necessity, which carries on events of its own will and energies without command."[22]

As more and more of the artifacts of nature, such as the solar system, came to be seen as products of natural law rather than divine miracle, defend-ers of design increasingly shifted their attention to the origin of the laws that had proved capable of such wondrous things. Many Christians concluded that these laws had been instituted by God and were evidence of His existence and wisdom. In this way, as John LeConte (1818–1891) of the University of Cali-fornia pointed out in the early 1870s, the cosmogony of Laplace helped to bring about a transformation in the application of the principle of design "from the region of facts to that of laws." The nebular hypothesis thus strengthened, rather than weakened, the argument from design, opening "before the mind a stupendous and glorious field for meditation upon the works and character of the Great Architect of the Universe."[23]

Christian apologists proved equally adept in modifying the doctrine of di-vine providence to accommodate the nebular hypothesis. Instead of pointing to the miraculous creation of the world by divine fiat, a "special" providential act, they emphasized God's "general" providence in creating the world by means of natural laws and secondary causes. While the Creator's role in the forma- tion of the solar system thus changed, it neither declined nor disappeared, as some timid believers had feared. Daniel Kirkwood (1814–1895), a Presbyterian astronomer who contributed more to the acceptance of the nebular hypothesis in America than anyone else, argued that if God's power is demonstrated in sustaining and governing the world through the agency of secondary causes, then it should not "be regarded as derogating from his perfections, to sup- pose the same power to have been exerted in a similar way in the process of its formation."[24]

God's reliance on secondary causes in the daily operation of the world made it seem only reasonable to suppose that He had at least sometimes used the same means in creating it. "God generally effects his purposes ... by interme- diate agencies, and this is especially the case in dead, unorganized matter," wrote one author:

> If, then, the rains of heaven, and the gentle dew, and the floods, and
> storms, and volcanoes, and earthquakes, are all products of mate-
> rial forces, exhibiting no evidence of miraculous intervention, there is
> nothing profane or impious in supposing that the planets and sat-
> ellites of our system are not the immediate workmanship of the great
> First Cause.... God is still present; but it is in the operation of un-
> changeable laws; in the sustaining of efficient energies which he
> has imposed on the material world that he has created; in the pres-
> ervation of powers, properties, and affinities, which he has trans-
> ferred out of himself and given to the matter he has made.[25]

To at least one observer, Laplace's cosmogony offered an even more con- vincing demonstration of divine providence than did the traditional view:

> How much more sublime and exalted a view does it give us of the
> work of creation and of the Great Architect, to contemplate him
> evolving a system of worlds from a diffused mass of matter, by the
> establishment of certain laws and properties, than to consider him as
> taking a portion of that matter in his hand and moulding it as it
> were into a sphere, and then imparting to it an impulse of motion.[26]

As we shall see in chapter 5, many Christians were so eager to baptize the nebular hypothesis, they even read it back into the first chapter of Genesis.

In 1829 the English astronomer John Herschel (1792–1871) published *A Preliminary Discourse on the Study of Natural Philosophy* (1830), described by one scholar as "the first attempt by an eminent man of science to make the methods of science explicit." Frequently extrapolating from astronomy, the paradigmatic science of the time, Herschel asserted that sound scientific knowledge derived exclusively from *experience*, "the great, and indeed only ultimate source of our knowledge of nature and its laws," which was gained by *observation* and *experiment*, "the fountains of all natural science." Natural philosophy and science (he used the terms interchangeably) recognized only those causes "having a real existence in nature, and not being mere hypotheses or figments of the mind." Although this stricture ruled out supernatural causes, Herschel adamantly denied that the pursuit of science fostered unbelief. To the contrary, he insisted that science "places the existence and principal attributes of a Deity on such grounds as to render doubt absurd and atheism ridiculous." Natural laws testified to God's existence; they did not make him superfluous.[27]

Efforts to naturalize the history of the earth followed closely on the naturalization of the skies—and produced similar results. When students of earth history, many of them Protestant ministers, created the new discipline of geology in the early nineteenth century, they consciously sought to reconstruct earth history using natural means alone. By the 1820s virtually all geologists, even those who invoked catastrophic events, were eschewing appeals to the supernatural. When the British geologist Charles Lyell (1797–1875) set about in the early 1830s to "free the science from Moses," the emancipation had already largely occurred. Nevertheless, his landmark *Principles of Geology* (1830–1833) conveniently summed up the accepted methods of doing geology, with the subtitle, *Being an Attempt to Explain the Former Changes in the Earth's Surface by Reference to Causes Now in Operation*, conveying the main point. As Lyell described his project to a friend, it would in good Herschelian fashion "endeavour to establish the principles of reasoning in the science," most notably the idea "that *no causes whatever* have from the earliest time to which we can look back to the present ever acted but those *now* acting & that they never acted with different degrees of energy from that which they now exert."[28]

Lyell applauded his geological colleagues for following the lead of astronomers in substituting "fixed and invariable laws" for "immaterial and supernatural agents":

Many appearances, which for a long time were regarded as indicating mysterious and extraordinary agency, are finally recognized as the necessary result of the laws now governing the material world; and the discovery of this unlooked for conformity has induced some geologists to infer that there has never been any interruption to the

same uniform order of physical events. The same assemblage
of general causes, they conceive, may have been sufficient to produce, by their various combinations, the endless diversity of effects,
of which the shell of the earth has preserved the memorials, and,
consistently with these principles, the recurrence of analogous
changes is expected by them in time to come.

The community of geologists, comprising mostly Christian men of science,
thus embraced "the undeviating uniformity of secondary causes"—with one
troubling exception.[29]

Like so many of his contemporaries, Lyell, a communicant of the Church
of England, for years stopped short of extending the domain of natural law
to the origin of species, especially of humans. At times he leaned toward attributing new species to "the intervention of intermediate causes"; on other
occasions he appealed to "the direct intervention of the First Cause," thus
transferring the issue from the jurisdiction of science to that of religion. He
used his *Principles of Geology* as a platform to oppose organic evolution, particularly the theories of the late French zoologist Jean-Baptiste Lamarck (1744–
1829), and he professed not to be "acquainted with any physical evidence by
which a geologist could shake the opinion generally entertained of the creation of man within the period generally assigned."[30]

The person most responsible for naturalizing the origin of species—and
thereby making the problem a scientific matter—was Lyell's younger friend
Charles Darwin (1809–1882). As early at 1838 Darwin had concluded that attributing the structure of animals to "the *will* of the Deity" was "no explanation—it
has not the character of a physical law & is therefore utterly useless." Within a
couple of decades many other students of natural history (or naturalists, as
they were commonly called) had reached the same conclusion. The British
zoologist Thomas H. Huxley, one of the most outspoken critics of the supernatural origin of species, came to see references to special creation as repre-
senting little more than a "specious mask for our ignorance." If the advocates
of special creation hoped to win a hearing for their views as science, he argued,
then they had an obligation to provide "some particle of evidence that the
existing species of animals and plants did originate in that way." Of course,
they could not. "We have not the slightest scientific evidence of such uncon-
ditional creative acts; nor, indeed, could we have such evidence," Huxley noted
in an 1856 lecture; "for, if a species were to originate under one's very eyes,
I know of no amount of evidence which would justify one in admitting it to be
a special creative act independent of the whole vast chain of causes and events
in the universe." To highlight the scientific vacuity of special creation, Darwin,

Huxley, and other naturalists took to asking provocatively whether "elemental atoms flash[ed] into living tissues? Was there vacant space one moment and an elephant apparent the next? Or did a laborious God mould out of gathered earth a body to then endue with life?" Creationists did their best to ignore such taunts.[31]

In his revolutionary essay *On the Origin of Species* (1859), Darwin aimed primarily "to overthrow the dogma of separate creations" and extend the domain of natural law throughout the organic world. He succeeded spectacularly—not because of his clever theory of natural selection (which few biologists thought sufficient to account for evolution), nor because of the voluminous evidence of organic development that he presented, but because, as one Christian reader bluntly put it, there was "literally nothing deserving the name of Science to put in its place." The American geologist William North Rice (1845–1928), an active Methodist, made much the same point. "The great strength of the Darwinian theory," he wrote in 1867, "lies in its coincidence with the general spirit and tendency of science. It is the aim of science to narrow the domain of the supernatural, by bringing all phenomena within the scope of natural laws and secondary causes."[32]

In reviewing the *Origin of Species* for the *Atlantic Monthly*, the Harvard botanist Asa Gray (1810–1888) forthrightly addressed the question of how he and his colleagues had come to feel so uncomfortable with a "supernatural" account of speciation. "Sufficient answer," he explained, "may be found in the activity of the human intellect, 'the delirious yet divine desire to know,' stimulated as it has been by its own success in unveiling the laws and processes of inorganic Nature." Minds that had witnessed the dramatic progress of the physical sciences in recent years simply could not "be expected to let the old belief about species pass unquestioned." Besides, he later explained, "the business of science is with the course of Nature, not with interruptions of it, which must rest on their own special evidence." Organic evolution, echoed his friend George Frederick Wright (1838–1921), a geologist and ordained Congregational minister (discussed at greater length in chapter 4), accorded with the fundamental principle of science, which states that "we are to press known secondary causes as far as they will go in explanation of facts. We are not to resort to an unknown (i.e., supernatural) cause for explanation of phenomena till the power of known causes has been exhausted. If we cease to observe this rule there is an end to all science and all sound sense."[33]

All of these statements welcoming Darwinism as a legitimate extension of natural law into the biological world came from Christian scientists of impeccable religious standing: Rice, a Methodist; Gray, a Presbyterian; Wright, a Congregationalist. Naturalism appealed to them, and to a host of other

Christians, in part because it served as a reliable means of discovering God's laws. As the Duke of Argyll, George Douglas Campbell (1823–1910), so passionately argued in his widely read book *The Reign of Law* (1867), the natural laws of science represented nothing less than manifestations of God's will. Christians could thus celebrate the rule of natural law as "the delight, the reward, the goal of Science." Even the evangelical theologian Benjamin B. Warfield (1851–1921), a leading defender of biblical inerrancy in turn-of-the-century America, argued that teleology (that is, belief in a divinely designed world) "is in no way inconsistent with . . . a complete system of natural causation."[34]

The adoption of naturalistic methods did not drive most nineteenth-century scientists into the arms of agnosticism or atheism. Long after God-talk had disappeared from the heartland of science, the vast majority of scientists, at least in the United States, remained Christians or theists. Their acceptance of naturalistic science sometimes prompted them, as Jon H. Roberts has pointed out, "to reassess the relationship between nature and the supernatural." For example, when the American naturalist Joseph LeConte (1821–1901), John's brother, moved from seeing species as being "introduced by the miraculous interference of a personal intelligence" to viewing them as the products of divinely ordained natural laws, he rejected all "anthropomorphic notions of Deity" for a God "ever-present, all-pervading, ever-acting." Nevertheless, LeConte, as we shall see in chapter 4, remained an active church-going Christian.[35]

The relatively smooth passage of naturalism turned nasty during the last third of the nineteenth century, when a noisy group of British scientists and philosophers, led by Huxley and the Irish physicist John Tyndall (1820–1893), began insisting that empirical, naturalistic science provided the *only* reliable knowledge of nature, humans, and society. Their anticlerical project, aimed at undermining the authority of the established Anglican church and dubbed "scientific naturalism" by Huxley, had little to do with naturalizing the practice of science but a lot to do with creating positions and influence for men such as themselves. They sought, as the historian Frank M. Turner has phrased it, "to expand the influence of scientific ideas for the purpose of secularizing society rather than for the goal of advancing science internally. Secularization was their goal; science, their weapon."[36]

For centuries men of science had typically gone out of their way to assure the religious of their peaceful intentions. In 1874, however, during his presidential address to the British Association for the Advancement of Science, Tyndall declared war on theology in the name of science. Men of science, he threatened, would "wrest from theology, the entire domain of cosmological theory. All schemes and systems which thus infringe upon the domain of science must, in so far as they do this submit to its control, and relinquish all thought of controlling it. Acting otherwise proved always disastrous in the past, and it is simply fatuous today." In contrast to most earlier naturalists, who had aspired simply to eliminate the supernatural from science while leaving religion alone, Tyndall and his crowd sought to root out supernaturalism from all phases of life and to replace traditional religion with a rational "religion of science." As described by one devotee, this secular substitute rested on "an implicit faith that by the methods of physical science, and by these methods alone, could be solved all the problems arising out of the relation of man to man and of man towards the universe." Despite the protests of Christians that the scientific naturalists were illegitimately trying to "associate naturalism and science in a kind of joint supremacy over the thoughts and consciences of mankind," the linkage of science and secularization colored the popular image of science for decades to come.[37]

The rise of the social sciences in the late nineteenth century in many ways reflected these imperialistic aims of the scientific naturalists. As moral philosophy fragmented into such new disciplines as psychology and sociology, many social scientists, insecure about their scientific standing, loudly pledged their allegiance not only to the naturalistic methods of science but to the philosophy of scientific naturalism as well. Most damaging of all, they turned religion itself into an object of scientific scrutiny. Having "conquered one field after another," noted an American psychologist at the time, science now entered "the most complex, the most inaccessible, and, of all, the most sacred domain—that of religion." Under the naturalistic gaze of social scientists the soul dissolved into nothingness, God faded into an illusion, and spirituality became, in the words of a British psychologist, " 'epiphenomenal,' a merely incidental phosphorescence, so to say, that regularly accompanies physical processes of a certain type and complexity." Here, at last, Christians felt compelled to draw the line.[38]

Reclaiming Science in the Name of God

By the closing years of the twentieth century naturalistic methods reigned supreme within the scientific community, and even devout Christian scientists scarcely dreamed of appealing to the supernatural when actually doing science. "Naturalism rules the secular academic world absolutely, which is bad enough," lamented one concerned layman. "What is far worse is that it rules much of the Christian world as well." Even the founders of scientific creationism, who brazenly rejected so much of the content of modern science, commonly ac-knowledged naturalism as the legitimate method of science. Because they nar-rowed the scope of science to exclude questions of origins, they typically limited it to the study of "present and reproducible phenomena" and left God and miracles to religion. Given the consensus on naturalism, it came as something of a surprise in the late 1980s and 1990s when a small group of so-called the-istic scientists and camp followers unveiled plans "to reclaim science in the name of God." They launched their offensive by attacking methodological nat-uralism as atheistic—or, as one partisan put it, "absolute rubbish"—and by asserting the presence of "intelligent design" (ID) in the universe.[39]

The roots of the intelligent design argument run deep in the soil of natural theology, but its recent flowering dates from the mid-1980s. The guru of ID, a Berkeley law professor named Phillip E. Johnson (b. 1940), initially sought to discredit evolution by demonstrating that it rested on the unwarranted as-sumption that naturalism was the only legitimate way of doing science. This bias, argued the Presbyterian lawyer, unfairly limited the range of possible explanations and ruled out any consideration of theistic factors. Johnson's writings inspired a Catholic biochemist at Lehigh University, Michael J. Behe (b. 1952), to speak out on the inadequacy of naturalistic evolution for ex-plaining molecular life. In his iconoclastic book, *Darwin's Black Box* (1996), Behe maintained that biochemistry had "pushed Darwin's theory to the limit...by opening the ultimate black box, the cell, thereby making possible our understanding of how life works." The "astonishing complexity of sub-cellular organic structure" led him to conclude—on the basis of scientific data, he asserted, "not from sacred books or sectarian beliefs"—that intelligent de-sign had been at work. "The result is so unambiguous and so significant that it must be ranked as one of the greatest achievements in the history of science," he gushed. "The discovery [of intelligent design] rivals those of Newton and Einstein, Lavoisier and Schroedinger, Pasteur and Darwin"—and by implica-tion elevated *its* discoverer to the pantheon of modern science.[40]

The partisans of ID hoped to spark "an intellectual revolution" that would rewrite the ground rules of science to allow the inclusion of supernatural ex-planations of phenomena. If Carl Sagan (1934–1996) and other reputable re-searchers could undertake a Search for Extra-Terrestrial Intelligence in the name of science, they reasoned, why should they be dismissed as unscientific for searching for evidence of intelligence in the biomolecular world? Should logical analogies fail to impress, ID advocates hoped that concerns for cul-tural diversity might win them a hearing. "In so pluralistic a society as ours," pleaded one spokesman, "why don't alternative views about life's origin and development have a legitimate place in academic discourse?"[41]

Personalities in the ongoing debates over evolution, creation, and in-telligent design, as depicted in a painting by Jody Nilsen that first appeared in the 1997 book issue of *Christianity Today* (April 28, 1997). Seated: Michael Behe and Charles Darwin. Standing (left to right): evolutionist Stephen Jay Gould, Richard Dawkins, the artist's father, the artist, and Phillip Johnson. Courtesy of Jody Nilsen.

This quixotic attempt to foment a methodological revolution in science created little stir within the mainstream scientific community. Most scientists either ignored it or dismissed it as "the same old creationist bullshit dressed up in new cloths." The British evolutionary biologist Richard Dawkins (b. 1941) wrote it off as "a pathetic cop-out of [one's] responsibilities as a scientist." Significantly, the most spirited debate over intelligent design and scientific naturalism took place among conservative Christian scholars. Having long since come to terms with doing science naturalistically, reported the editor of the evangelical journal *Perspectives on Science and Christian Faith*, "most evangelical observers—especially working scientists—[remained] deeply skeptical." Though supportive of a theistic worldview, they balked at being "asked to add 'divine agency' to their list of scientific working tools."[42]

As the editor's response so graphically illustrates, scientific naturalism of the methodological kind could—and did—coexist with orthodox Christianity. Despite the occasional efforts of unbelievers to use scientific naturalism to construct a world without God, it has retained strong Christian support down to the present. And well it might, for, as we have seen, scientific naturalism was largely made in Christendom by pious Christians. Although it possessed the potential to corrode religious beliefs—and sometimes did so—it flourished among Christian scientists who believed that God customarily achieved his ends through natural means.[43]

I began this chapter by asserting that nothing characterizes modern science better than its rejection of God in explaining the workings of nature. That statement is, I believe, true. It would be wrong, however, to conclude that the naturalization of science has secularized society generally. As late as the 1990s nearly 40 percent of American scientists continued to believe in a personal God, and, despite the immense cultural authority of naturalistic science, the overwhelming majority of Americans maintained an active belief in the super-natural. In the early years of the twenty-first century 46 percent of Americans affirm belief in the statement "God created man pretty much in his present form at one time within the last 10,000 years or so," and an additional 36 percent think that God has guided the process of evolution. Only 13 percent subscribe to purely naturalistic evolution. A whopping 82 percent of Americans trust "in the healing power of personal prayer," with 77 percent asserting that "God sometimes intervenes to cure people who have a serious illness." Science may have become godless, but the masses—and many scientists—privately cling tenaciously to the supernatural.[44]

3

Reading the Book of Nature through American Lenses

For centuries the book of nature rivaled the Bible as the most widely read work in North America. References to it abounded in the literature of the nineteenth century: in devotional tracts, scientific texts, marriage manuals, and memoirs.[1] Since at least the early eighteenth century, when the Puritan cleric Cotton Mather (1663–1728) of Boston published *The Christian Philosopher* (1721), the book of nature has been a common trope, especially, but not exclusively, in writings about science and religion. Mather attributed the metaphor to the fourth-century Christian bishop John Chrysostom, who, according to Mather's recollection, had mentioned "a *Twofold Book* of GOD; the Book of the *Creatures*, and the Book of the *Scriptures*." For Mather, the "Book of Nature" constituted a veritable "Publick Library" of information about the universe of natural things.[2]

Revelation for All

Throughout the next two centuries the phrase frequently adorned the titles of books: *Stray Leaves from the Book of Nature, The Two Books of Nature and Revelation Collated,* and *The Child's Book of Nature.*[3] It appeared on cheap tracts and on expensive leather-bound volumes devoted to "Bible lessons from the book of nature." Embossed on one of the latter was the most widely quoted biblical justification for assuming a natural revelation: "The heavens declare the glory of God" (Psalms 19:1).[4]

Although occasionally employed for nonreligious purposes—for example, to represent the antithesis of book learning—the metaphor most commonly appeared in religious works to designate God's revelation in the natural world. Despite its eighteenth-century connection with deism, this relationship elicited little concern. The Philadelphia Baptist cleric George D. Boardman (1828–1903) alluded to "a sort of secret feeling that to call Nature a Bible savors of irreverence" but assured readers that the God of Nature was in no way inferior to the God of Scripture and urged them to "take care lest our religiosity here be in fact a sort of infidelity under [the] guise of sanctity."[5]

The book of nature was no respecter of doctrine; it enjoyed popularity across the theological spectrum, wherever the flame of natural theology continued to flicker: in works by deists and Unitarians, Congregationalists and Presbyterians, Episcopalians and Lutherans, Baptists and Methodists, Mormons and Adventists.[6] The Seventh-day Adventist prophetess Ellen G. White (1827–1915) used it over five dozen times in her various writings. According to the godmother of creation science, "Both the book of nature and the written word make us acquainted with God by teaching us something of the wise and beneficent laws through which he works.... The things of nature speak to man of his Creator's love."[7]

Darwinists and anti-Darwinists, scientists and theologians, liberals and conservatives all found the book of nature useful, especially in interpreting ambiguous passages in the Bible.[8] In 1885 the prominent Congregational clergyman Henry Ward Beecher (1813–1887) devoted a Sunday-morning sermon to "The Two Revelations," which he playfully referred to as "the Old Testament and the New" and in which he called for a closer reading of "the book of the divine revelation of nature." Directing his listeners' attention to "the literature of the rocks written by the hand of God all over the earth," this leading voice among liberal American Protestants marveled at the "indifference with which good men have regarded this stupendous revelation of the ages past, and especially at the assaults made by Christian men upon scientific men who are bringing to light the long-hidden record of God's revelation in the material world." Although reared a Calvinist, he confessed that "the only religious feelings or impressions I had were those which were excited in my mind through the unconscious influence of God through nature." For liberals such as Beecher, the book of nature assumed an authority even greater than Scripture.[9]

Beecher's claim of neglect showed an abysmal ignorance of contemporary apologetical literature, written by men of science and men of the cloth

Interior of Plymouth Church in Mr. Beecher's day

The Reverend Henry Ward Beecher, who endorsed "The Two Revelations" in a sermon in 1885, preaching from the pulpit of his huge Congregational church in Brooklyn. From *Henry Ward Beecher as His Friends Saw Him* (1904), courtesy of the Department of Special Collections, Memorial Library, University of Wisconsin–Madison.

alike.[10] The ultraconservative Rochester minister and sometime mathematician Herbert W. Morris (1818–1897), one of the nation's best-selling authors on science and religion, defended the notion of two revelations with fervor equal to Beecher's. In demanding that the "days" of Genesis 1 be taken as literal twenty-four-hour periods, he repeatedly drew attention to God's "two great Volumes," nature and the Bible. "While in the Bible we have a *verbal* revelation of the wisdom and power and goodness of God," he declared, "in material Nature we have a *pictorial* revelation of the same."[11]

The American geologist John Wesley Powell (1834–1902), a Methodist preacher's son, vividly testified to the power of this pictorial revelation after exploring the Colorado River and its awe-inspiring Grand Canyon. A skilled observer of nature, he described the strata revealed in the rocky cliffs as an open "book," so clearly written that he could read it on the run. "One might imagine that this was intended for the library of the gods; and it was," he raved. "The shelves are not for books, but form the stony leaves of one great book. He who would read the language of the universe may dig out letters here and there, and with them spell the words, and read, in a slow and imperfect way, but still so as to understand a little, the story of creation."[12]

Just as Cotton Mather sometimes substituted the synonym "Publick Library" for the book of nature, nineteenth-century writers employed such phrases as "the Bible of the creation," "the Creation Archive," "this illuminated missal of the heavens," "a Natural Bible," "God's Unwritten Word," "a letter direct from the Father's own hand," and "elder Scripture writ by God's own hand."[13] Unlike Mather, however, most Americans showed little interest in the history of the metaphor. No one mentioned Galileo. The Reverend Boardman alluded to both Thomas Brown's *Religio Medici* (1642) and Bishop Joseph Butler's *The Analogy of Religion, Natural and Revealed, to the Constitution and Course of Nature* (1736), but such historical attributions were rare.[14]

Opposition to the use of the metaphor seems practically nonexistent, although the aging Mark Twain (1835–1910) insisted that "the Book of Nature tells us distinctly that God cares not a rap for us—nor for any living creature." Skeptics such as Robert Ingersoll (1833–1899) aimed their anti-Christian artillery at the "mistakes of Moses," not at natural theology.[15] Even the chemist-historian John William Draper (1811–1882), author of the notorious *History of the Conflict between Religion and Science* (1874), defended the integrity of the book of nature, arguing that for science "the volume of inspiration is the book of Nature."[16]

Modernists and Fundamentalists

By the early twentieth century the popularity of the book-of-nature metaphor was closely linked to the fate of natural theology. And in the years after the Great War the prospects for natural theology in the dominant Protestant culture of America appeared dim indeed. On the left end of the theological spectrum, liberals and modernists, dominant among the cultural elite since the late nineteenth century, followed the German theologians Friedrich Schleiermacher (1768–1834) and Albrecht Ritschl (1822–1889) in stressing religious experience and moral judgments over revelation, whether general or special. Having embraced evolution and abandoned a transcendent God for an immanent force, these liberals saw Darwinism as having undermined the traditional notion of divine design in nature, though they did not repudiate the notion of natural revelation in the laws of nature.

In the center were the so-called neo-orthodox, who rose to prominence in America during the interwar years. They restored the notion of a (nonpropositional) supernatural revelation but repudiated the idea that knowledge of God could be discovered in nature. Karl Barth (1886–1968), the Swiss doyen of neo-orthodoxy, described himself as "an avowed opponent of all natural theology," who, following the sixteenth-century Protestant reformers Martin Luther and John Calvin, saw "both the church and human salvation founded on the Word of God *alone*, on God's *revelation in Jesus Christ.*"[17] On the right stood the evangelicals, including the militant wing that came to be known as fundamentalists. Although the evangelicals no doubt constituted a majority of church-going Americans, their cultural authority was waning, or so they feared. Taking the Bible "to be the inspired Word of God ... inerrant, infallible, and God's revealed will for men ... the only rule for Faith and the only guide for practice," these conservatives seemed among the least likely to recommend reading the book of nature.[18]

Counter to expectations, however, no group did more in the twentieth century to keep the book of nature in circulation than the fundamentalists and their evangelical brethren. The fundamentalists launched their antimodernist movement with the publication of a series of pamphlets, *The Fundamentals* (1910–1915), defending orthodox Christianity. Most of the essays in these booklets dealt with nonscientific issues, but one article, on "Science and Christian Faith" by the Scottish divine James Orr (1844–1913), assured readers that, contrary to the loud assertions of John William Draper and Andrew Dickson White (1832–1918), science and the Bible were not in conflict. "Each book of God's writing," Orr declared, "reflects light upon the pages of the other, but neither contradicts the other's essential testimony."[19] Despite their growing focus on evolution as the archenemy of Christianity, fundamentalists, from the intellectual J. Gresham Machen (1881–1937) of Princeton Theological Seminary to the bombastic William Jennings Bryan (1860–1925), continued to preach this message (though neither Machen nor Bryan liked being called fundamentalists). While insisting on the uniqueness of the biblical revelation, Machen, for example, used its own authority—"The heavens declare the glory of God; and the firmament showeth his handiwork"—to confirm "the revelation of God in nature."[20] Bryan, who bears more responsibility than anyone for instigating the antievolution agitation of the 1920s, denied any conflict between truth "in the book of nature" and in "the Book of Books," for both came from God.[21]

American fundamentalists may have been united in their opposition to evolution but they remained deeply divided over the correct reading of the first chapters of Genesis. The most prominent exegetes from the three main hermeneutical camps all drew on the book of nature to assist with interpreting the Bible. Some of the movement's leaders, including Bryan, accommodated the evidence of the antiquity of life on earth by interpreting the "days" of Genesis 1 as eons, not solar days. William Bell Riley (1861–1947), the high-profile Baptist pastor from Minneapolis who founded the World's Christian Fundamentals Association, also defended this so-called day-age theory, in part because of the agreement between "the books of Nature and Grace, specifically the pages of geology," which clearly required a great deal of time. Although he expressed total confidence in the "perfect agreement between God's Word and God's Work," he feared that "the dust of false reasoning" might impair the vision of readers, making it difficult for them "to see the meaning of the open book of Nature."[22]

Other fundamentalists, perhaps the majority, followed Thomas Chalmers (see chapter 1) and the *Scofield Reference Bible* (1909) in accommodating the facts of geology and paleontology by inserting a gap lasting "an incalculable span of time" between the *two* creations described in the first verses of Genesis 1, the first "in the beginning," the second associated with the appearance of Adam and Eve. One of the most energetic advocates of this exegesis was the flamboyant Presbyterian evangelist and self-described research scientist Harry Rimmer (1890–1952), who affirmed belief in God's "two revelations," the first "in the page of nature," the second in the Bible. Because "heathen" nations in possession of the former but without the latter engaged in "abominable practices," it was clear to Rimmer that "the revelation of God in nature" was both inadequate and inferior to the Bible.[23]

Although most fundamentalists who wrote about Genesis during the first two-thirds of the twentieth century embraced either the day-age or gap interpretation of Genesis, a third view, advocated by the self-trained Seventh-day Adventist geologist George McCready Price (1870–1963, discussed in chapter 4), attracted considerable attention. Unlike most fundamentalists, Price, described by the editor of *Science* as "the principal scientific authority of the Fundamentalists," adamantly rejected the evidence of geological ages and hence the necessity of adopting either the day-age or gap theories to accommodate them. Instead, inspired by Ellen G. White's divine "testimonies" and an ultraliteral reading of the Mosaic record, he squeezed earth history into about six thousand years and collapsed virtually the entire geological column into the year of Noah's flood. This scheme, called "flood geology," would by the 1970s provide the intellectual foundation for "creation science."[24]

Finding two revelations—those of Moses and White—insufficient to buttress his radical scheme, Price invoked a third revelation: the book of nature. To resolve the apparent contradiction between science and Scripture, he urged God's people to "familiarize themselves with the truths now available from God's oldest testament, the book of nature," by which he meant his own theory of flood geology: "The only kind of record that could possibly prove an original creation would have to come from nature itself. Here is something that we can trust, if we can only read the record correctly; for nature itself is from God, and it is conceivable that God Himself might have planned all things in such a way that by studying nature man might himself become convinced of the truth of an original creation."[25] In a book called *Back to the Bible; or, The New Protestantism* (1916), Price ironically chided other Protestants for ignoring natural theology and not using "the Bible as a guide in the study of the book of nature": "Were it not for the blight of sin, nature would still be a perfect revealing of God's character and his law. And were it not for the beclouding and bewildering influence of sin upon our own faculties, we might even yet read unaided the message of our Father's love in cloud, and cell, and rock."[26]

As surprising as it may seem to those who view fundamentalists as distrustful of nature and science, Price devoted an entire volume to *God's Two Books; or, Plain Facts about Evolution, Geology, and the Bible* (1911), in which he argued for "the absolute harmony between the book of nature and God's written Word." Just as the Protestant reformers of the sixteenth century had "vindicated the Bible as the supreme spiritual authority, and restored it to its rightful place as the guide of the church," so Price aspired to "vindicate before the world the harmony of his two books" by showing the perfect correspondence between flood geology, revealed in the book of nature, and the revelation given in the first chapters of Genesis.[27]

The cover of George McCready Price's *God's Two Books: or, Plain Facts about Evolution, Geology, and the Bible* (1911), courtesy of the Department of Special Collections, Memorial Library, University of Wisconsin–Madison.

Such enthusiasm among fundamentalists for the book of nature did prompt occasional words of warning. Leander S. Keyser (1856–1937), the leading Lutheran fundamentalist, drew attention to the deist connection in explaining why some Christians emphasized the need for special revelation. "That God may be partly known by His works, no Christian would pretend to deny," he admitted, adding that "it would stand to reason that the God who originally 'created the heavens and the earth,' would reveal Himself, at least to some extent, therein. The Bible itself frequently appeals to nature as a proof of God's existence and greatness." Keyser cited not only Psalm 19:1 but Romans 1:20: "For the invisible things of Him from the creation of the world are clearly seen, being understood by the things that are made, even His eternal power and God head; so that they are without excuse."[28]

Similarly, Frank Lewis Marsh (1899–1992), an Adventist student of Price's and one of the earliest creationists to earn a graduate degree in biology, began to fret as he saw creationist friends deviate from the faith as a result of studying nature. "The creationistic philosophy," he warned, "does not admit an open-minded study of nature in the matter of origins.... God knew that a nature deranged by sin would require a guidebook. The Bible is that book, and through a careful study of its pages we vision the real harmony and significance of the things of nature as they portray God's love for us." It is significant that although Marsh believed that the Bible and nature served as complementary sources for the special creationist, he refrained (as far as I can tell) from referring to nature as a book.[29]

In 1941 a small group of evangelical men of science, encouraged by the Moody Bible Institute, organized the American Scientific Affiliation (ASA) to produce "accurate" information on the relationship of science and religion. By midcentury a number of fundamentalist and evangelical Christians were entering scientific fields, eager to harmonize their religious beliefs with what they were learning in science classrooms. Affiliation members signed a statement committing themselves to two revelations: "I believe in the whole Bible as originally given, to be the inspired word of God, the only unerring guide of faith and conduct. Since God is the Author of this Book, as well as the Creator and Sustainer of the physical world about us, I cannot conceive of discrepancies between statements in the Bible and the real facts of science." Members only occasionally referred to the "book of nature" as such, but they commonly wrote about the "Bible of Nature" and the "Book of Works," "the natural revelation of God" and "His revelation in creation." They often referred to God as "the Author of nature."[30]

Arguably no one influenced ASA members on their views of revelation more than the Baptist theologian and philosopher of science Bernard Ramm

(1916–1992). Searching for a middle way between the "hyper-orthodoxy" of fundamentalists such as Price, which allegedly made "the words of God and the work of God clash," and neo-orthodoxy and religious liberalism, which simply ignored science, he argued for a "very positive harmonization between science and evangelicalism." "God cannot contradict His speech in Nature by His speech in Scripture," he insisted. "If the Author of Nature and [of] Scripture are the same God, then the two books of God must eventually recite the same story."[31]

As the ASA was just getting off the ground, the Reverend Irwin Moon (1907–1986) of the Moody Institute of Science was producing a hugely successful series of scientific films aimed at showing the harmony between God's two books. Typical was the film *God of Creation*, released in 1946, with the ASA's seal of approval. As the historian James Gilbert has documented, in the years after World War II Americans flocked to see it; in 1947 and 1948

The Reverend Irwin Moon dramatically demonstrating the nature of electricity in one of his Sermons from Science. Courtesy of Joe Cataio and the Moody Bible Institute Library.

alone an estimated 1.4 million people viewed it, and twenty-four hundred became Christians as a result. The United States Air Force adopted it (and three other Moody films) to show to servicemen around the globe.[32]

Evidentialism versus Presuppositionalism

By the second half of the century fundamentalist apologists, once fairly comfortable with the notion of two revelations, were growing increasingly divided over evidentialism, which allowed for natural theology, and presuppositionalism, which held "that the self-attesting triune God revealed in Scripture is the authority in all things." Influenced by the conservative Dutch Calvinist Herman Dooyeweerd (1894–1977) and the Orthodox Presbyterian Cornelius Van Til (1895–1987), an American, presuppositionalists called for the rejection of all nonbiblical assumptions, including ones based on reason and nature, in the construction of an acceptable theology. Extreme presuppositionalists, such as the Christian Reconstructionist Rousas John Rushdoony (1916–2001), advocated a theocratic government that would reinstitute the death penalty for such Old Testament offenses as sodomy and Sabbath breaking and argued that "only on the presupposition of Christian theism is a valid science possible." Not surprisingly, presuppositionalists did not often refer positively to "the book of nature."[33]

In an unusually happy marriage of evidentialism and presuppositionalism, two fundamentalists, John C. Whitcomb Jr. (b. 1924), an Old Testament scholar, and Henry M. Morris (1918–2006), a civil engineer, in 1961 brought out *The Genesis Flood: The Biblical Record and Its Scientific Implications*. As self-described believers in "the verbal inerrancy of Scripture," they began their investigation of the Flood story by presupposing "that the Bible is the infallible word of God, verbally inspired in the original autographs." In contrast to Christian apologists who for centuries had reinterpreted the Bible in the light of modern science, they adopted the practice "of letting the Bible speak for itself and then trying to understand the geological data in the light of its teachings." While conceding that "God has given us two revelations, one in nature and one of the Bible," they maintained that "special revelation supersedes natural revelation, for it is only by means of special revelation that we can interpret aright the world about us."[34]

Thus on the major issues the coauthors stood united, but Whitcomb inclined toward presuppositionalism whereas Morris embraced evidentialism. On the basis of biblical authority, including Psalm 19:1, Whitcomb admitted that "God has given to men a revelation of Himself in the material university";

thus he accepted natural revelation. But he adamantly rejected the "Double-Revelation Theory," the version of natural theology held by believers in "the Bible of nature." For him the character and purposes of God could be found only through the Bible, the reliability of which he accepted on the basis of its own claims rather than on the basis of external evidence.[35] Having committed himself to *biblical* creationism, he strongly resisted the shift to *scientific* creationism, made by Morris and others about 1970 to squeeze creationism into the public schools of America.[36]

Morris, too, rejected the double-revelation theory, because he believed that it required theologians to defer to scientists in matters of natural fact; but he nevertheless believed that "God's revelation in nature" and "His revelation in Scripture" could be studied independently, if priority were given to the Scriptures. He devoted an entire section of one of his many books to the "controversial" subject of "The Book of God in the Heavens," opening it with Psalm 19:1. Humans, he speculated, had learned about God, including the plan of salvation, from the book of nature "long before there were any written Scriptures."[37]

The intellectual excitement in the fundamentalist community generated by *The Genesis Flood* led, in 1963, to the formation of the Creation Research Society (CRS), a group of flood geologists and young-earth creationists disaffected with the ASA. Although biblical claims (and sometimes personal conviction) prevented members of the CRS from denying God's revelation in nature, they instinctively subordinated nature to the Bible, not the other way around, as had been so common in the nineteenth century. According to the CRS statement of belief, "The Bible is the written Word of God, and because it is inspired throughout, all its assertions are historically and scientifically true in all the original autographs." Nevertheless, some of these creationists warmly embraced the book of nature. Morris, as we have seen, believed that God had revealed himself in nature; the geneticists William J. Tinkle (1892–1981) and Walter Lammerts (1904–1996), the two principal founders of the society, had written in 1948: "Since God is the author of both the Bible and nature, it is evident that there can be no discrepancies between them." In an early volume of the *Creation Research Society Quarterly* Tinkle defended natural theology against disapproving theologians. And a young University of Groningen contributor to the journal, Nicolaas A. Rupke (b. 1944), found both "the Work of God (Nature)" and "the Word of God (Scripture)" testifying to the truth of cataclysmal sedimentation.[38]

The prosperity of creation science prompted one critical scholar, Roland Mushat Frye (1922–2005), to call in the early 1980s for a revival of the belief in "the two books of God": "the book of God's word in Scripture, which concerns the ultimate nature and destiny of humanity, and the book of God's works in nature, which deals with the conditions of the created order." Apparently unaware that many creationists were themselves endorsing the two-books doctrine, he suggested that it needed "to be revived, disseminated, and applied in our time" as a corrective to the creationists' insistence on "a literal or semi-literal reading of the parabolic accounts of creation in the first chapter of Genesis."[39]

As I have suggested, the book-of-nature metaphor hardly needed resuscitation (except among creationists inclined to presuppositionalism). Evangelical scientists continued to invoke it in justification of their vocation, and evangelical preachers sermonized about it.[40] (The latter found sanction for its use in the still-published writings of the famous nineteenth-century English preacher Charles H. Spurgeon [1834–1892], who urged young ministers to draw on natural history in their sermons to illustrate the Scriptures, thus "explaining one of God's books by another volume that He has written.")[41] Liberals, too, joined the choir. One of them, Philip Hefner, the Lutheran editor of *Zygon: Journal of Religion and Science*, promoted the "Two Books" idea by arguing that "the message or communication that we receive from nature is parallel to the communication that we receive from our canonical Sacred Scriptures."[42] By the late 1980s and 1990s the billionaire philanthropist Sir John M. Templeton (b. 1912) was pouring millions of dollars into demonstrating that the universe, the "book of God's works," "does indeed have meaning and purpose, and we can *read the message*."[43] And Roman Catholics continued the Galilean tradition of venerating "the Book of Nature."[44]

Intelligent Design

The growing popularity in the 1990s of the intelligent design (ID) movement—associated with the Berkeley law professor Phillip Johnson (b. 1940) and led by the biochemist Michael J. Behe (b. 1952) and the mathematician-philosopher William A. Dembski (b. 1960)—gave a big boost to natural theology in some conservative circles. These critics of Darwinism and naturalism argued for setting aside the divisive effort of deciphering the Mosaic account of creation and focusing instead on the empirical evidence of design in nature, especially what Behe liked to call "irreducible complexity." Their formulation of design "as a scientific theory" led, in the opinion of one ID theorist, to "an explosive resurgence" of interest in the argument from design.[45]

The shift in attention away from Genesis-based young-earth creationism and to natural theology might have prompted an equally explosive adoption of the book-of-nature metaphor. Indeed, one clerical admirer of intelligent design, drawing on the Christian tradition of viewing "the created world itself as a kind of writing, a text for man's study," has maintained that "the discoveries of the pure sciences are forcing them [the ID theorists] to return to the ancient thesis that the structure of the world forms a kind of writing. The current study of chemistry, biology, and astrophysics testifies that the information within the universe presents us with a text."[46] However, a quick perusal of the canonical ID texts turns up little use of the book-of-nature metaphor, perhaps because it is too literary—or obviously religious—for the writers' scientific tastes.[47] After nearly two millennia as a stand-in for natural theology, the phrase may be losing some of its evocative power, but its resilience through the ages should caution us against premature declarations of its demise.

4

Experiencing Evolution

Psychological Responses to the Claims
of Science and Religion

In the early twentieth century the psychologist Sigmund Freud (1856–
1939) noted that science had already inflicted on humanity "two
great outrages upon its naïve self-love": the first, associated with the
sixteenth-century astronomer Nicholas Copernicus, "when it realized that our earth was not the centre of the universe, but only a tiny
speck in a world-system of a magnitude hardly conceivable"; the
second, associated with Charles Darwin, "when biological research
robbed man of his peculiar privilege of having been specially created,
and relegated him to a descent from the animal world." Conceit-
edly, Freud went on to observe that "man's craving for grandiosity
is now suffering the third and most bitter blow," this time at the
hands of psychoanalysts such as himself, who were showing that
humans behaved under the influence of unconscious urges.[1]

Freud need not have worried so much about the mental suffer-
ings inflicted by modern science. Copernicanism had indeed dis-
lodged humans from the center of the cosmos, but in the Aristotelian
world the center was the lowliest place in the universe; there is little evidence that humans felt diminished by being hurled into space.[2]
Psychoanalysis never achieved the prominence its founder dreamed
of, so never caused the trauma he anticipated. But what of Darwinism? How much emotional distress did the revelation of ancestral
apes cause humans? How often did their encounters with evolution produce spiritual crises? And what was the nature of the crises
that occurred?

Two of these queries can be dealt with quickly. Darwin's indelicate announcement in *The Descent of Man* (1871), that humans had "descended from a hairy quadruped, furnished with a tail and pointed ears," indeed attracted considerable attention. And some conservative Christians (as we saw in chapter 1) did express abhorrence at the notion of having apes for ancestors. There is no reason to believe, however, that diehard creationists ever took human evolution seriously enough to be more than rhetorically distressed.[3]

More revealing of genuine concern was the confession of the fundamentalist A. C. Dixon (1854–1925) to feeling "a repugnance to the idea that an ape or an orang outang was my ancestor." But even he promised not to let the "humiliating fact" stand in the way of accepting human evolution, "if proved." The Southern Baptist New Testament scholar A. T. Robertson (1863–1934) put the choice somewhat more colorfully in stating his openness to theistic evolution: "I can stand it if the monkeys can." Despite lots of humor about routing "the biological baboon boosters" and shaking "the monkey out of the cocoanut tree," I have found no evidence that the prospect of having monkeys for uncles caused emotional distress anywhere near the level of that created by biblical and philosophical concerns.[4]

Somewhat more surprising, given the widespread assumption that evolution played a major role in the secularization of Western thought, is the relative infrequency with which evolution became implicated in the loss of religious faith. Fairly typical of intellectuals who rejected Christianity was the experience of Charles Darwin himself. By the time he returned to England from the voyage of the *Beagle*, he was entertaining doubts about the reliability of the Bible. He tried to stanch these doubts, but, despite persistent effort, he reported in his autobiography that "disbelief crept over me at a very slow rate," causing "no distress." Instead, he came to find Christianity revolting: "I can indeed hardly see how anyone ought to wish Christianity to be true; for if so the plain language of the text seems to show that the men who do not believe, and this would include my Father, Brother and almost all my best friends, will be everlastingly punished. And this is a damnable doctrine." As these words suggest, and as the historian James Moore has shown, Darwin finally abandoned Christianity, not primarily because of his developing views on evolution but for moral concerns awakened by the death of his kind but unbelieving father in 1848 and the passing of his favorite child, lovable, delightful ten-year-old Annie, two and a half years later. How, reasoned the distraught father, could an omnipotent, benevolent God let such a perfect child suffer so much and die so young? Too broken even to attend Annie's funeral, Darwin turned his back on God.[5]

A number of years ago the sociologist Susan Budd studied the biographies of 150 British secularists or freethinkers who lived between 1850 and 1950, hoping to test the prevailing view that "the effects of developing scientific knowledge, especially Darwinism, and of the higher criticism have been... mainly responsible for weakening belief in the literal truth of scriptural religion for some, and for forcing others to abandon belief in God altogether." She discovered that only two of her subjects "mentioned having read Darwin or Huxley *before* their loss of faith." A few years back I examined the reactions of eighty prominent nineteenth-century American scientists to Darwinism and found no evidence to suggest that a single one of them severed his religious ties as a direct result of his encounter with evolution.[6] It is no wonder that in writing the sensational Victorian novel *Robert Elsmere* (1888), in which the clerical hero experiences a crisis of faith and abandons Christianity, Mrs. Humphry Ward (1851–1920) said nothing about Darwin or evolution. Although she had initially intended to invoke the "converging pressure of science & history," she decided in the end that it would be truer to the times to feature only the latter.[7]

Even personal testimonies about the corrosive effects of evolution on religious beliefs cannot always be taken at face value. The Victorian writer Samuel Butler (1835–1902) supposedly told a friend "that the *Origin of Species* had completely destroyed his belief in a personal God." But, as one of his biographers pointed out, "He had... already quarreled with his father [a cleric], refused to be ordained, thrown up his Cambridge prospects, and emigrated to New Zealand as a sheep-farmer before Darwin's book came out." He quit praying the night before he left for the Antipodes.[8]

In this chapter I explore the emotional experiences of some of the people who *did* suffer spiritual crises associated with Darwinism. Most historians of evolution and Christianity—indeed of science and religion generally—have focused on intellectual issues and have largely ignored or downplayed experiential factors; they have treated spiritual and emotional crises as mere "decorative episodes" in the lives of their subjects. But, as Robert J. Richards has argued in one of the few historical studies to highlight the importance of psychological crises in the lives of scientists, emotions have often been as significant as ideas.[9] To identify as clearly as possible some of the actual roles that evolution played in creating and resolving spiritual crises, I examine how four scientific Americans, who together nearly span the spectrum of reactions to evolution, wrestled with the teachings of Christ and Darwin: Joseph LeConte, George Frederick Wright, J. Peter Lesley, and George McCready Price.[10]

(Left) Joseph LeConte. Courtesy of University Archives, University of California, Berkeley. (Right) J. Peter Lesley. From *Biographical Memoirs of the National Academy of Sciences* 8 (1919).

(Left) George Frederick Wright in the early 1880s. Courtesy of the Oberlin College Archives. (Right) George McCready Price in 1906. Courtesy of the late Molleurus Couperus.

Joseph LeConte (1823–1901)

Joseph LeConte was arguably the most influential—and certainly one of the most interesting—American harmonizers of evolution and religion in late nineteenth-century America. His widely quoted definition of evolution as "(1) continuous *progressive change*, (2) *according to certain laws*, (3) and by means of *resident forces*" served for years as a standard. More of a popularizer than an original investigator, he took great pride in showing that "evolution is entirely consistent with a rational theism." But this achievement did not come without a struggle; for decades he repeatedly "wrestled in agony . . . with [the] demon of materialism."[11]

Young LeConte grew up in an "intensely religious" community in rural Georgia. His pious Presbyterian mother died when he was a toddler; his father, a medically trained plantation owner and unbeliever, passed away when Joseph was fourteen. The death of his father "outside the pale of the church" distressed him greatly and precipitated "a very great crisis," followed by a classic conversion to orthodox Christianity. For a time, while attending the University of Georgia, he considered becoming a Presbyterian minister. Instead, he studied medicine, then apprenticed himself to Louis Agassiz (1807–1873) at Harvard's Lawrence Scientific School. Early in his career he taught at both the universities of Georgia and South Carolina.[12]

In about the mid-1850s LeConte first encountered the "dragon of materialism," in the form of August Comte's positivism, which held that only physical phenomena were knowable, that God-talk was meaningless. As an ardent believer in the reliability of human reason, LeConte stood briefly on the "brink of the edge of materialism," only to pull back in horror when he recognized the full implications of this "degrading" philosophy, "which destroys [man's] spirituality, his immortality, every noble upward striving of his nature." For the rest of his life, he shunned materialism, a term he used synonymously with atheism and agnosticism.[13]

In 1861 LeConte experienced a life-altering loss: the death of his two-year-old daughter, Josie, from whooping cough. During her last hours, he cuddled her small body, wracked by spasms. So traumatic was her passing, it left him "prostrated" for several days. Decades later he could still felt the raw pain: "Little Josie, dear little Josie! I can not even mention her name without the tenderest emotions. She was the most beautiful child we ever had, with that rare combination of flaxen hair and dark eyes. Alas! We lost her just two years later. The light, the sunlight, the spiritual light seemed to have gone out of my house." As we have seen, Darwin's loss of his unbelieving, but Christ-like, physician father followed by the death of his favorite daughter had destroyed his faith in Christianity. Virtually identical events produced in LeConte a lifelong obsession with immortality. Late in life he was still reassuring himself of the impossibility "that the object of such love [Josie] can be other than immortal."[14]

By the early 1870s LeConte had passed through the trauma of the Civil War and relocated at the new University of California. In 1873, in a series of published lectures on religion and science, he announced that he had become a "reluctant evolutionist" of the theistic kind. Adopting the age-old argument (described in chapter 3) that God had revealed himself in *two divine books*," nature and Scripture, LeConte repeatedly alluded to the "distress and doubt" he had suffered as "one who has all his life sought with passionate ardor the truth revealed in the one book, but who clings no less passionately to the hopes revealed in the other":

> During my whole active life, I have stood just where the current runs swiftest. I confess to you, that, in my earlier life, I have struggled almost in despair with this swift current. I confess I have some-times wrestled in an agony with this fearful doubt, with this demon of materialism, with this cold philosophy whose icy breath withers all the beautiful flowers and blasts all the growing fruit of hu-manity. This dreadful doubt has haunted me like a spectre, which would not always down at my bidding.

He had come to reject the idea of "the creation of species *directly* and without secondary agencies and processes," but he believed that "the real cause of evolution" remained unknown.[15]

By the end of the decade he had evolved into a "thorough and enthusi-astic," if somewhat unorthodox, evolutionist. In what he regarded as "one of the most important" of his scientific contributions, he proposed in 1877 a theory of "paroxysmal" evolution, which correlated "rapid changes of physical conditions and correspondingly rapid movement in evolution." That same year he gave the first of many talks sharing his insights into the relationship between evolution and religion. Harmonizing religion and evolution, includ-ing the evolution of the human body, quickly became his great mission, his divine calling: "It is, indeed, glad tidings of great joy which shall be to all peoples. Woe is me, if I preach not the Gospel." His efforts along this line culminated in the publication of his oft-reprinted *Evolution and Its Relation to Religious Thought* (1888).[16]

To mitigate the "difficulty and distress" of coming to terms with evolution, LeConte insisted on two conditions: that it not promote godless materialism and that it not endanger his faith in immortality, "the most dearly cherished and most universal of all human beliefs." Thus he claimed not only that evolution and materialism were entirely distinct but that there was "not a single philosophical question connected with our highest and dearest religious and spiritual interests that is fundamentally affected, or even put in any new light, by the theory of evolution." On this point LeConte may have protested too much. Although it is difficult at this late date to sort out what orthodox doctrines he ditched because of evolution and which ones he abandoned for other reasons, we do know that by the last decade of his life he had come to reject the idea of a transcendent God, the notion of the Bible as "a direct revelation," the divinity of Christ, the existence of heaven and of the devil, the efficacy of intercessory prayer, the special creation and fall of humans, and the plan of salvation. Only the existence of an imminent, pantheistic God and personal immortality survived. Yet despite toying at times with leaving organized religion, till the end LeConte remained a nominal Presbyterian and an ecumenical Christian.[17]

In his early years as a harmonizer LeConte insisted that because science could "say absolutely nothing" about the soul and immortality, the field remained "open for evidence from any quarter, and of any degree." By the 1890s, however, he had concluded that science, particularly the doctrine of evolution, could indeed say something—and something positive—about immortality. "Do you not see," he asked fervently, *without immortality, the whole purpose is balked—the whole process of cosmic evolution is futile.* Shall God be so long and at so great pains to achieve a *spirit,* capable of communing with Him, and then allow it to lapse again into nothingness?" Besides, there was always Josie to think about. Even after Joseph's death his wife, Bessie, would write him letters on their birthdays and wedding anniversary. "How happy you must be dear to be with so many loved ones," she wrote tearfully on one of these occasions. Among those she mentioned was "our little Josie."[18]

LeConte's crises—especially those brought on by the loss of his daughter and his encounter with materialism—made it psychologically impossible for him to accept any nontheistic version of evolution, including Darwin's own. At the same time these traumatic experiences facilitated his identification with the emotional and theological needs of other liberal Christians struggling with evolution and thus helped in his becoming the reconciler of evolution and religion par excellence.

J. Peter Lesley (1819–1903)

During the last quarter of the nineteenth century the distinguished geologist and sometime minister J. Peter Lesley ranked among the most prominent scientists in America who rejected Darwinism; yet his experience, which included spiritual crises and mental breakdowns, remains little known. This is especially surprising because, unlike most antievolutionists, Lesley disliked orthodox Christianity even more than Darwinism and was among the first Americans to make the case for human evolution.

As a religiously devout youth who memorized most of the Bible, he studied at the University of Pennsylvania in anticipation of entering the Presbyterian ministry. But the first of numerous bouts of ill health, physical and mental, led to a postponement of his seminary studies, while he spent a few years as an assistant on the Geological Survey of Pennsylvania, headed by Henry Darwin Rogers (1808–1866). Hoping to become a missionary to rural Pennsylvania, he attended Princeton Theological Seminary for three years, then spent some time in Europe, exposing himself to German rationalism and higher criticism of the Bible. He returned with his faith pretty much intact and began working as a colporteur among the poor German settlers in the hills of Pennsylvania.[19]

The strenuous labor undermined his health, and after two years he rejoined the geological survey. By 1848, having received a ministerial license from the Presbytery of Philadelphia, he was pastoring a Congregational church in Milton, Massachusetts, near Boston, where he came under the influence of Unitarians, including his wife-to-be, Susan Lyman. Under circumstances that remain vague, the Presbytery charged him with harboring "infidel" sentiments and "denying the Inspiration of the Scriptures." He adamantly denied being an infidel but confessed to putting the truths of science above the teaching of the church. In May 1849 the Presbytery withdrew his license to preach. His "theological troubles" split the church and exacerbated his poor health. In 1851 he left the ministry yet again and returned to the geological survey. However, he soon developed an almost pathological hatred of his boss, Rogers. Finally, Lesley's behavior became so erratic and his temper so terrible that Rogers fired him, fearing that "insanity is evidently growing upon him."[20] For some time thereafter Lesley struggled to earn a living, but he eventually found financial success as a consulting geologist.[21]

Shortly after the end of the Civil War Lesley returned to Boston to deliver the prestigious Lowell Lectures, on "Man's Origin and Destiny, Sketched from the Platform of the Sciences." His liberal wife, perhaps sensing the manic mood of her husband, urged him not to offend his audience by unduly criticizing religion. Though he prided himself on always speaking the truth, he assured her that he had trimmed his language and made his *"statements of the opposi-tions of Science and Religion as mild as possible."* Despite his promise, he began his lectures sounding like an American Huxley or Tyndall, arguing that "Jew-ish Theology and Modern Science...are irreconcilable enemies" and that Genesis is "a poem, not a text-book." He dismissed theology as "science falsely so called" and blamed the "unchristian state of the theological and social sci-ences" for retarding the progress of science.[22]

Hearing such rhetoric, his auditors might have anticipated an early en-dorsement of Darwin's new theory. But no. Lesley professed to accept organic evolution only "if kept *within the regions of variety.*" Before admitting more extensive evolution—of genus, family, or class—he wanted to observe "nature in the very act of exchanging one species for another." Even then he was confident that the evidence would show not one but four lines of evolutionary development, each corresponding to one of Georges Cuvier's divisions of the animal kingdom: *Radiata, Articulata, Mollusca,* and *Vertebrata.* Addressing Dar-win, Lesley pointed out the resulting difficulties:

> My dear sir, you have four times as much to do as you thought you had. You must not only explain how a man came from a monkey, and a monkey from a squirrel, and a squirrel from a bat, and a bat from a bird, and a bird from a lizard, and a lizard from a fish; but you must suggest some possible means of transforming a verte-brate fish out of a shell fish, or out of a jelly fish, or out of a lob-worm or trilobite; then you must go on to show us how the first trilobite, or the first coral animal, or the first shizopod was ob-tained by your process of natural selection out of still earlier *vege-table* species. Nay, you cannot even stop there. You must explain the very first appearance of living tissue out of the inorganic elements of dead matter.

Darwinism, he concluded, remained "an open question...that ought to be no bugbear in the path of generous and truthful minds."[23]

Many early Darwinists, such as the Harvard botanist Asa Gray (1810–1888), accepted organic evolution in general but made a special exception for humans. Lesley—uniquely, as far as I can tell—rejected organic evolution but argued that humans had descended from apes. With Darwin, Lesley believed "that man is a developed monkey," but instead of one evolutionary track for humans he argued for three, each descending from a different type of "manlike ape, viz. the orang, the chimpanzee, and the gorilla, the three principal di-visions of the family of apes." The only barrier to accepting such a human history, he maintained, was the "tissue of absurdity, called the biblical history of the origin of mankind." No wonder he reported to his wife following this lecture, "You can't imagine what amusement my flat-footed advocacy of the monkey origin of man occasioned. There was no end to the jokes."[24]

Despite "threatening symptoms and occasional illness," Lesley had maintained a heavy workload. But shortly after completing his Lowell Lectures, he suffered from what a nephew described as a "completely broken down" nervous system, or what we would call severe depression. According to an intimate friend, a "black cloud of cerebral exhaustion" came over him, and his "brain-battery" ceased to function. A couple of years recuperating in Europe helped, but more years passed before he could put in a full day of work.[25] In 1872 the University of Pennsylvania appointed him professor of geology and mining and dean of the Scientific Department. Two years later he replaced Rogers as the state geologist of Pennsylvania. In the early 1890s his incapacitating depression returned, and this time he never recovered. It is unlikely that we will ever know what role religious and scientific doubts played in his repeated breakdowns, though indirect evidence suggests that they were not insignificant.[26]

Although Lesley occasionally attended a Unitarian church with his family, he, like LeConte, had become a pantheist, believing that "God is Nature, and Nature is God." He remained deeply spiritual but skeptical of, if not hostile to, virtually all theology and organized religion. For him, the ideal religion was "simply Morality and Philanthropy." Again like LeConte, he clung to the prospect of immortality.[27]

Late in life Lesley described evolution as "the prevalent epidemic scientific superstition of the day" and insisted in a letter to the editor of *Science* that he was "not a Darwinist, and [had] never accepted the Darwinian hypothesis so called." Yet his early advocacy of the evolution of humans from apes—to say nothing of his scorn for traditional religion—left even those close to him confused about his true views. His nephew found it ironic that during the 1860s and early 1870s, before the scientific community had reached a consensus, Lesley had seemed inclined toward Darwinism but never fully embraced it. "Twenty years later, when the theory had gained almost universal acceptance even among theologians, he was fully decided, and would at times express complete disapproval of it." Some friends attributed his late-life denunciations of evolution to "senile decay." But Lesley had never found the evidence for Darwinism sufficiently convincing to join the evolutionist camp.[28]

Lesley's precarious mental health and his idiosyncratic response to evolution make it hazardous to venture any generalization based on his experience. Because he lost his faith in traditional Christianity long before his encounter with evolution, it seems unlikely that his religious beliefs had much influence on his negative attitude toward Darwinism. And because his bouts of depression antedated the *Origin of Species*, his mental illness can hardly be blamed on the disturbing effects of contemplating evolution. The most that can be claimed in his case is that Darwinism sometimes irritated his sensitive psyche.

George Frederick Wright (1838–1921)

George Frederick Wright, a seminary-trained Congregational minister and amateur geologist, emerged in the 1870s as a leader of the so-called Christian Darwinists and a recognized expert on the ice age in North America. As a young minister he read Darwin's *Origin of Species* and Charles Lyell's *Geological Evidences of the Antiquity of Man* (1863), which clashed with the views he had been taught as a youth, but his autobiographical writings do not reveal the extent to which these books may have precipitated a crisis of faith. They do indicate, however, that he found in Asa Gray's theistic interpretation of Darwinism a compromise that allowed him simultaneously to embrace organic evolution and to retain his belief in a divinely designed and controlled universe.[29]

Wright especially appreciated a passage in which Gray described "the popular conception" of efficient cause: "Events and operations in general go on in virtue simply of forces communicated at the first, but that now and then, and only now and then, the Deity puts his hand directly to the work." This view of God's relationship to the natural world appealed to Wright as an ideal solution to the problem of reconciling the respective demands of science and Scripture. As he later wrote, it "allows us to retain our conceptions of reality in the forces of nature, makes room for miracles, and leaves us free whenever necessary, as in the case of the special endowments of man's moral nature, to supplement natural selection with the direct interference of the Creator."[30]

In making the case for the natural origin of species, Wright blunted the possible psychological shock of Darwin's theory by retaining such familiar concepts as God, miracles, and the special creation of humans. He also repeatedly used language that seemed to restrict natural selection to the lower end of the taxonomic scale while attributing kingdoms and the broader taxonomic groupings to special creation. According to Wright's paraphrase of Darwin's views, "The Creator first breathed life into one, or more probably, four or five, distinct forms," after which a process combining miraculous variations and natural selection split each "order" into families, genera, and species. Wright thought the appearance of humans might legitimately remain outside the evolutionary process, writing that "the miraculous creation of man

might no more disprove the general theory of natural selection than an ordinary miracle of Christ would disprove the general reign of natural law." Like
Gray, Wright derived great comfort from Darwin's inability to explain the origin of the variations preserved by natural selection, because this limitation
seemed to open the door for divine intervention. It "rob[bed] Darwinism of its
sting," "left God's hands as free as could be desired for contrivances of whatever sort he pleased," and preserved a "reverent interpretation of the Bible."[31]

Because he believed that the inspired writers intended only to state the
"fact of creation by divine agency"—not to provide a historically or scientifically
accurate account of creation—Wright professed to see "no difficulty at all in
adjusting the language of the first chapter of Genesis to that expressing the
derivative origin of species." But he remained too much of a biblical literalist
simply to dismiss the story of Eve's creation from one of Adam's ribs. And,
though he readily accepted the natural evolution of the human body, he insisted on a supernatural infusion of the soul. "No! man is not merely a developed
animal; but the inventive genius displayed in the rudest flint implement
stamps him as a new creation," he declared. "The new creation, however, is
spiritual rather than material or physical."[32]

As far as I can tell, Wright experienced little, if any, psychological trauma
in absorbing this watered-down version of Darwinism. A serious crisis of faith
did not erupt till the early 1890s, and then not from evolution but from
"higher criticism," which investigated the historical origins of the Bible using
naturalistic assumptions. Wright's long-festering fears about the implications
of higher criticism for an orthodox view of Scripture reached a critical level
when he fell under the "spell" of the eloquent and controversial Charles A.
Briggs (1841–1913), a Presbyterian theologian who rejected the inerrancy of
the original scriptural autographs and questioned the Mosaic authorship of
the first five books of the Bible. "So violent has been the shock," Wright can-
didly reported, "that out of self-respect I have found it necessary to turn a little
aside from my main studies to examine anew the foundations of my faith."
Wright emerged from this soul searching convinced more firmly than ever
in the Mosaic authorship of the Pentateuch and in a supernatural view of
history.[33]

In the wake of this episode Wright turned sharply rightward. He repudiated his earlier belief that Genesis was merely a protest against polytheism
and embraced Arnold Guyot's (1807–1884) widely held interpretation of the
days of Genesis as cosmic ages. Wright confessed that "in writing upon this
subject at previous times I have dwelt, I now believe, somewhat too exclusively upon the adaptation of the document to the immediate purpose of
counteracting the polytheistic tendencies of the Israelites and, through them,

of the world." The story of a six-day creation might not be literally true, but at least it was scientifically accurate.[34]

By this time Wright was also denouncing the evolutionists, such as Herbert Spencer (1820–1903) and John Fiske (1842–1901), who rashly pushed beyond Darwin's "limited conclusions" to construct a system of cosmic evolution. Wright frequently contrasted the modest, cautious Darwin, who had allegedly sought to explain only the origin of species and who had limited his theory of descent to no more than "all the members of the same great class or kingdom," with the impetuous—and often impious—souls who tried to explain the evolution of the entire world and who described development from "the first jelly speck of protoplasm to the brain of a Newton or a Gladstone" without any direct reference to the Creator. This, he declared, was "Darwinism gone to seed in barren soil."[35]

Even as a spokesman for Christian Darwinism in the 1870s and 1880s Wright had excluded the origin of matter, life, and the human soul from the rule of natural law; by the late 1890s he was sounding more and more like a special creationist. In discussing the origin of humans, Wright emphasized the great gap between "the highest animal and the lowest man," though he allowed that a divine miracle might have bridged the gap, thereby joining humans and animals. The opening years of the twentieth century found him damning "the antiquated Uniformitarian geology of Lyell and Darwin" and arguing for "the traditional view that man originated, through supernatural interference, at a comparatively recent time, somewhere in Central Asia."[36]

If Wright's identity as an evolutionist was in doubt at the turn of the century, it practically disappeared during the next two decades, when he joined forces with the leaders of the emerging fundamentalist movement. Writing on "The Passing of Evolution" for *The Fundamentals*, the founding documents of the movement, Wright stressed the special creation of the earliest forms of plants, animals, and, most important, humans. Man, he wrote, differed so greatly from the higher animals it was "necessary to suppose that he came into existence as the Bible represents, *by the special creation of a single pair*, from whom all the varieties of the race have sprung." Exactly how this "special creation" happened remained a mystery.[37]

Wright found his early encounter with Darwinism more exhilarating than spiritually threatening. His modification of Darwin's theory, especially the limitations on the extent of natural selection, allowed him to preserve his belief in an active Creator God—and temporarily to escape a spiritual crisis. But when theological danger appeared in the form of higher criticism, Wright found it theologically and psychologically soothing to abandon Christian Darwinism for fundamentalism.

George McCready Price (1870–1963)

George McCready Price, the founder of what in the 1970s came to be called "scientific creationism," was born in eastern Canada in 1870. When his widowed mother joined the Seventh-day Adventist church, he, too, at the age of fourteen, embraced that faith. Seventh-day Adventists not only commemorated a literal six-day creation by celebrating on the seventh day; they accepted as authoritative the "visions" and "testimonies" of the founder of the sect, Ellen G. White (1827–1915). On one occasion she claimed to be "carried back to the creation and was shown that the first week, in which God performed the work of creation in six days and rested on the seventh day, was just like every other week." White also endorsed the largely discarded view of Noah's flood as a worldwide catastrophe that had buried the fossils and reshaped the earth's surface.[38]

During the early 1890s young Price attended Battle Creek College for two years and subsequently completed a teacher-training course at the provincial normal school in New Brunswick, Canada. While serving as principal of a small high school in an isolated part of the province, he read for the first time about the paleontological evidence for evolution. To Price, the theory of evolution seemingly *all turned on its view of geology, and that if its geology were true, the rest would seem more or less reasonable.* On at least three occasions, he later recalled, he nearly succumbed to the lure of evolution, or at least to what he always considered its basic tenet: the progressive nature of the fossil record. Each time he was saved by sessions of intense prayer—and by reading Mrs. White's "revealing word pictures" of earth history. As a result of this experience, he decided on a career championing what he called the "new catastrophism," in contrast to the old catastrophism of the French naturalist Georges Cuvier (1769–1832).[39]

Still, he puzzled over ways to interpret the evidence that apparently indicated the earth's antiquity, which at first glance seemed "so strong and plausible." Only after poring over the standard geology texts and "almost tons of geological documents, government reports, memoirs, and monographs on special geological topics" did he discover "how the actual facts of the rocks and fossils, *stripped of mere theories*, splendidly refute this evolutionary theory of the invariable order of the fossils, *which is the very backbone of the evolution doctrine.*" This discovery not only resolved his intellectual crisis but determined his future course. Believing that he had found a fatal flaw in the logic of evolutionary geology, he grew increasingly convinced that God wanted him "to enter this unworked field; accordingly I threw myself into it with all the energy I possessed, constantly asking and receiving special help from the guiding and enlightening Spirit of God." Responding to this call not only satisfied his spiritual needs but also allowed him to fulfill his dream of becoming a writer.[40]

Price completed his first antievolution book, *Outlines of Modern Christianity and Modern Science*, in 1902, but instead of elation came desperation, as a sense of failure engulfed him. In the spring of that year he abandoned teaching in New Brunswick to become an Adventist evangelist on Prince Edward Island. His experiment in the pulpit proved disastrous, as did a brief stint as the administrator of a small boarding academy. Thoroughly discouraged and driven by guilt to earn a living for his wife and three children, he returned in the summer of 1904 to the one job that had brought him a measure of success: selling religious books. But as he pedaled his bicycle over the rough roads of eastern Canada, he continued to dream of a literary career, "the thing for which I am best fitted and which I thoroughly enjoy above everything else." He had tried various lines of church work only to find "black, dismal Failure" mocking him at every turn. By late summer he had grown so depressed by his situation that he was contemplating suicide. However, out of consideration for his family he decided instead to leave church employment and head for New York City to try his hand at writing "hack stuff for the Metropolitan newspapers and magazines." If life did not improve in the city, he planned to sell his watch, buy a revolver, and rid the world "of another useless, good-for-nothing man."[41]

In the city his circumstances only worsened. Unable to find steady work, he suffered unspeakable privations—and the torment of knowing that his family was "destitute and almost starving" back in Canada. Since his conversion to Adventism he had derived strength from his religious faith, but now in his neediest hour he quit even attending church. His wife, fearing the worst, wrote to church headquarters in Takoma Park, Maryland, begging for help for her husband. Moved by the family's plight, the president of the church personally offered the estranged worker a temporary construction job. Price gratefully accepted the offer, noting that he was willing to go anywhere and do anything, "even if it means hard manual labor."[42]

By 1906, still "heartbroken" over his failure in life, Price was living in southern California and working as a handyman at the Adventists' Loma Linda Sanitarium. That year he published a slim volume entitled *Illogical Geology: The Weakest Point in the Evolution Theory*, in which he confidently offered a $1,000 reward "to any who will, in the face of the facts here presented, show me how to prove that one kind of fossil is older than another." In brief, he argued that Darwinism rested "logically and historically on the succession of life idea as taught by geology" and that "if this succession of life is not an actual scientific fact, then Darwinism ... is a most gigantic hoax."[43]

During the next fifteen years Price taught in several Adventist schools and authored six more books attacking evolution, particularly its geological foundation. Although not unknown in fundamentalist circles before the early 1920s, he did not begin attracting widespread national attention until then. Shortly after the fundamentalist controversy entered its antievolution phase, Price published *The New Geology*, the most systematic and comprehensive of his two dozen or so books. In it, he restated his "great 'law of conformable stratigraphic sequences' ... by all odds the most important law ever formulated with reference to the order in which the strata occur." According to this law, "any kind of fossiliferous beds whatever, 'young' or 'old,' may be found occurring conformably on any other fossiliferous beds, 'older' or 'younger.'" To Price, "deceptive conformatives" (where strata seem to be missing) and "thrust faults" (where the strata are apparently in the wrong order) proved that there was no natural order to the fossil-bearing rocks, all of which he attributed to Noah's flood.[44] Despite repeated attacks from the scientific establishment, Price's influence among non-Adventist fundamentalists grew rapidly. By the mid-1920s the editor of *Science* could accurately describe Price as "the principal scientific authority of the Fundamentalists," and Price's byline was appearing with increasing frequency in a broad spectrum of religious periodicals.[45]

Price's success as an internationally known spokesman for creationism unquestionably fulfilled a craving for public recognition, though for the rest of his life he chafed at the failure of fellow fundamentalists to abandon their old-earth creationism for his "flood geology." His uncompromising creationism remained on the fringes of fundamentalism until 1961, when John C. Whitcomb Jr. and Henry M. Morris brought out their landmark book, *The Genesis Flood*, which launched the revival of young-earth creationism in the late twentieth century. Designed as a defense of Price against his critics, it was, as one perceptive reader described it, "a reissue of G. M. Price's views brought up to date." Flattered by the attention he was finally receiving, Price, then in his early nineties, uncharacteristically ignored the near absence of his name in the book.[46]

Among the four individuals we have been examining, Price seems to have suffered the most intensely as a result of entertaining evolution, largely because, as an Adventist, he had so little room for theological compromise. For him, unlike for LeConte, Lesley, or Wright, the acceptance of evolution would have meant a virtually complete rejection of his religious faith, or so it seemed. Yet his deepest psychological crisis, which prompted thoughts of suicide, apparently resulted more from his failure to find a satisfying job than from fear of succumbing to Darwinism. In the end, his thoroughgoing rejection of evolution gave direction to his life and served as the foundation of a rewarding career.

Fleeing Fundamentalism

Over a quarter-century ago the well-known science writer and skeptic Martin Gardner (b. 1914) published a wonderfully evocative, quasi-autobiographical novel called *The Flight of Peter Fromm* (1973). It tells the story of a young creationist from Oklahoma who fell hard for Price's flood geology. In the late 1930s he packed up his copy of *The New Geology* and went to Chicago to attend divinity school. As a dyed-in-the-wool fundamentalist, he joined the Moody Memorial Church and hung out with friends in the Chicago Christian Fellowship. During his second year at the University of Chicago "his fundamentalism was dealt a mighty death blow"—not from any of his seminars in the divinity school but from a course he had decided to audit on historical geology. When Fromm asked the professor, named Blitz, if all of the sedimentary rock could have been deposited during Noah's flood, the geologist was "dumbfounded." He "didn't want to embarrass the kid by arguing with him in front of the class," but, nevertheless, he devoted "the rest of the hour going over all the evidence [he] could think of that proves sedimentation has been going on for hundreds of millions of years." In so doing, he

> had driven the point of a geological hammer into the rock of Peter's fundamentalism. He had opened the first tiny fissure through which the waters of modern science could begin their slow erosion. Now the metaphor breaks down. It may take a million years for a boulder to crumble. A religion can crumble in a few centuries. A man's faith can crumble in less than a year.... Peter threw away his copy of *The New Geology*.

Despite his growing distrust of biblical science and history, Peter continued to believe in the Bible as God's inspired word. But he began sliding down the path of unbelief: from fundamentalism to Roman Catholicism and eventually to a vague theism. Finally, after the war, while preaching an Easter sermon at the liberal Midway Community Church in Hyde Park, he suffered a psychotic break and had to be taken from the pulpit to a nearby hospital—which is where the novel begins.[47]

Minus the mental breakdown, my own experience closely paralleled Fromm's. Growing up as the son and grandson of Adventist ministers, I attended church schools from first grade through college and unquestion-ingly accepted the authority of both the biblical prophets and the Adventist prophetess, Ellen G. White. Although I majored in physics and mathematics at Southern Missionary College, an Adventist institution, I do not recall ever doubting that God had created the world within the past six or seven thousand years or that virtually all of the fossil-bearing rocks had been deposited during the year of Noah's flood. The first serious book I remember buying with my own money was *Studies in Creationism*, a defense of young-earth creationism by one of Price's disciples, Frank Lewis Marsh (1899–1992). For years I felt nothing but sorrow for evolutionists, theistic and otherwise, who failed to rec-ognize the "truth" about the history of life on earth.

Then, in the mid-1960s, I found myself at Berkeley studying for a doc-torate in the history of science. No godless professors challenged my beliefs, which I kept pretty much to myself. But learning to read and think critically proved my spiritual undoing. One night a friend of mine, Joe Willey, an Ad-ventist graduate student in neurophysiology, and I attended a slide presen-tation on the famous fossil forests of Yellowstone National Park, where some two dozen layers are stacked one on top of the other. The speaker argued that even using the most rapid rates of volcanic decomposition and tree growing, the sequence of forests could not be explained in under thirty thousand years. It seems like a minuscule number today, but then it was huge. For me, it challenged the divine authority of both Moses and Mrs. White. My friend Joe and I wrestled with the implications of this knowledge for hours that night following the talk. By early in the morning we had decided to trade in the teachings of inspired writers for the authority of science. We knew we were making a momentous decision, but we had no idea where it would lead, intel-lectually or otherwise. Despite repeated prayers for divine guidance, I quickly moved from young-earth creationism to old-earth creationism and then on to theistic evolutionism and finally to agnosticism. The journey proved to be mostly liberating, but punctuated at times by episodes of fear, pain, and iso-lation. Hopes of eternal life faded, and relationships with many Adventist friends and family members became frayed.[48]

I soon learned that I was not alone. I discovered that a number of other conservative Christians had passed through equally trying circumstances. One was J. Frank Cassel (1916–2004), a leader in the evangelical American Sci-entific Affiliation (ASA), who had graduated from a conservative Christian col-lege, earned a PhD in biology, and gone on to a successful academic career. His autobiographical testimony poignantly captured some of the emotional turmoil he and his friends in the ASA experienced coming to grips with the evidence for evolution in the 1950s:

First to be overcome was the onus of dealing with a "verboten" term
and in a "non-existent" area. Then, as each made an honest and
objective consideration of the data, he was struck with the validity and
undeniability of datum after datum. As he strove to incorporate
each of these facts into his Biblico-scientific frame of reference, he
found that—while the frame became more complete and satisfying—
he began to question first the feasibility and then the desirability of
an effort to refute the total evolutionary concept, and finally he became impressed by its impossibility on the basis of existing data. This
has been a heart-rending, soul-searching experience for the committed Christian as he has seen what he had long considered the
raison d'être of God's call for his life endeavor fade away, and he
has struggled to release strongly held convictions as to the close limitations of Creationism.

The distress suffered by Cassel and his liberal friends elicited little sympathy
from conservatives within the ASA, who thought the affiliation had, in the
colorful phrase of one member, "gone to the apes." In the opinion of the conservatives, the drift toward evolution was motivated not by intellectual hon-
esty but by "the malignant influence of 'that old serpent, called the Devil, and
Satan, which deceiveth the whole world' (Revelation 12:9)."[49]

Before closing, I should note that occasionally Darwinism resolved as well as
induced spiritual crises. A good example of this is the experience of the psychologist William James (1842–1910), who suffered through a protracted crisis, accompanied by such debilitating depression that it pushed him to "the
continual verge of suicide" and briefly through the doors of an insane asylum.
Then he discovered in Darwinism what he interpreted as evidence that "mind
acted irrespectively of material coercion." This realization, the historian Robert
Richards has suggested, "helped heal his emotional sickness."[50]

The life stories I have presented, whether representative or not, show the
historical poverty and incompleteness of a purely intellectual account of science and religion. Feelings count—often more than facts. That is why even today
we have so many varieties of evolutionists and why the majority of Americans still prefer to consider themselves "creationists" rather than "evolutionists"
(with nearly half of them believing that "God created human beings pretty much
in their present form at one time within the last 10,000 years or so").[51]

ours, I try to situate his beliefs within the religioscientific world in which he lived and worked. To do so, I have drawn extensively on essays and reviews that appeared in the *Princeton Review* during his long tenure as editor. These sources may not tell us exactly what Hodge thought about particular topics, but, because of his disinclination to publish views that diverged from his own, they reflect the direction of his thinking. On one of the few occasions when he did accept an essay at odds with his own beliefs, he attached an editorial note alerting readers that the accompanying article should not "be regarded as presenting the estimate of the *Princeton Review*." Except for pieces attributed to Hodge in the published index to his journal, we have no way of identifying what came from his own pen.[7] The portrait that emerges from my reading of the available sources reveals an unusually complex man, both rigid and flexible, dogmatic and open-minded, torn between his genuine love of natural knowledge and his loathing for what sometimes passed as science.

The Nature of Science and Religion

In 1863 the *Princeton Review* published an anonymous essay on "The Scepticism of Science," later attributed to a Pennsylvania cleric-businessman named Joseph Clark. Clark repeatedly warned of an impending attack on Christianity by modern science, which in recent years had "realized more than the wildest dream of poet, seer, or madman." "It has come to be generally conceded among discerning men, that the great battles of Christianity henceforth are to be fought with the various forms of unbelief generated by scientific inquiry," he wrote ominously. "And it has come to be boldly, and even boastfully declared, that the positive claims of Christianity, so far, at least, as they are founded upon the infallibility of Scripture, must now assuredly succumb under the last great assault, slowly but steadily, as with the tread of destiny, preparing against them." Rather than urging Christians to fight to the death against the menace of science, he recommended that the church "avoid ill-natured and unbecoming abuse of science and scientific men" and grant them "the largest liberty . . . to carry on the pursuits and investigations of their respective sciences according to their legitimate mode." After all, he noted, the coming conflict would pit Christianity not against true science but false science, "against ignorant pretenders, sciolists, and vain boasters."[8]

An upset reader of Clark's article brought it to the attention of the editor of the staunchly conservative Presbyterian *Observer*, complaining that "the whole drift and tendency of it is to depreciate the Bible and exalt Science," to make "Science *lead* the way and the Bible *follow*." The *Observer* editor agreed that the *Princeton Review* had gone too far toward elevating science above revelation. He especially disliked Clark's claim that "the discoveries of science rest upon a basis peculiarly their own—a basis of actual experiment and observation—and nothing can claim authority in a scientific view which does not so rest." To his way of thinking this statement was a "distinct declaration that in *scientific* matters, faith in Moses and Paul must yield to Humboldt and Agassiz."[9]

This public charge of "abetting infidelity" provoked Hodge into writing a defense that spelled out his view of the relationship between science and Scripture, a message he reiterated in his monumental *Systematic Theology*. The *Princeton Review*, he insisted, had always "asserted the plenary inspiration of the Bible, in such sense that what the sacred writers say, the Holy Ghost said." This meant that the Bible could "teach no error, whether in reference to doctrines, morals, or facts; whether those facts be historical, geographical, geological, or astronomical." However, because God had revealed himself through nature as well as the Bible, the *Review* had simultaneously taught that "this infallible Bible must be interpreted by science." Thus when sixteenth- and seventeenth-century astronomers demonstrated that the Earth revolves around the Sun, the church abandoned its long-standing commitment to geocentrism and reinterpreted the Scriptures to harmonize with science. As a believer in God's dual revelations, nature and the Bible, Hodge also held that true science could never contradict "the clear teachings of the Scripture." Although others sometimes found it difficult to distinguish between clear teachings and allegories, Hodge never doubted the perspicuity of Scripture, especially as it related to the plan of salvation.[10]

As a young man at Princeton and later in Europe Hodge had imbibed of the notion that theology was as much a science as geology or zoology, and as editor of the *Princeton Review* he had published a number of essays identifying induction as the distinctive method for doing science. In 1831 the *Review* called for "the full application of the inductive philosophy," commonly associated with the seventeenth-century English philosopher Francis Bacon (1561–1626) and his eighteenth-century Scottish commonsense disciples. Adopting the Baconian method meant stressing the primacy of facts, which served as a vivid "line of demarcation" between true science and pseudo-science and linked the science of theology with the sciences of nature. "The Bible is to the theologian what nature is to the man of science," wrote Hodge in his *Systematic Theology*. "It is his store-house of facts; and his methods of ascertaining what the Bible teaches, is the same as that which the natural philosopher adopts to ascertain what nature teaches."[11] As we shall see, the passage of time soon undermined the common ground shared by science and religion, but in the meantime Hodge took satisfaction in their fundamental unity.

Pseudo-Science

The first signs of discomfort over scientific developments appeared in the *Princeton Review* in the 1830s, when phrenology (described in chapter 1) reached America. Although individuals could influence the strength of a particular mental organ by exercising it, the basic thrust of phrenology lay in the direction of psychological determinism, materialism, and infidelity. On occasion phrenology merged into another German import of the 1830s, mesmerism, the practitioners of which put their subjects into hypnotic trances. Like phrenology, mesmerism raised doubts about the doctrine of free will and aroused concern among Christians.[12]

Writers for the *Princeton Review* typically dealt with these potential threats to the harmony between science and religion by dismissing them as "quackery," "pseudo-science," or "a miserable abortion of folly," representative not of modern times but "the days when astrology and the theory of 'herbal signatures' were sciences." They described mesmerism as simply "so absurd and incredible, that it cannot be true." Only persons "liable to be hoaxed" needed to be concerned. Though phrenology at first attracted some distinguished scientific supporters in America—Yale's revered Benjamin Silliman (1779–1864), the founding editor of the *American Journal of Science*, personally hosted the celebrated phrenologist Johann Gaspar Spruzheim (1776–1832) in New Haven—after a while the best scientific and theological minds tended not to take it seriously. Thus Hodge risked little by publishing attacks on its scientific standing.[13]

The sciences of the mind continued to attract critical attention in the 1840s, especially in connection with debates over the relationship between religion and insanity. Excessive religious enthusiasm had long been a topic of medical and theological interest, but the level of concern grew in the wake of the Finneyite revivals of the 1820s and 1830s, which sometimes reduced entire congregations to wailing and writhing, behaviors that could be interpreted as either pathological or spiritual. An epidemic of "religious insanity" reached its apex in the 1840s, when the excitement generated by William Miller's prediction of the imminent end of the world accounted for half of all religion-related admissions to some insane asylums in the Northeast. The prospect of widespread hereditary insanity resulting from such madness prompted the prominent asylum superintendent Amariah Brigham (1798–1849) to rank Millerism above even yellow fever and cholera as a threat to the public's health. Brigham attributed the "outward signs" associated with revivals to overstimulation of the nervous system rather than to the "*special outpouring of the Spirit of God.*"

His implication that clergymen could not distinguish between "the ravings of the insane or semi-insane and the operations of the Holy Spirit" did not go unchallenged. As Frederick A. Packard (1794–1867) explained in the *Princeton Review,* "An enthusiast preaching wildly would at once pass among us for an insane man, and his influence would extend but little if at all beyond those who are predisposed to the same class of mental aberrations or already under their power." Packard granted that some Millerites among the thousands duped by "the false prophet" from upstate New York had become "crazed" by the excitement of preparing for the imminent Second Coming of Christ—or by the disappointment experienced when Christ failed to appear on the appointed date in 1844. However, Packard and other contributors to the *Princeton Review* emphatically denied that "true religion" played any role in the epidemic of insanity sweeping the northeastern part of the nation, and they resented the impertinence of medical men who suggested otherwise. "The subject trenches so closely upon the domain of theology, and enters so far into that of experimental and spiritual religion," wrote one, "that it requires more than mere medical knowledge to do it justice."[14]

As early as 1839 Hodge himself entered "the labyrinth of medico-metaphysical speculations about nervous diseases" and their relations to religion. As a cerebral Calvinist skeptical of highly emotional religious displays, he offered no defense of the "fainting, convulsions, jerking, etc." commonly associated with rabble-rousing Methodists. Instead, he proposed a naturalistic explanation of their bizarre behavior and recommended medical treatment for its victims. "I am persuaded," he wrote to his physician brother, "that such phenomena

> are nothing but one form of an infectious nervous disease, gener-
> ated by strong impressions on the imagination and lively emotions. If
> so they have nothing to do, properly speaking, with religion, and
> instead of being encouraged or tolerated, as they almost always have
> been by good men to the great injury of religion, they ought by
> all means to be guarded against and suppressed as much as epi-
> lepsy or hysterics.

Clearly, scientific naturalism in the defense of religion was no vice.[15]

Despite this one medicalizing venture, Hodge and his circle kept a wary eye out for the encroachment of naturalistic psychology on the territory of moral philosophers. They strongly condemned the midcentury notion of "moral insanity," according to which outwardly normal persons charged with heinous crimes could be judged insane. "We regard the notion of 'moral insanity,' lately promulgated, as a device for the protection of wicked and ungovernable men from the just punishment of their crimes," declared Pack-ard. The concept of moral insanity reminded Lyman H. Atwater (1813–1883) too much of phrenological theory, which explained sinful behavior anatomi-cally rather than theologically, and he suspected that the advocates of moral insanity had "been influenced by the method of phrenology."[16]

By the late 1860s the *Princeton Review* was lashing out at the propa-gandists for physiological psychology, such as Herbert Spencer (1820–1903), Charles Darwin (1809–1882), and Thomas H. Huxley (1825–1895), who were attempting to create a scientific psychology devoid of spiritual elements—and doing so in a "loud, if not blatant," manner. The materialist advocates of the new psychology, noted one author with alarm, "propose to reconstruct edu-cation, society, morals, and religion in accordance with it; to make physical science, pure and applied, the chief element in education; to banish from it the classics, psychology, metaphysics, ethics, Christianity, and to replace them with physiology, biology, and a semi-brutish sociology, founded on mere bestial gregariousness." With so much at stake, accommodation seemed out of the question.[17]

The desire of many midcentury physiologists to explain the workings of biological organisms, including the human body, in mechanical and chemical terms without invoking "vital forces" was also an occasion for alarm. One re-viewer for Hodge's quarterly blamed comparative physiology for "converting the well-taught and religiously disposed youth, into the bold, careless, and sceptical physiologist or physician." Fearing that Christians did not fully ap-preciate the subversive influence of this science, he called on the "friends of religion . . . to baptize this new, brilliant, and fascinating science, into its legit-imate discipleship to Christianity, to compel it . . . to bring its tribute of wor-ship to the great Creator." Hodge consoled himself with the thought that a number of prominent men of science, including his trusted friend Joseph Henry, had not bowed to the feet of this materialistic science, which, in Henry's words, denied "the immediate presence of a direct, divine, and spir-itual essence."[18]

Genesis, Geology, and Astronomy

Hodge and the authors whose works he published in the *Princeton Review* op-posed the new psychology and physiology because they represented the cutting edge of naturalism, seemingly drove God out of the scientific enterprise, pro-moted infidelity, and undermined the biblical doctrines of the soul and free will. Their fears were well founded: midcentury men of science were indeed trying to erase the last traces of religion from the domain of science. As we have seen in chapter 2, methodological naturalism rather than Baconian inductivism was rapidly emerging as the chief distinguishing characteristic of modern science. Under such circumstances, Hodge saw little room for compromise—except, surprisingly, in dealing with the disciplines of astronomy and geology, which challenged the traditional reading of the Mosaic story of creation.

Beginning in about the second decade of the nineteenth century geologists on both sides of the Atlantic, most of them Christians and some of them clerics, abandoned the speculative theories of the earth that had typified so much of eighteenth-century scholarship in favor of empirical investigations that took them out of their studies and into the mountains and valleys around them. Using their knowledge of fossils, they constructed the so-called geological column and reconstructed the history of life on earth. In place of the Mosaic account of a recent creation in six twenty-four-hour days that was destroyed by a worldwide deluge at the time of Noah, they found compelling evidence of vast geological ages and no signs of a great flood that wiped out all but eight of the earth's inhabitants. By the early 1840s no geologist of note, Christian or otherwise, could be found still defending a six-thousand-year-old creation of the world or a geologically significant universal flood.[19]

In quick order many Americans harmonized the new geological findings with biblical description of the creation. Many adopted the "gap" interpretation associated with Thomas Chalmers (1780–1847) of Scotland. As described by its foremost American advocate, the cleric-geologist Edward Hitchcock (1793–1864), Chalmers's explanation "supposed that Moses merely states that God created the world in the beginning, without fixing the date of that beginning; and that passing in silence an unknown period of its history, during which the extinct animals and plants found in the rocks might have lived and died, he describes only the present creation, which took place in six literal days, less than 6000 years ago." An "extension of this interpretation," as Hitchcock phrased it, was advanced by the British theologian John Pye Smith (1774–1851) in 1839. Like Chalmers, Smith believed that Moses had described two separate creations, but he argued that the latter had been a local event, restricted to *the part of our world which God was adapting for the dwelling of man and the animals connected with him.*"[20]

Other harmonizers favored the "day-age" scheme, advocated in America by Benjamin Silliman of Yale. Silliman divided the period of the earth's development into six epochs, each corresponding to a day of the creation week. During the fourth epoch the previously made sun and moon had begun to measure time, and at the end of the sixth epoch—approximately six thousand years ago—God had created humans. Interpreting Genesis in this manner did not imply, for Silliman at least, that the Bible was in error. Geology and the Mosaic record remained in full accordance, he assured his readers, "but more time is required for the necessary events of the creation than is consistent with the common understanding of the days. The history therefore is true, but it must be understood so as to be consistent with itself and with the facts."[21]

In the early 1850s Hodge's Princeton colleague Arnold Guyot (1807–1884), a physical geographer recently arrived from Switzerland, modified the day-age theory to incorporate into the scheme Laplace's nebular hypothesis about the origin of the solar system. The French mathematician and astronomer had explained the birth of the solar system in terms of physical laws acting on a gaseous nebula. As the nebula cooled and contracted, it abandoned a series of rings along its equator (much like the rings of Saturn), which then broke up to form the individual planets. In like manner, the planets spun off their respective satellites. Greatly taken with this idea, Guyot, instead of equating all of the creative days with *geological* epochs, assigned the first days to *astronomical* developments. If the formless "waters" created by God in the beginning symbolized gaseous matter, then the light of the first day undoubtedly had been produced by the chemical action resulting from the concentration of this matter into nebulae. The dividing of the waters on the second day represented the breaking up of the nebulae into various planetary systems, of which ours was but one. During the third epoch the earth had condensed to form a solid globe, and during the fourth, the nebulous vapors surrounding earth had dispersed to allow the light of the sun to shine through. The fifth and sixth epochs had witnessed the population of the earth with living creatures. "Such is the grand cosmogonic week described by Moses," declared Guyot. "To a sincere and unprejudiced mind it must be evident that these great outlines are the same as those which modern science enables us to trace, however imperfect and unsettled the data afforded by scientific researches may appear on many points." Although the Swiss naturalist, who suffered from a severe case of writer's block, proved to be a poor publicist for his views, his message reached the book-reading masses through the works of Silliman's son-in-law, James Dwight Dana (1813–1895), and John William Dawson (1820–1899), the principal of McGill College in Montreal.[22]

Of immense significance to Hodge and his Princeton colleagues in evaluating these radical departures from the commonsense reading of Genesis were the identities of their leading promoters. Virtually all of the men mentioned above were pious Christians in the Reformed tradition: Chalmers, a noted Presbyterian minister and writer on natural theology; Hitchcock, an evangelical Congregational minister and accomplished geologist; Silliman, a devout geologist of Congregational persuasion; Guyot, a Presbyterian geographer and geologist who had once studied for the ministry; Dana, a widely respected Congregational geologist and contributor to theological journals; and Dawson, an internationally acclaimed geologist, known for both his Presbyterian piety and his scientific accomplishments. Even Smith, by far the most radical of the group, was a Bible-believing British theologian. With exegetes such as these, one could scarcely argue that the efforts to adjust the Mosaic narrative of creation to the finding of modern geology and astronomy represented the work of skeptics and infidels.

Besides, such views were being taught right in Princeton, both in the college and in the seminary. At least by the fall of 1841 Joseph Henry was not only endorsing geologists' efforts to lengthen the history of life on earth but also praising the nebular hypothesis as "one of the boldest and most sublime conceptions of the human mind." His brother-in-law Stephen Alexander (1806–1883), a former seminarian who taught mathematics and astronomy in the college from 1833 to 1877, devoted more energy to promoting the nebular hypothesis than any other American astronomer but one, the Presbyterian Daniel Kirkwood (1814–1895). By the late 1840s Alexander was describing the nebular hypothesis as God's method of creating the solar system. For years he devoted the last lecture of his popular astronomy course to the subject, drawing crowds of admiring auditors from both college and town. After joining the college faculty in 1854 as professor of physical geography and geology, Guyot, too, promoted the nebular hypothesis, and for several years he lectured at the seminary on the harmony of Genesis with modern science.[23]

In view of the above, we can see why biblical inerrantists such as Hodge and his colleagues at the *Princeton Review* generally supported the geologists and astronomers who were rewriting the story of creation. In fact, contributors to the *Review* repeatedly defended these men of science against conservative Christian critics, who worried that the Princeton harmonizers were giving precedence to science over the Bible, as indeed it seemed. From the earliest essay on geology, in 1841, *Review* authors generally defended both the facts of geology, though "totally incompatible with the belief, that the material of the earth was created only a few days before man and congenera," and the interpretation of those facts by Christian geologists. Invoking the authority of early church fathers who had deviated from the conventional reading of Genesis 1, as well as "eminent biblical scholars of our own age," one contributor concluded that there was not "much ground for apprehension." Another assured the faithful that there was "no need to be much concerned about the age of the globe on which our race resides. The chronology of Moses is that of the human race, and not of the material part of the earth." For the time being such writers defended a universal deluge at the time of Noah because "the fact is asserted in scripture as positively and clearly as it possibly could be in words," while noting that "no practical geologist, of any school whatever,... refers the formation of the geological strata *solely* to the action of Noah's flood."[24]

When some "zealous friends of revelation," such as the Lord brothers, Eleazar (1788–1871) and David (1792–1880), attacked geologists for violating the Scriptures, the *Princeton Review* put them in their place. Joseph Henry, dismissing Eleazar Lord's archconservative *Epoch of Creation* (1851) as gratuitous and unscientific, pointed to the "remarkable fact, that every practical geologist known to us, whatever his religious belief, and whatever his prior convictions may have been, is brought to the conclusion, by a thorough and minute study of the facts, that there were races of organic beings on the earth living, and succeeding one another on definite and settled principles, before the existence of the human race." For him, that settled the matter. Perhaps because of the lingering association of the nebular hypothesis with the notoriously atheistic Laplace, some contributors to the *Princeton Review* urged greater caution in embracing it. However, one reminded readers that "very few scientific theories are essentially impious" and that, regardless of Laplace's own opinions, "any old-fashioned Christian, beginning with the nebular hypothesis and resolving the fire-mist into chaos, might, if need be, proceed to the creation of the world in six ordinary days."[25]

Although Hodge's early views on pre-Adamic history remain uncertain, his published opinions from the 1870s closely reflect those of his associates. Relegating the question of *how* the world was made to "minor importance," he nevertheless devoted space in his *Systematic Theology* to describing the nebular hypothesis. While conceding that the original Laplacian version of the cosmogony left little work for God to do, he deemed it common knowledge "that there is a form in which the nebular hypothesis is held by many Christian theists." Along with Guyot, he felt that the first verses of Genesis "clearly intimated that the universe, when first created, was in a state of chaos, and that by the life-giving, organizing power of the spirit of God, it was gradually moulded into the wonderful cosmos which we now behold." His studies over the years had convinced him that development from preexisting material fell "within the Scriptural idea of creating." He declined, however, to pick the correct interpretation of Genesis 1, preferring to leave that matter an "open question," to be settled in the future by "duly authenticated" facts. Though open to using the latest astronomical and geological data in deciphering the meaning of the first chapter of Genesis, he drew the line at naturalistic explanations of the origin of present-day plants and animals. The introduction of life, he believed, necessitated the acceptance of "the Scriptural doctrine of an immediate creation ex nihilo by the power of God."[26]

When Hodge drafted his *Systematic Theology* in the early 1870s he gave his imprimatur to Guyot's (and Dana's) hermeneutic scheme, which viewed the "days" of Genesis 1 as cosmic ages and fully incorporated both the nebular hypothesis and the findings of historical geology. "The best views we have met with on the harmony between science and the Bible," he quoted Dana as saying, "are those of Professor Arnold Guyot, a philosopher of enlarged comprehension of nature and a truly Christian spirit." Since the mid-1850s Hodge had come to know and trust Guyot as both a first-rank naturalist and a discerning Christian. "Friends of the Bible," wrote Hodge, owed the Princeton professor and his Yale publicist, Dana, "a debt of gratitude for the able vindication of the sacred record." Several years later, when Princeton was looking for someone to take over Guyot's duties in geology, Hodge eagerly sought the services of Dawson of Montreal, one of Guyot's leading exegetical disciples.[27]

The Unity of Races

The relative ease with which Hodge succeeded in dismissing phrenology, mesmerism, and materialistic physiology as pseudo-sciences and in bringing once-suspect theories in astronomy and geology into harmony with the Bible gave him confidence that the same methods would work in the future. True, astronomy had once given cause for concern, but "no man now pretends that there is a word in the Bible, from Genesis to Revelation, inconsistent with the highest results of astronomy." Indeed, the agreement between the cosmogonies of Laplace and Moses was so great that men of science were now bowing "with wonder before the prescience of Moses." Geology, too, had raised some alarms, "but any one who has attended to the progress of this new science, must be blind indeed not to see that geology will soon be found side by side with astronomy in obsequiously bearing up the queenly train of God's majestic word." If scientific men could prove the antiquity of the earth, "the Bible will be found not only to agree with it, but to have anticipated it." Despite such optimism in the late 1850s, Hodge fretted that one science, anthropology, would not so easily be brought into harmony with the clear teachings of the Bible. As one of his book reviewers predicted, "The last of the long series of battles against the inspiration of the scriptures, pitched upon the ground of the natural sciences," would probably be fought on the field of anthropology.[28]

For decades Americans had been speculating about the origin of the various human races. Some attributed racial differences to supernatural intervention, such as God's curse on Noah's son Ham, which had allegedly produced the Negro race. Others, such as Princeton College President Samuel Stanhope Smith (1751–1819), suspected that natural factors, such as climate, had played a crucial role. In the late 1830s, in a book called *Crania Americana*, the Philadelphia naturalist-physician Samuel George Morton (1799–1851) had drawn on his comparative study of human skulls to offer still another explanation: that God had created each racial group separately and, therefore, that all human beings had not descended from Adam and Eve. Morton soon enlisted two vocal supporters, George R. Gliddon (1809–1857), the U.S. consul at Cairo, who collected Egyptian skulls for him, and Josiah Clark Nott (1804–1873), a physician from Mobile, Alabama, both of whom possessed a zeal to free anthropology, like astronomy and geology before it, from the shackles of Scripture. Together in 1854 they brought out a 738-page treatise, *Types of Mankind*, dedicated to the late Dr. Morton and devoted to the propagation of the polygenetic origin of humans. Included in the volume was a contribution from Louis Agassiz (1807–1873), the leading naturalist in America, who had embraced polygenetic theory a few years after emigrating from Switzerland in the mid-1840s.[29]

Gliddon and Nott might easily be dismissed as "heretics" and "charlatans," but the same could hardly be said of Agassiz or even Morton, whose very presence in the polygenesist camp made it difficult to dismiss their anthropology as pseudo-science. Hodge clearly felt uncomfortable criticizing Agassiz, who, he said, belonged to "a different class" from that of his collaborators and who had simply lent his name to the polygenesist project "as a jewel to be worn as on a stage and for a night." Hodge hoped that readers would not accuse him "of the presumption of even sitting at the feet of Agassiz as a naturalist." His quarrel was with "the logic and metaphysics of [Agassiz's] speculations," not with his scientific facts. Hodge did, however, find fault with Morton's sloppy techniques for determining the skull sizes of the different racial groups, such as ignoring the substantial differences in size between the skulls of men and women.[30]

In explaining the distinctive characteristics of the human races, Hodge followed his former teacher Smith in attributing them to "the differences of climate, diet, and mode of life, and to the effect of propagation in case of acquired peculiarities." However, he insisted that natural causes alone had not produced the defining characteristics of race, because those causes had been "intelligently guided by God for the accomplishment of some wise purpose." By secondary means God had fashioned "the different races of men in their peculiarities to suit them to the regions which they inhabit." In response to the ethnologists' argument that distinctive racial features could be seen in primitive art dating to thousands of years before Christ, and that there was too little time between the creation and the appearance of these features for them to have developed naturally, Hodge cited the work of his seminary colleague William Henry Green (1825–1900), whose study of biblical chronology (described in chapter 6) had led him in the early 1860s to argue for extending the post-Edenic time scale beyond six thousand years.[31]

Hodge's refusal to compromise with the anthropologists, even in the face of Agassiz's formidable authority, resulted from his conviction that the pluralist doctrine threatened the foundations of both Christianity and the social order, the latter by providing a scientific justification for slavery. Unlike questions about the antiquity of the earth and the structure of the solar system, he argued, the anthropologists' speculations about the origins of the human races contradicted "the explicit declarations of the Bible, as it subverts the great doctrines of the common apostasy and redemption of the race, and is opposed to the universal faith of the church." The developments in astronomy and geology had been assimilated "on the ground that the scriptures were not given to man for the purpose of teaching science," explained a contributor to the *Princeton Review*. But the same reasoning could not be applied to anthropology, because "the very object of the Bible was to clear up the history of the fall of man, to explain the condition in which he is found, and to reveal a plan for his recovery." Another essayist echoed these sentiments. "Whether the sun moves around the earth, or the earth round the sun; how many continents and what mountain ranges were above the surface of the ocean in Noah's day; are questions which seem to lie beyond the scope of those for the solution of which the aid of the spirit of God is promised to believers," he declared. "But questions which include the spiritual relations of the races of men to Adam or Christ, or which involve the connection between the sin of man and death, are of a very different nature."[32]

Complicating the issue for Hodge was his well-founded suspicion that some of the anthropologists were simply using their theory to undermine biblical authority. "It is indeed principally for the sake of disproving the Scriptural statement that all men are the children of Adam, and to break up the common brotherhood of man," he claimed, "that diversity of species is insisted upon." Hodge also resented the anthropologists' claim of exclusive rights to interpret early human history while warning "the theologian off of this ground as a trespasser." The "recklessness" displayed by some men of science in discussing the unity of mankind he found "not only lamentable but revolting." However, Hodge's "grand objection" to the hypothesis of multiple human races always remained its opposition "to the authority of the Bible, and to the facts of our mental, moral, and spiritual nature."[33]

Development

Even the despised anthropologists did not "advocate the same origin...for man and the monkey," Hodge noted in 1862. "This belongs to the opposite pole of sceptical speculation in natural history; of which the latest form appears in a remarkable book, from a very high authority," the English naturalist Charles Darwin (1809–1882). Since the appearance of the anonymous *Vestiges of the Natural History of Creation* in 1844, which chronicled the history of the world from nebula to humans by way of apes, Hodge and the *Princeton Review* had carefully monitored so-called theories of development (or what came to be called evolution). Fortunately for them, most men of science repudiated the thesis of *Vestiges* and continued to insist on the permanence of species. Even the Irish physicist John Tyndall (1820–1893), whom Hodge described as "one of the highest authorities in the scientific world," was reputed to have said that "if matter be what all the world believes it to be, materialism, spontaneous generation, and evolution, or development, are absurdities 'too monstrous to be entertained by a sane mind.'" But then in 1859 came Darwin's *Origin of Species*, aimed specifically at overthrowing "the dogma of separate creations" and establishing the theory of natural selection in its place.[34]

In his first extended discussion of the *Origin of Species* (and the subsequent *Descent of Man*, 1871) Hodge in his *Systematic Theology* credited Darwin with standing "in the first rank of naturalists...respected not only for his knowledge and his skill in observation and description, but for his frankness and fairness." Hodge also granted that Darwin himself was not an atheist and that it was possible to be a theistic evolutionist. Nevertheless, in opposition to the Harvard botanist Asa Gray (1810–1888), he insisted that Darwin's theory was essentially atheistic, because it removed God from the work of creation. It was also antibiblical, because it contradicted the statements in Genesis that "man was created in the image of God" and that "each species was specially created," and unscientific, because instead of dealing with the facts and laws of nature in Baconian fashion, it offered only unverifiable probabilities.[35]

Gray, a fellow Presbyterian who had been working on Darwin's behalf in America by giving his theory a theistic gloss, faulted Hodge for examining only the atheistic version of Darwinism and for pronouncing Darwin's "whole system 'thoroughly atheistic.'" Appealing to the previous experience with physics and geology, Gray argued that theologians had already conceded what evolutionists demanded, namely, "that there is a system of Nature with fixed laws." Hodge's complaint that Darwin was trying to account for developments that could be known only by revelation represented, in Gray's opinion, a fundamental misunderstanding of Darwin's goal. "For the very object of the evolutionists, and of Mr. Darwin in particular, is to remove these subjects from the category of origination, and to bring them under the domain of science by treating them as questions about how things go on, not how they began."[36]

On October 6, 1873, while attending the Sixth General Conference of the Evangelical Alliance being held in New York City, Hodge attended a session in which the president of Princeton College, James McCosh (1811–1894), presented a paper on "Religious Aspects of the Doctrine of Development." In the ensuing discussion Hodge pushed the participants to answer "the great question which divides theists from atheists—Christians from unbelievers. . . . Is development an intellectual process guided by God, or is it a blind process of unintelligible, unconscious force, which knows no end and adopts not means?" His own view, he explained, was that Darwinism teaches that "all the forms of vegetable and animal life, including man and all the organs of the human body, are the result of unintelligent, undesignating forces; and that the human eye was formed by mere unconscious action." If so, Darwinism clearly opposed both Scripture and reason.[37]

Hodge returned to Princeton the next day and almost immediately began writing down his thoughts about the development hypothesis, which he published the next year under the title *What Is Darwinism?* In it he expanded on the themes he had raised at the meeting of the Evangelical Alliance. Once again he praised Darwin as "a careful and laborious observer; skillful in his descriptions, and singularly candid in dealing with the difficulties in the way of his peculiar doctrine." He correctly identified "the heart of Mr. Darwin's theory" as his exclusive reliance on "natural laws" to explain the development of life on earth, from a primordial germ to humans. And he argued that Darwin, by denying "design in any of the organisms in the vegetable or animal world," including the eye, had brought his system "into conflict not only with Christianity, but with the fundamental principles of natural religion." Although Hodge had never attached great apologetical weight to natural theology, and denied that "the knowledge of God derived from his works [was] sufficient to lead fallen men to salvation," he strongly condemned Darwin's rejection of teleology. More important, Hodge failed to "see how the theory of evolution [could] be reconciled with the declarations of the Scriptures." In his opinion, "the grand and fatal objection to Darwinism" was its antibiblical denial of God's role in "the production of living organisms." Hodge concluded his tract with one of the most memorable phrases to come out of the nineteenth-century debates over evolution: "What is Darwinism? It is Atheism."[38]

This blunt verdict did not represent an obscurantist distortion of Darwin's views. It more accurately reflected the British naturalist's own feelings than

did the sugar-coated versions of his theory presented by Christian evolutionists such as Gray. The religious press in America overwhelmingly applauded
Hodge's effort. As one Methodist author aptly noted, the Princeton theologian's
"spirit is courteous, his statements accurate, his logic conclusive." The most
negative assessment came from Gray, who worried that Hodge's little book
would "not contribute much to the reconcilement of science and religion"—
and that it would undermine his own efforts to convince the reading public of
the compatibility between Darwinism and theism. Even Gray, who privately
complained to Darwin of the "uphill work I have in making a theist of you,"
grudgingly conceded the accuracy of Hodge's description of Darwinism. That
was sufficient to satisfy the aging Hodge. "Gray admits that I have stated Darwin's position fairly," he told his grandson. "I don't care about the rest."[39]

Hodge's uncompromising opposition to Darwin's theory stands in stark
contrast to his openness toward Laplace's nebular hypothesis. Both ideas originated with men notorious for their disavowal of Christianity; both promoted
creation by natural law; both contradicted what had long been regarded as
clear teachings of Scripture; and both, as countless Christian apologists had
shown, could be harmonized with natural and revealed religion. Why, then,
did Hodge go out of his way to portray Darwin's theory, but not Laplace's,
as atheistic? In contrasting the nebular hypothesis and Darwinism, Hodge
stressed Darwin's denial of all design. But Laplace, too, had denied design.
The difference, I think, can be traced to the implications of Darwinism for
the place of humans in nature. Early in *What Is Darwinism?* Hodge quoted
Thomas Huxley as saying "The question of questions for mankind—the problem which underlies all others, and is more interesting than any other—is the
ascertainment of the place which Man occupies in nature and of his relation
to the universe of things." Hodge could not have agreed more. As he pointed
out, the "grand conclusion" of Darwinism, found in *The Descent of Man*, was
that "man (body, soul, and spirit) is descended from a hairy quadruped, furnished with a tail and pointed ears, probably arboreal in its habits, and an
inhabitant of the Old World." Though the quotation was Darwin's, the par-
enthetical commentary was Hodge's, added to heighten the contrast between
Darwin's views and those of the Bible.[40]

Timing also proved important. Hodge had labored for years to grant science its due, even when it meant abandoning cherished readings of the Bible.
He had defended science and scientific men. As a theologian, he had adopted
the methods of science. However, as he observed in *What Is Darwinism?* the
rules of engagement had changed. Interpreters of the Bible and interpreters of
nature no longer relied on a common inductive method; they now employed
"different rules of evidence" that inevitably led to "different conclusions." To

Hodge's way of thinking, the "main root of the trouble" between science and religion could be traced to this epistemological shift:

> If science be the knowledge of the facts perceived by the senses, and scientific evidence, evidence addressed to the senses, then the senses are the only sources of knowledge. Any conviction resting on any other ground than the testimony of the senses, must be faith.... Now as religion does not rest on the testimony of the senses, that is on scientific evidence, the tendency of scientific men is to ignore its claims.

The very word *science* was "becoming more and more restricted to the knowledge of a particular class of facts, and of their relations, namely, the facts of nature or of the external world." Theology thus lost its scientific status, and its practitioners, such as Hodge, found themselves increasingly regarded as objects of suspicion. To make matters worse, Hodge noted bitterly, scientific men tended to denigrate metaphysicians and theologians such as himself. In such strained circumstances, Hodge felt disinclined to continue granting men of science the benefit of the doubt in their encounters with religion. Though he desired peace, he feared it would prove elusive. Religion, he sadly concluded, was in a "fight for its life against a large class of scientific men."[41]

6

"The Most Important Biblical Discovery of Our Time"

William Henry Green and the Demise of Ussher's Chronology

In 1650 the distinguished church historian Archbishop James Ussher (1581–1656) of Ireland announced his meticulously calculated time of the Creation: early Saturday evening, October 22, 4004 B.C., a date immortalized in the margins of countless Bibles for nearly three centuries. Among evangelical Protestants who believed in the inerrancy of Scripture this date came to mark the beginning of human history. For some believers it remained a landmark until the late twentieth century; others abandoned it as early as the 1860s. Among American evangelicals no one played a more important role in discrediting Ussher's chronology than William Henry Green (1825–1900), an Old Testament scholar at Princeton Theological Seminary. One of Green's Princeton colleagues called his demonstration of Ussher's fallacy "the most important biblical discovery of our time."[1] In some ways it was, although its full impact did not come until the second half of the twentieth century.

The Colenso Controversy

Green's interest in biblical chronology emerged in the context of a transatlantic controversy. Early in the fall of 1862 John William Colenso (1814–1883), an Anglican bishop from Natal in colonial South Africa, scandalized the English-speaking religious world with a

William Henry Green. Courtesy of Andrew Moody (www.Reformation Art.com).

thin volume entitled *The Pentateuch and the Book of Joshua Critically Examined.* Biblical critics had been busily deconstructing the purported writings of Moses since Jean Astruc (1684–1766) and J. G. Eichhorn (1752–1827) in the eighteenth century, but their work had attracted little public interest. The bishop's blast against Moses—following closely on the heels of Charles Darwin's recasting of the creation story in *The Origin of Species* (1859) and the efforts of the Anglican contributors to *Essays and Reviews* (1860) to reinterpret the Bible in the light of continental scholarship—created a mighty stir, rousing "the Anglo-Saxon world," as one contemporary described it, "from its uncritical condition."[2]

Colenso, a Cambridge-educated former schoolmaster and author of various widely used mathematics and science texts, had abandoned belief in the inerrancy of the Bible before journeying to Africa, where he began to read the German critics and their detractors. He experienced an epiphany while working with an African convert on a translation of Genesis into the Zulu language. As the bishop explained in the introduction to his book, "a simple-minded, but intelligent, native" asked him if he truly believed the story of Noah and a worldwide flood. Possessing some knowledge of geology from having read the British geologist Charles Lyell (1797–1875), Colenso understood "that a *Universal* Deluge, such as the Bible manifestly speaks of, could not possibly have taken place in the way described in the Book of Genesis." And he knew that he should not "speak lies in the Name of the Lord." His dilemma launched the missionary bishop on a quest to reexamine the Pentateuch in detail, or so he said.[3]

Colenso began by investigating the story of the Exodus, only to discover "the absolute, palpable, self-contradictions of the narrative." He thus devoted the first of an eventual seven volumes to exposing "the unhistorical character" of that story, often using arithmetical calculations to highlight textual difficulties. The following examples illustrate his method of attack:

> The Bible (Lev. 8:14) says that "the Assembly," comprising more than 600,000 able-bodied men plus women and children, "was gathered unto the door of the Tabernacle of the Congregation." But Colenso's calculations showed that the court of the Tabernacle, "when thronged, could only have held 5,000 people."

> The Bible (Deut. 1:1) says that "Moses spake unto all Israel," which numbered upward of 2,000,000 people. "Surely," reasoned Colenso, "no human voice, unless strengthened by a miracle of which the Scripture tells us nothing, could have reached the ears of a crowded mass of people, as large as the whole population of London." Crying babies alone would have made it impossible to hear Moses at great distances.

> The Bible (Ex. 16:16) says that the Israelites dwelt in tents in the wilderness. But "allowing ten persons for each tent, (and decency would surely require that there should not be more than this,—a Zulu hut in Natal contains on an average only *three and a half*,)—two millions of people would require 200,000 tents," plus "a prodigious number of trained oxen" to transport them.[4]

Numerous biblical scholars rushed to defend Moses against the bishop's charges, disseminated in books that circulated in the tens of thousands in inexpensive editions. Among the Mosaic defenders was the thirty-eight-year-old William Henry Green, who found Colenso's reasoning revolting. "Is it for this we are to give up faith in the Bible?" he scribbled while reading the book, stopping occasionally to jot such marginalia as "Whole thing garbled," "Bah!" "What outrageous representation," and "ALL FUDGE!"[5]

Although inclined at times to dismiss Colenso's book as "too childish to merit a serious reply," Green decided to wade through the "bog," mud and all. Within months he penned a scathing 195-page response, *The Pentateuch Vindicated from the Aspersions of Bishop Colenso* (1863). In it Green accused Colenso of proposing "by arithmetic to overthrow the Mosaic record" and of building his case on "a few superficial difficulties in the sacred record." He denounced Colenso as a mere "caviller" suffering from a "disordered brain" and an "utter incapacity to deal with the questions which he professes to handle." He ridiculed Colenso for making an astronomical error that no "schoolboy" would make (but in so doing, he committed one himself, as he reluctantly confessed in a note hurriedly added before publication). He dismissed Colenso's arguments as "punctilious," "dishonest," "absurd," and "clumsy" and derided them as "arithmetical pedantry," "outrageous misrepresentation," and "miserable sophisms"—all the while congratulating himself for refraining from the use of any "epithets" or "denunciation."[6]

As one who viewed the Scriptures as "an infallible communication from God," Green found Colenso's "utter want of confidence in Jesus and reverence for his words"—"Moses wrote of me," said Jesus (John 5:46)—particularly galling. As Green saw it, Colenso had raised a question "of life or death." "We will not, we can not give up our faith in the Bible," pledged Green. "To do so is to surrender ourselves to blank despair. It is to blot out the sun from the heavens and extinguish at once the very source of light and life and holiness."[7]

Colenso had only tangentially addressed the reliability of the Pentateuchal genealogies and had written nothing about Ussher's chronology. Nevertheless, Green went out of his way to note that "some links have been omitted in tracing the line of Moses' descent." Even casual biblical scholars, he alleged, knew that the biblical genealogies were "frequently abbreviated by the omission of unimportant names. In fact abridgment is the general rule, induced by the indisposition of the sacred writers to encumber their pages with more names than were necessary for their immediate purpose." A comparison of 1 Chronicles 6:3–14 with Ezra 7:1–5, which gave the identical genealogy minus six names, illustrated the practice.[8]

1 Chron. 6:3–14	Ezra 7:1–5
1. Aaron	Aaron
2. Eleazar	Eleazar
3. Phinehas	Phinehas
4. Abishua	Abishua
5. Bukki	Bukki
6. Uzzi	Uzzi
7. Zerahiah	Zerahiah
8. Meraioth	Meraioth
9. Amariah	
10. Ahitub	
11. Zadok	

12.	Ahimaaz	
13.	Azariah	
14.	Johanan	
15.	Azariah	Azariah
16.	Amariah	Amariah
17.	Ahitub	Ahitub
18.	Zadok	Zadok
19.	Shallum	Shallum
20.	Hilkiah	Hilkiah
21.	Azariah	Azariah
22.	Seraiah	Seraiah
		Ezra

At that point in his rebuttal to Colenso, Green initiated the evangelical assault on Ussher's chronology by inserting a note that would alter the course of Christian apologetics:

We may here be indulged with a remark aside from the special topic before us, viz.: that if scientific research should ever demonstrate what it cannot be said to have done as yet, that the race of man has existed upon the earth for a longer period than the ordinary Hebrew Chronology will allow, we would be disposed to seek the solution in this frequent, if not pervading, characteristic of the Scriptural genealogies. The Septuagint chronology, to which many have fled in their desire to gain the additional centuries which it allots to human history, is, we are persuaded, a broken reed. The weight of evidence preponderates immensely in favour of the correctness of the Hebrew text, and against the accuracy of the deviations of the Septuagint. But it must not be forgotten that there is an element of uncertainty in a computation of time which rests upon genealogies, as the sacred chronology so largely does. Who is to certify us that the ante-diluvian and ante-Abrahamic genealogies have not been condensed in the same manner as the post-Abrahamic? If Matthew omitted names from the ancestry of our Lord in order to equalize the three great periods over which he passes, may not Moses have done the same in order to bring out seven generations from Adam to Enoch, and ten from Adam to Noah? Our current chronology is based upon the *prima facie* impression of these genealogies. This we shall adhere to, until we see good reason for giving it up. But if these recently discovered indications of the antiquity of man, over which scientific circles are now so excited, shall, when carefully inspected and thoroughly weighed, demonstrate all that any have imagined they might demonstrate, what then? They will simply show that the popular chronology is based upon a wrong interpretation, and that a select and partial register of ante-Abrahamic names has been mistaken for a complete one.[9]

As Green's reference to the "recently discovered indications of the antiquity of man" suggests, the age of humanity had of late become a contentious topic. Since about the 1820s Christian scholars had been extending prehuman history to accommodate the finding of geologists and paleontologists, but, with few exceptions, human history had been left untouched. As one British writer noted in 1863, it was "remarkable how chary Geologists have until recently been of disturbing the popular notion that the creation of Man took place in the year 4004 B.C. It has seemed as if they had purchased their right to speculate freely on the anterior history of the Earth, by promising to leave untouched that which the theologian claims as his proper province, the origin and early history of the Human Race." Sustained scientific (as opposed to literary) discussion of human antiquity began in the 1840s, with the finding of stone implements mixed with the bones of extinct animals in gravel pits at Abbeville in northwestern France. Still, belief in ancient humans remained relatively rare until 1858, when human flint knives were discovered among the bones of extinct mammals in Brixham Cave in southwestern England. By 1863, when Charles Lyell brought out his *Antiquity of Man*—and Green published his reply to Colenso—the scientific community was rapidly coming to a consensus on the issue. As the historian Thomas Trautmann has noted, "*the* intellectual revolution" of Green's generation "was the explosion of the traditional biblically based chronology" for human history. "The last great battle between science and dogmatism . . . has now commenced," the anticlerical physician-anthropologist Josiah Nott gleefully announced.[10]

William Henry Green

Just who was this conservative revolutionary who sought to turn American evangelicals away from Ussher's chronology? Historians of religion in America rarely mention him, and the few who do almost never mention his fundamental contribution to primeval chronology. (Mark A. Noll's half-sentence in *Between Faith and Criticism* stands, I believe, as a unique exception.)[11] In apologetical literature, where Green's name still occasionally appears, we are likely to find his name misspelled, his death misdated, his training misconstrued, and his contributions misidentified.[12]

Henry Green, to use his common name, was born in 1825 in rural New Jersey, near Princeton, into a family distinguished by its learning and wealth. At the age of twelve he entered Lafayette College in Pennsylvania. After graduating with honors at age fifteen, he remained at the college for two years as a tutor in mathematics before enrolling in Princeton Theological Seminary in 1842. Early on he displayed impressive linguistic skills. As one of his fellow students later recalled, young Green "took to Greek as if he had been born at Athens; he took to Hebrew as if he had been the son of a rabbi in Jerusalem." In view of his aptitude for foreign languages, it is not surprising that immediately following his graduation from the seminary, he accepted an appointment as instructor in Hebrew at Princeton. Except for two years, spanning 1849 to 1851, when he pastored the Central Presbyterian Church in Philadelphia, he remained on the Princeton seminary faculty, becoming in 1851, at age twenty-six, professor of biblical and Oriental literature, a title later changed to professor of Oriental and Old Testament literature. For seventeen years he served as president of the seminary. Generations of students, impressed equally by his knowledge and his severity, privately called him Rabbi. Although a frequent contributor to the *Biblical Repertory and Princeton Review* before replying to Colenso, he had written only one book, a Hebrew text. Unlike so many other prominent biblical scholars of his day, he never studied in Germany, though during a honeymoon trip to Europe in the summer of 1858 he did take time out to audit two of Ernst Wilhelm Hengstenberg's lectures in Berlin (which has misled a couple of historians into describing him as a student and protégé of Hengstenberg's).[13]

Little in his published writings, either before or after 1863, suggests that he took much of an interest in issues relating to science and religion. Sermon notes from his days as a minister in Philadelphia, however, reveal something of his early views on the subject. He welcomed modern science as a bulwark against infidelity and as "a powerful auxiliary in the overthrow of heathenism." Although happy to let science determine the early history of the earth—to the extent of accepting both its nebular origin and the existence of geological ages that "may have been going on for periods that years can scarcely number"—he insisted that the world's "present inhabitants . . . were formed by the immediate creative power of God at a period not very remote,—a period which revelation dates for us exactly, but which Science can only venture to approximate." Still wedded to Ussher's chronology for human history, he believed that "if we found authentic records or monuments any where reaching back for millions of years or even for ten thousand years that wd. be of course in flat contradiction to the Mosaic record." By the time he delivered his inaugural discourse at the seminary, in the fall of 1851, he was warning of

a "grand battle" over the integrity of the Bible in which "enthusiasm for science" and "foreign researches" (that is, German biblical scholarship) were on
the antibiblical side.[14]

Although Green did not believe that the Bible taught or anticipated modern science, he did, like many fellow Christians, think that science and the
Bible could not, if properly understood, conflict, because God had created both.
"Abandon neither the evidence of your senses on the one hand, nor the
assurance of a well-established faith on the other," he advised the faculty and
students of his alma mater, on the occasion of the laying of the cornerstone
for a new chemistry building at Lafayette College, "but calmly abide in the
confident anticipation that in this, as in hundreds of instances before, an
increase of knowledge will reveal the mutual consistency of the word and
works of God." Throughout his life Green rejected the notion that Genesis 1
and 2 represented two distinct creation narratives, though from his earliest
writings he granted that the "days" of the first chapter represented "successive
periods," not literal days. Indirect evidence suggests that he adopted the harmonizing scheme advocated by his Princeton colleague Arnold Guyot (1807–
1884) and John William Dawson (1820–1899) of McGill University, whom
Green brought to the seminary to lecture on the harmony of science and
the Bible and later tried to lure to Princeton permanently. As noted in chapter 5, Dawson, following Guyot, interpreted the "days" of Genesis as vast
epochs spanning the development of the earth from nebulous mass to Edenic
perfection.[15]

Amid the uproar over Colenso—additional volumes, a sensational heresy
trial, and a successful legal fight to retain his bishopric—Green's reply attracted relatively little attention besides a few notices that commented on the
"vein of quiet ridicule" running through the tract or on the author's humor and wit. As far as I can tell, only one reviewer, in the *Methodist Quarterly
Review*, saw the significance of Green's note on primeval chronology. After
quoting the entire passage, the critic conceded that the time gained from the
incomplete genealogies might "meet all the difficulties arising from historic
and linguistic evidences of human antiquity." But, he asked skeptically, will
they "solve the difficulty of the *'fossil man'*?"[16]

By far the most significant endorsement of Green's chronological ex-
pansion of Genesis came from his senior colleague at the seminary, Charles
Hodge (1797–1878), who welcomed Green's insight as an exegetical lifesaver.
The famous theologian's son Alexander Hodge recalled his father's reaction to
Green's suggestion: "I can well remember my father walking up and down in
his study when he heard [about it] and saying, 'What a relief it is to me that he
should have said that.'" In his immensely influential three-volume work the

elder Hodge put Green's insight to work to resolve the discrepancy between the Egyptian and Hebrew chronologies. "The chronology of the Bible is very uncertain," he wrote in a passage citing Green. "The data are for the most part facts incidentally stated; that is, not stated for the purposes of chronology. . . . Under these circumstances it is very clear that the friends of the Bible have no occasion for uneasiness. If the facts of science or of history should ultimately make it necessary to admit that eight or ten thousand years have elapsed since the creation of man, there is nothing in the Bible in the way of such concession. The Scriptures do not teach us how long men have existed on the earth."[17]

Still, Green's major contribution to biblical interpretation languished in obscurity, while his reputation as America's leading defender of traditional views of the Bible soared, especially in the years after the German publication in 1878 of Julius Wellhausen's *History of Israel*, which for Green reduced the Pentateuch "to a compilation, by no one known, of legends gathered from diverse and contradictory sources originating no one knows how," and whose author Green dismissed as a trickster whose interpretation of the Bible came largely from his "own exuberant fancy." For a man who believed that "the Old Testament contains no errors that require correction, no mistakes due to the inadequacy of the organ employed to transmit the divine will," the times were indeed troubling. And the battle was only heating up. By the early 1880s the Scottish critic William Robertson Smith (1846–1894) was introducing English readers to the new criticism, hitherto largely inaccessible to the public by virtue of being "locked up in German." Worse yet, whereas in the past friends of the Bible had defended it "against pagans, infidels, and sceptics," they were now being called on to protect it against prominent churchmen. Biblical scholars no longer contented themselves with merely determining what God taught in the Bible; the most radical among them were now questioning whether the Bible even came from God. "The battle rages around the citadel," Green observed with alarm in 1883. "No drones or cowards are wanted now."[18]

Meanwhile, his reputation as an evangelical scholar and administrator continued to grow. Although he declined the presidency of Princeton College in 1868, he presided over the seminary for seventeen years. During the 1870s and early 1880s he chaired the ecumenical Old Testament section of the American Bible Revision Committee and, in 1891, served as moderator of the Presbyterian General Assembly. Even his critics grudgingly conceded his intelligence and tenacity. Smith, who counted Green among the driest writers he knew, nevertheless regarded him as "the most scholarly by far of my assailants." The editors of the widely read *Sunday School Times* lauded Green as one of "the foremost biblical scholars on either side of the Atlantic" and

invited him in 1887 to contribute six months' worth of commentary to ac-
company the Sunday school lessons on the Old Testament. When the liberal
Baptist critic William Rainey Harper (1856–1906) sought a worthy conservative to debate the merits of higher criticism in the pages of his journal *Hebraica*, he selected Green, who ably, if tendentiously, defended the traditional
point of view. Green's two classic books, *The Unity of the Book of Genesis*
(1895) and *The Higher Criticism of the Pentateuch* (1895), promptly appeared in
German translations.[19]

Among progressives at home and abroad Green's reputation plummeted
as higher criticism prospered. The publication of his books in German led to
an outcry from critics there, offended by his "perfidious" habit of attributing
the "worst motives" to his opponents. The Edinburgh-based *Expository Times*
identified him as the last remaining "Old Testament scholar who rejects
the results of criticism" and described his "battle-flag" as "the Pentateuch, the
whole Pentateuch, and nothing but the Pentateuch." Green's prominent role
in the heresy trial of his sometime friend and fellow Presbyterian, Charles
Augustus Briggs (1841–1913), the leading American higher critic, prompted
outraged liberals to tag him a "heresy hunter." Briggs himself dubbed Green
"the American Hengstenberg" (after the most prominent German tradition-
alist) and belittled him for using "the method of an advocate, and not of a
scholar." Another critic thought it "pathetic" that "in appealing to authorities
in support of his views, Professor Green is obliged to call a roll of the dead."
Indeed, by the 1890s Green stood virtually alone as a major scholar opposing
the higher criticism, much as his friend Dawson stood alone among scientists
in defending the Bible against Darwin.[20]

Primeval Chronology

While liberal biblical critics were dismissing Green as a scholarly dinosaur,
Bible-believing evangelicals such as George Frederick Wright (1838–1921),
editor of *Bibliotheca Sacra*, were turning to Green for help in dealing with
the increasingly convincing evidence of human antiquity. Wright, an accomplished geologist and Congregational cleric, had risen to prominence in the
1870s and 1880s as one of the leading American advocates of theistic evolution. During that time he had appealed to Green and Hodge for help in
harmonizing the accumulating evidence of human antiquity with the apparently short chronology given by the Old Testament genealogies. The elasticity
of these records, he concluded, allowed "the geologist and the archaeologist
and the Egyptologist and the linguist to work peaceably at their several prob-

lems." It was "already high time," he declared in 1882, to "remove the mis-
leading dates of Archbishop Usher [sic] from the margins of our 'authorized'
translation." By the late 1880s Wright was moving increasingly to the right
theologically, so much so that when he brought out his magnum opus, *The
Ice Age in North America: And Its Bearing upon the Antiquity of Man* (1889),
he expressed concern that anthropological and archaeological evidence was
pushing human antiquity back to at least the end of the glacial period, eight
thousand to ten thousand years ago (which he later extended to sixteen thousand to twenty thousand years). For help in resolving this tension, he turned
to B. B. Warfield (1851–1921), a biblical inerrantist at the Princeton Theological Seminary, who shared Wright's openness to biological evolution. Warfield
wisely suggested that Wright talk to Green, which he did. The two men con-
versed until "the small hours of the night," and Wright emerged from the
dialogue feeling reassured that the biblical genealogies did indeed provide the
wiggle room he needed to harmonize his findings about human antiquity
with his belief in the accuracy of the Genesis record.[21]

A grateful Wright invited Green to share his insights with the readers
of *Bibliotheca Sacra* by expanding the note he had inserted in his reply to
Colenso into a full article. Thus in 1890 the journal featured a nineteen-page
fleshed-out version simply titled "Primeval Chronology," in which Green offered evangelical scholars "the needed relief" from the uncomfortable—and
unnecessary—constrictions imposed on them by Ussher's chronology. He
assured them "that the Scriptures furnish no data for a chronological computation prior to the life of Abraham; and that the Mosaic records do not fix
and were not intended to fix the precise date either of the Flood or of the
creation of the world." The following year he prepared a condensed version of
his essay for the popular religious weekly *The Independent*, framed explicitly as
a refutation of the charge, circulated by John William Draper and others, that
science conflicted with the Bible.[22]

Green's recalculation of the primeval chronology led to immediate calls
for the repudiation of Ussher's chronology. "In the face of these admissions,"
declared one academic, "it is, to say the least, a misfortune that Bible houses
and tract societies should continue to print Usher's [sic] chronology in the
Bible margin." No one contributed more to popularizing Green's discovery
than Wright, who effusively praised his new mentor for showing that "the
forms of speech in Genesis permit us to place Adam as far back as the earliest
date for which we shall find satisfactory and specific evidence." To publicize
Green's work, as well as to cloak himself in the mantle of Green's unquestioned orthodoxy, Wright devoted eight pages of his *Scientific Confirmations of
Old Testament History* (1906) to summarizing Green's argument against

Ussher, reprinted Green's "Primeval Chronology" in its entirety in his *Origin and Antiquity of Man* (1912), and frequently alluded to Green in other publications.[23]

Despite Wright's efforts to popularize Green's declaration of freedom from Ussher, many, if not most, turn-of-the-century evangelicals remained unappreciative, even unaware, of Green's contribution. When friends and colleagues from around the country met in Princeton in 1896 to celebrate Green's fifty years of service to the seminary, no one mentioned his path-breaking chronological work. And when he died four years later, those who noted his passing remained equally silent. No wonder Princeton's professor of natural history, George Macloskie (1834–1920), complained to Wright in 1904 that "Green's work on the chronology is still unknown to the public," despite its being, in his opinion, "the most important Biblical discovery of our time." Perhaps Macloskie, an ordained Irish Presbyterian minister, did more harm than good to the anti-Ussher cause by going around proclaiming that "all our theologians had gone wrong on every important scientific question, until Dr. W. H. Green saved the Bible from Colenso by showing that Ussher had misinterpreted the Bible." Macloskie felt that at the very least Green's discovery gave the lie to Charles Hodge's infamous boast, at the celebration of *his* fifty years of service to Princeton Theological Seminary, that "a new idea never originated in this Seminary."[24]

Hodge's public adoption in the early 1870s had given Green's chronology its biggest boost in the late nineteenth century; its embrace by Green's junior colleague B. B. Warfield produced a similar effect in the early twentieth century. Warfield, the foremost biblical inerrantist of his time, took to praising Green for showing "that it is precarious in the extreme to draw chronological inferences from [the biblical] genealogies." Although he figured that twenty thousand years would sufficiently accommodate the needs of science, he expressed a willingness to go up to two hundred thousand years if necessary, arguing that the biblical genealogies were "so elastic that they may be commodiously stretched to fit any reasonable demand on time." Warfield may have been stretching inerrancy to its limits, but endorsements did not come any better in fundamentalist circles.[25]

It is difficult to assess Green's status between the early 1910s and the late 1950s, because there was little public discussion of his views on chronology, and evangelicals, if anything, became less interested than before in accommodating evidence of human antiquity. Most of his influence on chronological discussions came indirectly through the writings of Hodge, Wright, and Warfield. One contributor to *The Fundamentals* (1910–1915) hailed Green as "perhaps the strongest of the scholarly opponents of the rationalistic Higher

Critics" but said nothing about his chronology. Neither did such evangelical stalwarts as James Orr (1844–1913) and Oswald T. Allis (1880–1973), who frequently invoked Green's name in other contexts. One of the few promoters of Green's chronology during the interwar years was Melvin G. Kyle (1858–1933), Wright's fundamentalist successor to the editorship of *Bibliotheca Sacra*. Convinced by anthropological and archaeological discoveries of "the stupendous antiquity of man," he resurrected Green's long-"ignored" work to prove that the Old Testament chronology remained trustworthy.[26]

The full impact of Green's anti-Ussherian chronology did not come until the second half of the twentieth century, when it became an exegetical hot potato in certain sectors of the evangelical community. Virtually all parties, even the strictest fundamentalists, came to agree with Green that human history had begun earlier than 4004 B.C. The divisive issue was how much earlier: thousands or millions of years? In the contest to resolve that issue Green became an icon.[27]

A symbolic turning point came in 1948 with the publication of Byron C. Nelson's *Before Abraham: Prehistoric Man in Biblical Light*. A prominent minister in the Norwegian Lutheran Church of America, Nelson (1893–1972) had during the previous two decades earned a reputation as the Lutheran apostle of flood geology, a scheme devised by the Seventh-day Adventist George McCready Price (1870–1963) for squeezing all of earth history into about six thousand years. During the mid-1930s Nelson had served as vice president of the short-lived Religion and Science Association, an ill-fated effort to form a united creationist front against evolution. Within a few years, however, a growing acquaintance with geology and anthropology had convinced him that human history dated back at least forty thousand to fifty thousand years and that the continued reliance on Ussher's chronology was "probably the most common and injurious error which is fastened on the Bible." Following a decade-long struggle for church approval to disseminate his suspect views, he finally brought out *Before Abraham* in 1948. Nelson opened chapter 1 with a long quotation from Green's "Primeval Chronology," casting doubt on Ussher's "erroneous" chronology. "It is very essential that the world know" that Ussher's dates are undependable, "because what Dr. William Green said fifty years ago might come to pass, namely, that some day a scientific discovery might be made which would clearly demonstrate that mankind is older than Ussher's interpretation has allowed." By this time Nelson was privately entertaining the possibility of "the creation being back maybe a million years—a literal 7 day week creation—and a Deluge which changed the face of the whole earth correspondingly ancient."[28]

During the 1950s the so-called neo-evangelicals associated with *Christianity Today* and the American Scientific Affiliation also discovered Green and the utility of his unimpeachable orthodoxy in their fight against fundamentalist "hyperorthodoxy." The Baptist theologian and philosopher Bernard Ramm (1916–1992), a self-styled progressive creationist, led the charge in 1954 with the publication of his landmark *Christian View of Science and Scripture*. Although eager himself to reject Ussher's chronology, he feared that less cautious exegetes might try to wedge too much time into the Genesis narrative between Adam and Abraham. Exactly that seemed to happen when evangelical anthropologists began wrestling with the implications of Louis B. Leakey's discovery in 1959 of a 1.75 million-year-old fossil man, *Zinjanthropus*, in East Africa. When Donald R. Wilson (b. 1931), an anthropologist at Calvin College, shared this finding with the readers of *Christianity Today*, he called on Green and Warfield to assure them that Christians had nothing to fear theologically. "It may not be necessary as yet to think of the age of man in terms of millions of years," he wrote. "But it certainly is necessary to think of man's origin in terms of tens of thousands of years and with very high probability in terms of hundreds of thousands."[29]

Such Christian generosity prompted Carl F. H. Henry (1913–2003), the founding editor of the magazine, to complain in 1965 that Christian anthropologists might be too hastily caving in to "the inordinate pressures of contemporary scientific theory about the antiquity of man." James O. Buswell III (b. 1922), a Wheaton College anthropologist, tried to deflect Henry's rebuke by arguing in effect that with "theologians of the orthodoxy of Green and Warfield" on their side, Christian anthropologists need not worry about mere mortals such as Henry. "It seems to me," he wrote in a published letter to Henry, "that those who oppose an antiquity of man of hundreds of thousands of years *must* take" the statements of Green and Warfield into account. Later that year Buswell delivered much the same message in an effort aimed at convincing members of the American Scientific Affiliation that they should, for scientific reasons, and could, for biblical reasons discovered by Green, embrace Leakey's early man. For years to come evangelical anthropologists almost instinctively shielded themselves behind Green and Warfield whenever they felt threatened by less open-minded believers.[30]

During the 1970s and 1980s Green became a favorite of evangelical scientists wanting more time and biblical scholars wanting more respect. In 1972 Baker Book House brought out an anthology edited by Walter C. Kaiser Jr. of "the fourteen best evangelical essays in the field of Old Testament studies." Thanks in part to Kaiser's inclusion of Green's "Primeval Chronology," this essay, infrequently noticed in Green's own lifetime, became a "classic," the thinking evangelical's antidote to Ussher. Robert C. Newman and Herman J. Eckelmann Jr. reprinted it as an appendix to *Genesis One and the Origin of the Earth*, published by InterVarsity Press. The evangelical guru Francis A. Schaeffer (1912–1984), the Old Testament scholar Ronald Youngblood (b. 1931), and the geologist Davis A. Young (b. 1941) all followed Green. "Perhaps more than any other evangelical of his generation," wrote Youngblood, "he demonstrated the fact that wholly satisfactory, conservative answers could be given to questions being raised by liberal higher critics with respect to the origin and nature of the Pentateuch."[31]

About the same time so-called young-earth creationists such as John C. Whitcomb Jr. (b. 1924) and Henry M. Morris (1918–2006), authors of the immensely influential *The Genesis Flood: The Biblical Record and Its Scientific Implications* (1961), were fighting to limit the time gained by Green's insight, preferring what Morris called "a modified Ussher chronology." Although they readily conceded small gaps in the Genesis genealogies—and acknowledged Green's discovery of such—they refused to push the date of creation back farther than 10,000 B.C. and preferred a much more recent date. It struck Whitcomb as "an utter absurdity" to allow "100,000 years between *each* of the twenty patriarchs of Genesis 5 and 11," as some evangelicals, such as Buswell, seemed to be doing. "Our understanding of *the basic outline of man's earliest history* must come from Scripture rather than from science," he insisted. On occasion Morris lamented that "the much-maligned Usher [sic] chronology ... may have been discarded too quickly."[32]

Certainly that was the opinion of the contentious Canadian creationist Arthur C. Custance (1910–1985), who denied the existence of any genealogical gaps at all, arguing speciously that the alleged gaps were only apparent, because the Bible itself actually filled them in elsewhere. Despite an extensive familiarity with biblical languages and anthropology—and a willingness to concede immense amounts of time *before* Adam—Custance regarded Ussher's chronology as "a serious contribution to understanding the Bible," defective only "in small details." Green he condemned for abandoning Ussher's time scale "on biblical grounds" and for thus disastrously admitting "the thin edge of the evolutionary wedge."[33]

Green may not have opened the door for evolution, but the hyperbolic Canadian was correct in asserting that Green had facilitated the accommodation of modern anthropology through biblical means. That in itself was unusual. Throughout the nineteenth century discoveries in geology and astronomy had driven Christian apologists to reinterpret the Scriptures, for example, reading the "days" of Genesis 1 as ages or shrinking Noah's flood to a regional event. Those who did so often sought the sanction of biblical scholarship, but the impetus came from science. Just the opposite occurred with anthropology. Green provided a rationale for rejecting Ussher's chronology *before* Christian anthropologists began demanding more time, thus smoothing the way for the acceptance of discoveries yet to come. In that sense, and for evangelical Christians in America, he may well have made the most important biblical discovery of his time.

7

Science, Secularization, and Privatization

A Concluding Note

Social scientists and historians have long pointed to modern science as one of the most secularizing influences in Western society. As the sociologist Rodney Stark has noted, in virtually all versions of the secularization thesis "it is science that has the most deadly implications for religion." Typical of past claims is the overstated generalization of the distinguished British historian Keith Thomas. As the mechanical philosophy pushed God further and further into the distance, he wrote in 1971, it "killed the concept of miracles, weakened the belief in the physical efficacy of prayer, and diminished faith in the possibility of direct divine inspiration." At about the same time, the American anthropologist Anthony F. C. Wallace brashly predicted the "extinction" of religion at the hands of scientists. It might take "several hundred years," he granted, but "belief in supernatural powers is doomed to die out, all over the world, as a result of the increasing adequacy and diffusion of scientific knowledge and of the realization by secular faiths that supernatural belief is not necessary to the effective use of ritual." Before long, supernaturalism would be nothing more than "an interesting historical memory."[1]

Contrary to such wishful prophecies, supernaturalism not only persisted but flourished. Instead of becoming more rational and liberal, world religions in the late twentieth century became more fideistic and militant. "Fundamentalism"—whether Christian, Muslim, or Hindu—thrived. At the turn of the millennium an estimated 27.7 percent of the roughly 2 billion Christians in the world identified themselves as Pentecostals or charismatics, speaking in tongues and healing the sick. The heart of Christianity moved ever southward, and rightward. In the words of one African scholar, "The centers of the church's universality [are] no longer in Geneva, Rome, Athens, Paris, London, New York, but Kinshasa, Buenos Aires, Addis Ababa, and Manila."[2]

At first glance Western Europe seemed to be an exception to worldwide trends, but even for that region it is hazardous to generalize. The historian Hugh McLeod, who makes one of the best cases for the secularization of Western Europe, nevertheless warns that "secularization has come about for different reasons in different countries and at different times, and there is no master-factor—whether 'science,' 'modernisation' or any other—which can account for this pattern." Besides, as others have observed, popular religion has remained a booming enterprise even among Europeans. To give just one example: in the decade 1991 to 2001 the number of pilgrims traveling to the Lourdes healing shrine in the French Pyrenees grew from 4 million to 6 million.[3]

Bowing to the evidence, however unexpected or unwelcome, many sociologists of religion (who have theorized the most about secularization) quickly began reversing field. One erstwhile prophet of secularization, Peter Berger, openly recanted. "The world today is massively religious, is *anything but* the secularized world that had been predicted (whether joyfully or despondently) by so many analysts of modernity," he confessed in the late 1990s. Even scholars who continued to advocate the secularization thesis tended no longer to implicate science. The British sociologist Steve Bruce, for example, argues in his recent book *God Is Dead* for the reality of secularization in the West— but anachronistically absolves science of playing a major role, in part because the mass media have so devalued "the status of science." Furthermore, Bruce insists that "no contemporary sociologist of religion argues that Christianity has been fatally undermined by science."[4]

Notwithstanding the new sociological consensus, the notion of science as an agent—or victim—of secularization will not die. Despite the warnings of John Hedley Brooke against conflating the occasional use of science for purposes of secularization with the notion "that modern science has been largely responsible for the secularization of society," many American intellectual historians, for instance, keep stressing the link between science and secularization. George M. Marsden, writing self-consciously as an evangelical Christian, fingers the "methodological secularization" or "naturalism" of the sciences as one of the chief villains in his mournful tale of how the American university lost its soul. "The natural scientific model for research which dominated the new academic profession," he writes, "proclaimed . . . the irrelevance of religious belief." In telling the same story behind a mask of cold-eyed impartiality, Jon H. Roberts and James Turner nevertheless follow Marsden in emphasizing the secularizing role of scientific specialization and methodological naturalism.[5]

Elsewhere Roberts has argued not only that science has become secular-ized but that this secularized science at least partially explained why "fewer and fewer members of the American intellectual community, at least, have continued to call attention to the link between nature and nature's God." David A. Hollinger, who readily acknowledges that most Americans have re-mained resolutely religious, attributes the "de-Christianization" of elite Amer-ican culture after World War II in part to the role of "an informal alliance among liberal Protestants, ex-Protestants, religious Jews, and freethinking Jews" attracted by "the cognitive superiority of science." James Gilbert asserts that "secularization...proceeded rapidly" in twentieth-century America as "science, along with its technological applications," came to define the future. R. Laurence Moore blames the social sciences for helping "to destroy Protes-tant claims to be the dominant cultural authority in the United States." Where so many accomplished historians smell smoke, there surely must be a fire worth investigating.[6]

Before proceeding, I should say a word about the vexed meaning of sec-ularization. In explaining "the secularization of the European mind in the nineteenth century," Owen Chadwick famously reduced secularization to the axiom *"Miracles do not happen."* Others have associated secularization with a range of behaviors and beliefs, from dwindling church ownership to declining church attendance. To avoid quibbling over what counts as religious, Hol-linger (as indicated above) has suggested substituting "de-Christianization" for secularization to capture what happened to elite American culture in the twentieth century. Regardless of which term we use, it strikes me as un-necessary to go beyond Hans Blumenberg's commonsense observation that secularization implies "a long-term process by which a disappearance of re-ligious ties, attitudes to transcendence, expectations of an afterlife, ritual per-formances, and firmly established turns of speech is driven onward in both private and daily public life."[7]

Decades ago the historian of science Alexandre Koyré cleverly portrayed science as both "the root and the fruit" of secularization.[8] In this chapter I focus primarily on science as the fruit of secularization and only secondarily on the scientific roots of secularization. I readily grant that secularization some-times occurred and that science was occasionally implicated in the process, but if the concept of secularization is to retain any historical value, it must be contextualized in terms of specific times, places, and actors. In chapter 2 on

"Science without God" I explored one of the most significant developments associated with the disappearance of God-talk from science: methodological naturalism. Here I briefly examine the process of privatization, which, like naturalization, has been implicated in the process of secularization. But, as we shall see, the privatization of religious views did not necessarily reflect a diminution of religious belief among the practitioners of science.

The claims of intelligent design theorists to the contrary notwithstanding, the adoption of methodological naturalism, as we have seen, did not drive most nineteenth-century scientists to agnosticism or atheism. Long after appeals to God had disappeared from the heartland of science, the vast majority of scientists, at least in the United States, remained Christians or at least theists. But increasingly, manifestations of their religious convictions retreated from the professional sphere into personal space. (Although some scientists continued to share their metaphysical views with a large lay public, I refer to the virtual disappearance of religious language from professional literature as privatization.) The extensive retreat of religion into the nonprofessional world resulted from a diverse array of factors, including such religious factors as a desire to quarantine sectarian differences and to avoid crossing confessional lines. The secularizing agenda of nonbelievers may have contributed to the process, but not in a major way.[9]

Compared to the millennia-long narrative of naturalism, the history of privatization began fairly recently. The distinguished evolutionist Ernst Mayr, in a paroxysm of hyperbole, once claimed that Charles Darwin's *Origin of Species* (1859) "almost single-handedly effected the secularization of science," but he was dead wrong. Darwin himself concluded his book with an invocation of "the Creator": "To my mind it accords better with what we know of the laws impressed on matter by the Creator, that the production and extinction of the past and present inhabitants of the world should have been due to secondary causes, like those determining the birth and death of the individual." During the early years of the Darwinian debates it was not unusual for even scientific participants to allude occasionally to God. But the time was fast approaching when such "Pentateuchal" language, as Darwin called it, would virtually vanish from scientific works.[10]

Unfortunately, the process of privatization is difficult to document. Published references to the growing silence among scientific authors about their religious views are rare, but I have found a few. Just a year after the appearance of *The Origin of Species* the merchant-naturalist Samuel Elliott Coues (1797–1867) penned an essay on geological and meteorological phenomena, *Studies of the Earth*, which listed fourteen ways of calculating the distance of the sun from the earth. In presenting the fourteenth method, based on the structure of the heavens and earth given in Genesis 1, Coues noted self-consciously, "The author was advised by a friend to omit the fourteenth method...on the ground that the method would be deemed altogether un-satisfactory; and also, because a reference should never be made in scientific works to the Bible." He conceded that the Bible primarily revealed spiritual matters, but asked readers to remember "that the Prophets and Patriarchs were the astronomers of their times." This note caught the attention of a contributor to the *Princeton Review*, who interpreted it as a disturbing sign of the increasingly secular times.[11]

By the 1880s references to God were seldom appearing in the specialized literature of science. The "scientific etiquette of the day," as David L. Hull has termed it, dictated that even in public debates over evolution scientists avoided dragging religion into the discussion. In 1885 the science popularizer John Fiske (1842–1901) remarked that scientific texts were "no proper place" to refer to the Divine Architect or the Great Designer. That same year Enoch Fitch Burr (1818–1907), a scientifically trained Congregational minister who wrote numerous popular works on science and religion, contrasted the new policy of privatization, which declared that it was "not scientific to mix up science and religion in the same book," with the views of the "most eloquent expounder of science in this country during the last generation," Benjamin Silliman (1779–1864): "I can truly declare that in the study and exhibitions of science to my pupils and fellowmen I have never forgotten to give all honor and glory to the infinite Creator—happy if I might be the honored interpreter of a portion of his works and of the beautiful structure and beneficent laws discovered therein by the labors of many illustrious predecessors." Advocates of privatization argued that separation would "be for the comfort and advan-tage of both" science and religion. But Burr suspected that such separation would make "God himself...unscientific, for he has so largely and legibly written himself into that Book of Nature that contains all the sciences that even the heathen 'are without excuse for not reading his eternal power and godhead in the things that are made.'"[12]

The deletion of religious references—by both Christians and unbelievers—went hand in hand with the depersonalization of scientific rhetoric, such as avoiding the first person and adopting the passive voice. The disappearance of God from scientific treatises makes it difficult for historians to assess the religiosity of the authors of scientific works after the late nineteenth century and creates problems for scholars who generalize on the basis of what does not appear. The virtual silence about religion in scientific publications has led the historian of science Peter Bowler, for example, to argue—erroneously, I believe—that theistic evolution went into eclipse in the late nineteenth century and that Darwinism "established a complete break between science and religion."[13]

In truth, many American scientists remained extremely fond of theistic evolution and repudiated attempts to sever the mutually supportive relationship between science and religion. But they rarely said so in their professional writings. Scattered evidence supports this observation. During the antievolution agitation of the 1920s, for instance, members of the scientific community repeatedly went out of their way to assert the harmony of evolution and Christianity. As Edward B. Davis has recently discovered, such stellar scientists as Robert Millikan, Arthur Holly Compton, Kirtley Mather, and Michael Pupin each contributed to the mass-circulated pamphlets in the "Science and Religion Series" underwritten by the Rockefeller Foundation. The Tennessee Academy of Sciences, in a brief submitted in connection with the appeal of the Scopes decision in 1926, declared, "Innumerable numbers of our greatest Christian scientists, philosophers, educators and ministers firmly believe in the truth of the origin of man as taught by evolution."[14]

The evangelical physicist Howard J. Van Till (b. 1938), one of the foremost advocates of theistic evolution during the late twentieth century, has argued that doing science "can be as religiously neutral as dialing a telephone"—so much so that scientific publications in professional journals seldom betray their authors' religious allegiances. "One could, for example, read the *Astrophysical Journal* for days on end," claims Van Till, "without detecting the religious commitments of any authors, many of whom are Christians." To discover religious values, one had to turn to popular literature written for a lay audience. Addressing the public rather than their peers, scientists "usually choose to speak as complete persons, and therefore not only report the technical results of natural science but also seek to place those scientific results in the framework of their worldview."[15]

Some teleologically inclined scientists have skirted the ban on religious language by letting nature do the work previously attributed to God. A Christian biochemist once asked a prominent colleague "why he was willing to ascribe to nature a personality and an intelligence, rather than to say that God created or set the course of things in a particular way." His colleague "replied that it was acceptable in scientific parlance to refer to nature in this way, whereas reference to God would be construed as mixing science and religion."[16] Such circumlocutions gave the appearance of secularity while leaving open the possibility of substantial spirituality.

If science were as corrosive of religious sentiments as some scholars have suggested, then we should expect to see increasing numbers of scientists falling victim to unbelief. In this respect, however, the evidence is ambiguous.

Opinion surveys did not become available before the twentieth century, but my own retrospective assessment of the religious beliefs of the leading American biologists, geologists, and anthropologists in the years 1863 to 1900 shows that three-quarters of them remained theists, with the overwhelming majority identifying themselves as Christians.[17]

On the eve of World War I, the American psychologist James Leuba (1867–1946) conducted a pioneering survey of one thousand American men of science and found that 41.8 percent affirmed belief in a personal God "to whom one may pray in expectation of receiving an answer." Because he did not ask how many endorsed a less personal divinity, such as a God who did not answer intercessory prayers, it is impossible to determine the percentage of theists. Of the same group, 50.6 percent subscribed to the notion of individual human immortality. In general, the more distinguished the scientist, the greater the likelihood of disbelieving in these "two fundamental dogmas" of Christianity. Belief was lower among biological scientists than among physical scientists—and, as subsequent surveys showed, lowest of all among social scientists such as psychologists and sociologists. The relationship between science and religious faith remained unclear, but Leuba interpreted it negatively, which led him to predict a growth in skepticism as more and more Americans encountered science.[18]

Eighty years later, however, Edward Larson and Larry Witham replicated his survey and discovered virtually no additional loss of faith among scientists. Using the same crude instrument Leuba had employed, they found that approximately four in ten American scientists (39.3 percent) continued to embrace a prayer-answering God, and 38 percent believed in an afterlife.[19] Leuba's prophecy about growing skepticism had clearly failed, but it remained unclear whether the widely touted 40 percent of believers counted for or against secularization.

Among the general public in the West, respect for science soared in the nineteenth century and most of the twentieth, but its growing cultural authority did not necessarily come at the expense of religion. In the United States, one of the most scientifically literate nations on earth at the end of the twentieth century, nearly 90 percent of the population remained devoted to theism. Despite the stunning progress of naturalistic science, approximately 80 percent of adults continued to believe in the efficacy of intercessory prayer for healing, and 57 percent of all Americans claimed to believe in or lean toward "creationism." Modern science may have altered the way that theists pictured God operating in the world, but it did not necessarily reduce their sense of God's presence in the universe. Such people live more or less comfortably in what Martin E. Marty has called a "religio-secular" world, in which they "blur, mesh, meld, and muddle together elements of both the secular and the religious, the worldly and the other-worldly." In this intellectual environment about the only people who continue to worry about secularization—besides academics, of course—are the militantly secular, who pray for the eradication of religion, and the militantly religious, who need "secular humanism" as a bogeyman to arouse the faithful.[20]

Notes

INTRODUCTION

I am indebted to Jon Roberts and Frank Turner for their feedback on the chapters in this book, to David Livingstone for his encouragement, and to Cynthia Read, my editor at Oxford University Press, for seeing merit in this project.

1. Andrew Dickson White, "The Battle-Fields of Science," *New-York Daily Tribune*, December 18, 1869, 4; Jon H. Roberts, " 'The Idea That Wouldn't Die': The Warfare between Science and Christianity," *Historically Speaking* 4 (February 2003): 21–24. Still the best critique of the warfare thesis is James R. Moore, *The Post-Darwinian Controversies: A Study of the Protestant Struggle to Come to Terms with Darwin in Great Britain and America, 1870–1900* (Cambridge, UK: Cambridge University Press, 1979), 19–122. On White and Draper, see David C. Lindberg and Ronald L. Numbers, "Beyond War and Peace: A Reappraisal of the Encounter between Christianity and Science," *Church History* 55 (1986): 338–354; and Ronald L. Numbers, "Science and Religion," in *Historical Writing on American Science: Perspectives and Prospects*, ed. Sally Gregory Kohlstedt and Margaret W. Rossiter (Baltimore: Johns Hopkins University Press, 1985), 59–80.

2. David C. Lindberg, *The Beginnings of Western Science: The European Scientific Tradition in Philosophical, Religious, and Institutional Context, 600 B.C. to A.D. 1450* (Chicago: University of Chicago Press, 1992); J. L. Heilbron, *The Sun in the Church: Cathedrals as Solar Observatories* (Cambridge, MA: Harvard University Press, 1999), 3. Among the growing body of writings on Catholics and science, see, e.g., J. L. Heilbron, "Science in the Church," *Science in Context* 3 (1989): 9–28; J. L. Heilbron, *Electricity in the 17th and*

18th Centuries: A Study of Early Modern Physics (Berkeley: University of California Press, 1979); Steven J. Harris, "Transposing the Merton Thesis: Apostolic Spirituality and the Establishment of the Jesuit Scientific Tradition," *Science in Context* 3 (1989): 29–65; and Florence C. Hsia, "Jesuits, Jupiter's Satellites, and the *Académie Royale des Sciences*," in *The Jesuits: Cultures, Sciences, and the Arts, 1540–1773*, ed. John W. O'Malley et al. (Toronto: University of Toronto Press, 1999), 241–257.

3. Alfred North Whitehead, *Science and the Modern World* (New York: Macmillan, 1925); Rodney Stark, *For the Glory of God: How Monotheism Led to Reformations, Science, Witch-Hunts, and the End of Slavery* (Princeton, NJ: Princeton University Press, 2003), 123. See also Rodney Stark, *The Victory of Reason: How Christianity Led to Freedom, Capitalism, and Western Success* (New York: Random House, 2005), and the critique of it by a panel of historians in *Historically Speaking* 7 (March–April 2006): 2–18. Similar arguments appear in M. B. Foster, "The Christian Doctrine of Creation and the Rise of Modern Natural Science," *Mind* 43 (1934): 446–468; M. B. Foster, "Christian Theology and Modern Science of Nature," *Mind* 44 (1935): 439–66 and 45 (1936): 1–17; Reijer Hooykaas, *Religion and the Rise of Modern Science* (Grand Rapids, MI: Eerdmans, 1972); Eugene M. Klaaren, *Religious Origins of Modern Science: Belief in Creation in Seventeenth-Century Thought* (Grand Rapids, MI: Eerdmans, 1977); and Stanley L. Jaki, *The Road of Science and the Ways to God* (Chicago: University of Chicago Press, 1978). It is only fair to mention that not all scholars who have argued for a connection between Christianity and science are apologists. Prominent exceptions include Robert K. Merton, "Science, Technology and Society in Seventeenth-Century England," *Osiris* 4 (1938): 360–632; and Charles Webster, *The Great Instauration: Science, Medicine and Reform, 1626–1660* (London: Duckworth, 1975). In *The Post-Darwinian Controversies*, Moore suggests a "non-violent and humane" interpretation.

4. David C. Lindberg and Ronald L. Numbers, eds., *God and Nature: Historical Essays on the Encounter between Christianity and Science* (Berkeley: University of California Press, 1986); John Hedley Brooke, *Science and Religion: Some Historical Perspectives* (Cambridge, UK: Cambridge University Press, 1991). See also John Hedley Brooke and Geoffrey Cantor, *Reconstructing Nature: The Engagement of Science and Religion* (Edinburgh: T & T Clark, 1998); and John Hedley Brooke, "A Call for Complexity," available at www.science-spirit.org. For the origin of "the complexity thesis," see Ronald L. Numbers, Review of *Science and Religion*, by Brooke, *Metascience*, new ser. 1 (1992): 35–39, quotation on 36.

5. Moore, *Post-Darwinian Controversies*, ix; David L. Hull, "Darwinism and Historiography," in *The Comparative Reception of Darwinism*, ed. Thomas F. Glick (Austin: University of Texas Press, 1974), 388–402, quotation on 391.

6. Jon H. Roberts, *Darwinism and the Divine in America: Protestant Intellectuals and Organic Evolution, 1859–1900* (1988; Notre Dame, IN: University of Notre Dame Press, 2001), x; David N. Livingstone, *Darwin's Forgotten Defenders: The Encounter between Evangelical Theology and Evolutionary Thought* (Grand Rapids, MI: Eerdmans, 1987); Ronald L. Numbers, *The Creationists* (New York: Knopf, 1992), 7–36; Ronald L. Numbers, *Darwinism Comes to America* (Cambridge, MA: Harvard University Press, 1998), 24–48. Livingstone detects less hostility toward theistic evolution than Roberts

and I do. See also Jon H. Roberts, "Darwinism, American Protestant Thinkers, and the Puzzle of Motivation," in *Disseminating Darwinism: The Role of Place, Race, Religion, and Gender*, ed. Ronald L. Numbers and John Stenhouse (Cambridge, UK: Cambridge University Press, 1999), 145–172. Regarding Seventh-day Adventists and Pentecostals, see Numbers, *Darwinism Comes to America*, chap. 5, " 'Sciences of Satanic Origin': Adventist Attitudes toward Evolutionary Biology and Geology," and chap. 6, "Creation, Evolution, and Holy Ghost Religion: Holiness and Pentecostal Responses to Darwinism." The pioneering study of American Protestant responses to Darwinism also emphasized denominational differences; see Windsor Hall Roberts, *The Reaction of American Protestant Churches to the Darwinian Philosophy, 1860–1900* (Chicago: University of Chicago Libraries, 1938).

7. Harry W. Paul, "Religion and Darwinism: Varieties of Catholic Reaction," in Glick, *Comparative Reception of Darwinism*, 403–436, quotation on 408; Mariano Artigas, Thomas F. Glick, and Rafael A. Martinez, *Negotiating Darwin: The Vatican Confronts Evolution, 1877–1902* (Baltimore: Johns Hopkins University Press, 2006). On the reaction of Catholics to evolution, see also Thomas F. Glick, "The Reception of Darwinism in Uruguay," in *The Reception of Darwinism in the Iberian World: Spain, Spanish America and Brazil*, ed. Thomas F. Glick, Miguel Angel Puig-Samper, and Rosaura Ruiz (Dordrecht: Kluwer Academic, 2001), 29–52, especially 43–47; John Lyon, "Immediate Reactions to Darwin: The English Catholic Press' First Reviews of the 'Origin of the Species,' " *Church History* 41 (1972): 78–93; Jacob W. Gruber, *A Conscience in Conflict: The Life of St. George Jackson Mivart* (New York: Columbia University Press, 1960); Noor Giovanni Mazhar, *Catholic Attitudes to Evolution in Nineteenth-Century Italian Literature* (Venice: Istituto Veneto di Scienze, Lettere ed Arti, 1995); Harry W. Paul, *The Edge of Contingency: French Catholic Reaction to Scientific Change from Darwin to Duhem* (Gainesville: University Presses of Florida, 1979); R. Scott Appleby, "Exposing Darwin's 'Hidden Agenda': Roman Catholic Responses to Evolution, 1875–1925," in Numbers and Stenhouse, *Disseminating Darwinism*, 173–208; and Ralph E. Weber, *Notre Dame's John Zahm: American Catholic Apologist and Educator* (Notre Dame, IN: University of Notre Dame Press, 1961).

8. Glick, "The Reception of Darwinism in Uruguay," 29–52, quotations on 47 (enemy) and 52 (crucial variable); Pietro Corsi and Paul J. Weindling, "Darwinism in Germany, France and Italy," in *The Darwinian Heritage*, ed. David Kohn (Princeton, NJ: Princeton University Press, 1985), 683–729, quotation on 725–726.

9. David N. Livingstone, "Science, Region, and Religion: The Reception of Darwinism in Princeton, Belfast, and Edinburgh," in Numbers and Stenhouse, *Disseminating Darwinism*, 7–38; David N. Livingstone and Mark A. Noll. "B. B. Warfield (1851–1921): A Biblical Inerrantist as Evolutionist," *Isis* 91 (2000): 283–304; Peter Monaghan, interview with David Livingstone, *Chronicle of Higher Education*, September 19, 2003, A19. See also David Livingstone, "Darwinism and Calvinism: The Belfast-Princeton Connection," *Isis* (1992): 408–428; and David Livingstone, *Putting Science in Its Place: Geographies of Scientific Knowledge* (Chicago: University of Chicago Press, 2003), especially 116–123.

10. Glick, *Comparative Reception of Darwinism*; David L. Hull, "Evolutionary Thinking Observed," *Science* 223 (1984): 923–924. See also Kohn, *Darwinian Heritage*, part 3, "Towards the Comparative Reception of Darwinism"; Numbers and Stenhouse, *Disseminating Darwinism*; and Glick et al., *Reception of Darwinism in the Iberian World*, an English translation of most of the essays in *El Darwinismo en España e Iberoamérica* (México: Universidad Nacional Autónoma de México, 1999), by the same editors. See also Miguel Ángel Puig-Samper, Rosaura Ruiz, and Andrés Galera, eds., *Evolucionismo y cultura: Darwinismo en Europa e Iberoamérica* (México: Universidad Nacional Autónoma de México, 2002). National studies include Alvar Ellegård, *Darwin and the General Reader: The Reception of Darwin's Theory of Evolution in the British Periodical Press, 1859–1872* (Göteborg, Sweden: Acta Universitatis Gothoburgenis, 1958), which antedated Glick's book; Yvette Conry, *L'introduction du darwinisme en France au XIXe siècle* (Paris: Vrin, 1974); Alfred Kelly, *The Descent of Darwin: The Popularization of Darwinism in Germany, 1860–1914* (Chapel Hill: University of North Carolina Press, 1981); Eve-Marie Engels, ed., *Die Rezeption von Evolutionstheorien im 19. Jahrhundert* (Frankfurt am Main: Suhrkamp, 1995); Robert J. Richards, *The Tragic Sense of Life: Ernst Haeckel and the Battle over Evolutionary Theory in Germany* (Chicago: University of Chicago Press, forthcoming); Giuliano Pancaldi, *Darwin in Italy: Science across Cultural Frontiers*, trans. Ruey Brodine Morelli (Bloomington: Indiana University Press, 1991), 163–166; Francisco Pelayo, *Ciencia y creencia en España durante el siglo XIX: La paleontología en el debate sobre el darwinismo* (Madrid: Consejo Superior de Investigaciones Científicas, 1999); Alexander Vucinich, *Darwin in Russian Thought* (Berkeley: University of California Press, 1988), 240–248; James Reeve Pusey, *China and Charles Darwin* (Cambridge, MA: Harvard University Press, 1983); Roberto Moreno, ed., *La Polémica del darwinismo en Mexico: Siglo XIX* (México: Universidad National Autónoma de México, 1989); Pedro M. Pruna and Armando García González, *Darwinismo y sociedad en Cuba: Siglo XIX* (Madrid: Consejo Superior de Investigaciones Científicas, 1989); Bernardo Marquez Breton, *Origenes del darwinismo en Chile* (Santiago: Editorial Andres Bello, 1982); Adriana Novoa and Alex Levine, *¡Darwinistas! Evolution, Race, and Society in Nineteenth Century Argentina* (Lincoln: University of Nebraska Press, 2007). On evolution and Eastern Orthodoxy, see George L. Kline's pioneering essay, "Darwinism in the Russian Orthodox Church," in *Continuity and Change in Russian and Soviet Thought*, ed. Ernest J. Simmons (Cambridge, MA: Harvard University Press, 1955), 307–328.

The literature on non-Christian responses to evolution is smaller but growing. On Jews and Darwinism, see Marc Swetlitz, "American Jewish Responses to Darwin and Evolutionary Theory, 1860–1890," in Numbers and Stenhouse, *Disseminating Darwinism*, 209–246; Geoffrey Cantor, *Quakers, Jews, and Science: Religious Responses to Modernity and the Sciences in Britain, 1650–1900* (Oxford: Oxford University Press, 2005), 321–345; and Geoffrey Cantor and Marc Swetlitz, eds., *Jewish Tradition and the Challenge of Darwinism* (Chicago: University of Chicago Press, 2006). For Islam, see Adel A. Ziadat, *Western Science in the Arab World: The Impact of Darwinism, 1860–1930* (New York: St. Martin's Press, 1986); Najm A. Bezirgan, "The Islamic World," in Glick, *Comparative Reception of Darwinism*, 375–387; and Marwa Elshakry,

"Darwin's Legacy in the Arab East: Science, Religion, and Politics, 1870–1914," PhD diss., Princeton University, 2003. Pusey, *China and Charles Darwin*, contains some information on Confucian, Taoist, and Buddhist responses to evolution. On Shintoists and Buddhists in Japan, see Eikoh Shimao, "Darwinism in Japan, 1877–1927," *Annals of Science* 38 (1981): 93–102. Masao Watanabe, *The Japanese and Western Science*, trans. Otto Theodor Benfey (Philadelphia: University of Pennsylvania Press, 1976), devotes considerable attention to Darwinism.

11. Suzanne Zeller, "Environment, Culture, and the Reception of Darwin in Canada, 1859–1909," in Numbers and Stenhouse, *Disseminating Darwinism*, 91–122; John Stenhouse, "Darwinism in New Zealand, 1859–1900," in Numbers and Stenhouse, *Disseminating Darwinism*, 61–89.

12. Adrian Desmond, *The Politics of Evolution: Morphology, Medicine, and Reform in Radical London* (Chicago: University of Chicago Press, 1989), 4, 21. Adrian Desmond and James Moore, *Darwin* (London: Michael Joseph, 1991), continues the class emphasis. See also Robert M. Young, *Darwin's Metaphor: Nature's Place in Victorian Culture* (Cambridge, UK: Cambridge University Press, 1985).

13. James A. Secord, *Victorian Sensation: The Extraordinary Publication, Reception, and Secret Authorship of* Vestiges of the Natural History of Creation (Chicago: University of Chicago Press, 2001), 220.

14. Frank J. Sulloway, *Born to Rebel: Birth Order, Family Dynamics, and Creative Lives* (New York: Pantheon Books, 1996), quotation on 237. In an analysis of American participants in the Darwinian debates, I found a similar, though less striking, pattern; Numbers, *Darwinism Comes to America*, 44–46.

15. Ronald L. Numbers and Lester D. Stephens, "Darwinism in the American South," in Numbers and Stenhouse, *Disseminating Darwinism*, 123–143, especially 131; Eric D. Anderson, "Black Responses to Darwinism, 1859–1915," in Numbers and Stenhouse, *Disseminating Darwinism*, 247–266; Jeffrey P. Moran, "Reading Race into the Scopes Trial: African American Elites, Science, and Fundamentalism," *Journal of American History* (2003): 891–911; Jeffrey P. Moran, "The Scopes Trial and Southern Fundamentalism in Black and White: Race, Region, and Religion," *Journal of Southern History* 70 (2004): 95–120.

16. Numbers, *Darwinism Comes to America*, 92–93 (White), 119 (McPherson); Jeffrey P. Moran, *The Scopes Trial: A Brief History with Documents* (Boston: Bedford/St. Martin's, 2002), 199–204 (mothers). For an introduction to women and Darwinism that says little about religion, see Sally Gregory Kohlstedt and Mark R. Jorgensen, " 'The Irrepressible Woman Question': Women's Responses to Evolutionary Ideology," in Numbers and Stenhouse, *Disseminating Darwinism*, 267–293.

CHAPTER I

This chapter is appearing simultaneously in *Modern Christianity to 1900*, ed. Amanda Porterfield, vol. 6 of *A People's History of Christianity*, ed. Denis R. Janz, 7 vols. (Minneapolis: Augsburg Fortress, 2007). I am indebted to Stephen E. Wald for his assistance in tracking down sources used in this chapter and for his critical comments. I also want to thank Ted Davis, Aileen Fyfe, Randy Maddox, Jon Roberts, and Mike Shank for their comments and suggestions.

1. Johannes Kepler, *Mysterium Cosmographicum: The Secret of the Universe,* trans. A. M. Duncan (New York: Abaris Books, 1981), 55–57; Frank E. Manuel, *Isaac Newton, Historian* (Cambridge, MA: Harvard University Press, 1963), 260; Larry Stewart, *The Rise of Public Science: Rhetoric, Technology, and Natural Philosophy in Newtonian Britain, 1660–1750* (Cambridge, UK: Cambridge University Press, 1992), xxviii, quoting Joseph Glanville. I am grateful to Robert S. Westman for bringing the Kepler quotation to my attention.

2. One discovers little about popular views in John Hedley Brooke's influential *Science and Religion: Some Historical Perspectives* (Cambridge, UK: Cambridge University Press, 1991), or, I regret to say, in the two collections I have coedited with David C. Lindberg, *God and Nature: Historical Essays on the Encounter between Christianity and Science* (Berkeley: University of California Press, 1986) and *When Science and Christianity Meet* (Chicago: University of Chicago Press, 2003). Slightly more inclusive is Gary B. Ferngren et al., eds., *The History of Science and Religion in the Western Tradition: An Encyclopedia* (New York: Garland, 2000).

3. H[erbert] Butterfield, *The Origins of Modern Science, 1300–1800,* rev. ed. (1949; London: G. Bell and Sons, 1968), 190.

4. Lisa Jardine and Alan Stewart, *Hostage to Fortune: The Troubled Life of Francis Bacon* (New York: Hill and Wang, 1999), 439 (criticisms); Adrian Johns, *The Nature of the Book: Print and Knowledge in the Making* (Chicago: University of Chicago Press, 1998), 536–538 (editors).

5. Robert S. Westman, "The Astronomer's Role in the Sixteenth Century: A Preliminary Study," *History of Science* 18 (1980): 105–147. For an overview of religious responses to Copernicus, see Robert S. Westman, "The Copernicans and the Churches," in Lindberg and Numbers, *God and Nature,* 76–113.

6. Maurice A. Finocchiaro, *Retrying Galileo, 1633–1992* (Berkeley: University of California Press, 2005), 72 (Galileo); Rienk Vermij, *The Calvinist Copernicans: The Reception of the New Astronomy in the Dutch Republic, 1575–1750* (Amsterdam: Koninklijke Nederlandse Akademie van Wetenschappen, 2002), 103 (1629), 370 (1772). Vermij provides the best account of the popularization of Copernicanism in one county; see especially 103–111, 202–206, 330, 369–370. See also Isabelle Pantin, "New Philosophy and Old Prejudices: Aspects of the Reception of Copernicanism in a Divided Europe," *Studies in History and Philosophy of Science* 30 (1999): 237–262.

7. Finocchiaro, *Retrying Galileo,* 26 (Inquisition), 30 (Cologne), 77 (Milton), 222 (nineteenth century). On the Galileo affair in the American colonies, see Perry Miller, *The New England Mind: The Seventeenth Century* (Boston: Beacon Press, 1961), 221, quoting Mather.

8. Brooke Hindle, *David Rittenhouse* (Princeton, NJ: Princeton University Press, 1964), 119. See also Harry Woolf, "Science for the People: Copernicanism and Newtonianism in the Almanacs of Early America," *Colloquia Copernicana* 1 (1972): 293–309; David Jaffee, "The Village Enlightenment in New England, 1760–1820,"

William and Mary Quarterly 47 (1990): 327–346; and J. Rixey Ruffin, "'Urania's Dusky Vails': Heliocentrism in Colonial Almanacs, 1700–1735," *New England Quarterly* 70 (1997): 306–313.

9. Carlo Ginsberg, *The Cheese and the Worms: The Cosmos of a Sixteenth-Century Miller*, trans. John and Anne Tedeschi (Baltimore: Johns Hopkins University Press, 1980), quotation on 52–53.

10. C. Scott Dixon, "Popular Astrology and Lutheran Propaganda in Reformation Germany," *History* 84 (1999): 403–418, quotation on 415.

11. Sara Schechner Genuth, *Comets, Popular Culture, and the Birth of Modern Cosmology* (Princeton, NJ: Princeton University Press, 1997), 5–8, 66–67, 111, 217. See also Sara Schechner Genuth, "Devils' Hells and Astronomers' Heavens: Religion, Method, and Popular Culture in Speculations about Life on Comets," in *The Invention of Physical Science: Intersections of Mathematics, Theology and Natural Philosophy Since the Seventeenth Century: Essays in Honor of Erwin N. Hiebert*, ed. Mary Jo Nye, Joan L. Richards, and Roger H. Stuewer (Dordrecht: Kluwer, 1992), 3–26.

12. Keith Thomas, *Religion and the Decline of Magic: Studies in Popular Beliefs in Sixteenth and Seventeenth Century England* (London: Weidenfeld and Nicolson, 1971), 329–330, 358–385, especially 358 (wicked art) and 383 (God's will). On Galileo as an astrologer, see H. Darrel Rutkin, "Galileo Astrologer: Astrology and Mathematical Practice in the Late-Sixteenth and Early-Seventeenth Centuries," *Galilæana: Journal of Galilean Studies* 2 (2005): 107–143. According to John McManners, popular astrology by the eighteenth century was "mainly confined to calendars"; McManners, *Church and Society in Eighteenth Century France*, 2 vols. (Oxford: Clarendon Press, 1998), 2: 196.

13. William R. Newman, *Promethean Ambitions: Alchemy and the Quest to Perfect Nature* (Chicago: University of Chicago Press, 2004), 110–111 (impostors); Charles Webster, "Alchemical and Paracelsian Medicine," in *Health, Medicine and Mortality in the Sixteenth Century*, ed. Charles Webster (Cambridge, UK: Cambridge University Press, 1979), ed. Webster, 301–334; Bruce T. Moran, *Distilling Knowledge: Alchemy, Chemistry, and the Scientific Revolution* (Cambridge, MA: Harvard University Press, 2005), 47–56, 83–84, quotation regarding house fathers on 53; Ole Peter Grell, ed., *Paracelsus: The Man and His Reputation, His Ideas and Their Transformation* (Leiden: Brill, 1998); Neil Kamil, *Fortress of the Soul: Violence, Metaphysics, and Material Life in the Huguenots' New World, 1517–1751* (Baltimore: Johns Hopkins University Press, 2005), 175. For a brief overview, see Lawrence M. Principe, "Alchemy," in Ferngren et al., *History of Science and Religion*, 541–546.

14. Paul H. Kocher, "The Idea of God in Elizabethan Medicine," *Journal of the History of Ideas* 11 (1950): 3–29, quotation from English cleric on 7; Carlo M. Cipolla, *Faith, Reason, and the Plague in Seventeenth-Century Tuscany* (Ithaca, NY: Cornell University Press, 1979), 12–13; *Letters to Father: Suor Maria Celeste to Galileo (1623–1633)*, trans. Dava Sobel (New York: Walker, 2001), 233. For a survey of medicine and religion since the sixteenth century, see Ronald L. Numbers and Ronald C. Sawyer, "Medicine and Christianity in the Modern World," in *Health/Medicine and the Faith Traditions: An Inquiry into Religion and Medicine*, ed. Martin E. Marty and Kenneth L. Vaux (Philadelphia: Fortress Press, 1982), 133–162. On the spiritual treatment of

mental disturbances, see David Lederer, *Madness, Religion and the State in Early Modern Europe: A Bavarian Beacon* (Cambridge, UK: Cambridge University Press, 2006).

15. William Eamon, *Science and the Secrets of Nature: Books of Secrets in Medieval and Early Modern Culture* (Princeton, NJ: Princeton University Press, 1994), 96–102, quotation on 99.

16. Lissa Roberts, "Going Dutch: Situating Science in the Dutch Enlightenment," in *The Sciences in Enlightened Europe*, ed. William Clark, Jan Golinski, and Simon Schaffer (Chicago: University of Chicago Press, 1999), 350–388. The lines were written by the well-known Dutch poet Casparus Barlaeus.

17. Marian Fournier, *The Fabric of Life: Microscopy in the Seventeenth Century* (Baltimore: Johns Hopkins University Press, 1996), 1–5, 195 (quoting Hooke).

18. Katharine Park and Lorraine J. Daston, "Unnatural Conceptions: The Study of Monsters in Sixteenth- and Seventeenth-Century France and England," *Past and Present* 92 (1981): 20–54; Lorraine J. Daston and Katharine Park, *Wonders and the Order of Nature, 1150–1750* (New York: Zone Books, 1998), 180, 361. For the American context, see Herbert Leventhal, *In the Shadow of the Enlightenment: Occultism and Renaissance Science in Eighteenth-Century America* (New York: New York University Press, 1976); and David D. Hall, *Worlds of Wonder, Days of Judgment: Popular Religious Belief in Early New England* (New York: Knopf, 1989).

19. Johns, *Nature of the Book*, 111–112 (quoting Gilbert), 184–185; Stewart, *Rise of Public Science*, 61, quoting Thomas Sprat. See also Terence D. Murphy, "Religion, Science, and the Public Imagination: The Restoration of Order in Early Modern France," in *Experiencing Nature: Proceedings of a Conference in Honor of Allen G. Debus*, ed. Paul H. Theerman and Karen Hunger Parshall (Dordrecht: Kluwer Academic, 1997), 113–161.

20. Stewart, *Rise of Public Science*, 102 (not one man). On the limited readership of Newton's *Principia*, see Steven Shapin, *The Scientific Revolution* (Chicago: University of Chicago Press, 1996), 123.

21. Stewart, *The Rise of Public Science*, 64 (dozed), 85; Alfred Owen Aldridge, *Benjamin Franklin and Nature's God* (Durham, NC: Duke University Press, 1967), 12–13. On the Boyle lectures, see Margaret C. Jacob, *The Newtonians and the English Revolution, 1689–1720* (Ithaca, NY: Cornell University Press, 1976), 143–200.

22. Mordechai Feingold, *The Newtonian Moment: Isaac Newton and the Making of Modern Culture* (New York: Oxford University Press, 2004), 95–105; James A. Secord, "Newton in the Nursery: Tom Telescope and the Philosophy of Tops and Balls, 1761–1838," *History of Science* 23 (1985): 127–151, quotation on 136. For colonial America, see Frances Herman Lord, "Piety, Politeness, and Power: Formation of a Newtonian Culture in New England, 1727–1779," PhD diss., University of New Hampshire, 2000. See also R. L. Walters, "Voltaire, Newton, and the Reading Public," in *The Triumph of Culture: Eighteenth-Century Perspectives*, ed. Paul Fritz and David Williams (Toronto: A. M. Hakkert, 1972), 133–155; Marta Fehér, "The Triumphal March of a Paradigm: A Case Study of the Popularization of Newtonian Science," *Tractrix: Yearbook for the History of Science, Medicine, Technology, and Mathematics* 2 (1990):

93–110; and Massimo Mazzotti, "Newton for Ladies: Gentility, Gender, and Radical Culture," *British Journal for the History of Science* 37 (2004): 119–146.

23. Stewart, *Rise of Public Science*, 146; Schechner Genuth, *Comets*, 5–8, 66; Raymond Phineas Stearns, *Science in the British Colonies of America* (Urbana: University of Illinois Press, 1970), 489–490; Thomas, *Religion and the Decline of Magic*, 666, quoting the Anglican author. See also Mary Fissell and Roger Cooter, "Exploring Natural Knowledge: Science and the Popular," in *Eighteenth-Century Science*, ed. Roy Porter, vol. 4 of *The Cambridge History of Science*, ed. David C. Lindberg and Ronald L. Numbers (Cambridge, UK: Cambridge University Press, 2003), 129–158; and Richard A. Overfield, "Science in the *Virginia Gazette*, 1736–1780," *Emporia State Research Studies* 16, no. 3 (1968): 5–53.

24. Michael N. Shute, "Earthquakes and Early American Imagination: Decline and Renewal in Eighteenth-Century Puritan Culture," PhD diss., University of California, Berkeley, 1977, 74–75.

25. I. Bernard Cohen, *Benjamin Franklin's Science* (Cambridge, MA: Harvard University Press, 1990), chap. 8, "Prejudice against the Introduction of Lightning Rods," 118–158, quotations on 141–142.

26. Thomas W. Laqueur, *Solitary Sex: A Cultural History of Masturbation* (New York: Zone Books, 2003), 13–14, 18, 26, 37–39; Antoinette Emch-Dériaz, *Tissot: Physician of the Enlightenment* (New York: Peter Long, 1992), 59–72. On the scientific and religious war against masturbation in nineteenth-century America, see Stephen Nissenbaum, *Sex, Diet, and Debility in Jacksonian America: Sylvester Graham and Health Reform* (Westport, CT: Greenwood Press, 1980); and Ronald L. Numbers, "Sex, Science, and Salvation: The Sexual Advice of Ellen G. White and John Harvey Kellogg," in *Right Living: An Anglo-American Tradition of Self-Help Medicine and Hygiene*, ed. Charles E. Rosenberg (Baltimore: Johns Hopkins University Press, 2003), 206–226.

27. Philip W. Ott, "John Wesley on Health: A Word for Sensible Regimen," *Methodist History* 18 (1980): 193–204; Samuel J. Rogal, "Pills for the Poor: John Wesley's *Primitive Physick*," *Yale Journal of Biology and Medicine* 51 (1978): 81–90; Owen Davies, "Methodism, the Clergy, and the Popular Belief in Witchcraft and Magic," *History: Journal of the Historical Association* 82, no. 266 (1997): 252–265, quotation about "extravagancies" on 253. On Wesley and masturbation, see James G. Donat, "The Rev. John Wesley's Extractions from Dr. Tissot: A Methodist *Imprimatur*," *History of Science* 39 (2001): 285–298. See also G. S. Rousseau, "John Wesley's *Primitive Physic* (1747)," *Harvard Library Bulletin* 16 (1968): 242–256; J. W. Haas Jr., "John Wesley's Views on Science and Christianity: An Examination of the Charge of Antiscience," *Church History* 63 (1998): 378–392; and Randy L. Maddox, "A Heritage Reclaimed: John Wesley on Holistic Health and Healing," in *A Living Tradition: Critical Recovery and Reconstruction of Wesleyan Traditions*, ed. Mary Elizabeth Moore (Nashville, TN: Kingswood Books, forthcoming).

28. Robert Heller, " 'Priest-Doctors' as a Rural Health Service in the Age of Enlightenment," *Medical History* 20 (1976): 362–376; Numbers and Sawyer, "Medicine and Christianity in the Modern World," 140–144, on which this paragraph is largely based; George M. Marsden, *Jonathan Edwards: A Life* (New Haven: Yale

University Press, 2003), 493–494. Regarding smallpox inoculation, see John Duffy, *Epidemics in Colonial America* (Baton Rouge: Louisiana State University Press, 1953), 30–32; Otho T. Beall Jr. and Richard H. Shryock, *Cotton Mather: First Significant Figure in American Medicine* (Baltimore: Johns Hopkins Press, 1954), 104–105; Timothy Tackett, *Priest and Parish in Eighteenth-Century France: A Social and Political Study of the Curés in a Diocese of Dauphiné, 1750–1791* (Princeton, NJ: Princeton University Press, 1977), 162; and Max Bihan, "Mandement de l'Archevêque de Paris en faveur de la vaccination antivariolique," *Histoire des Sciences Médicales* 6 (1972): 169–172. On preacher-physicians, see also Patricia Ann Watson, *The Angelical Conjunction: The Preacher-Physicians of Colonial New England* (Knoxville: University of Tennessee Press, 1991); and Renate Wilson, *Pious Traders in Medicine: A German Pharmaceutical Network in Eighteenth-Century North America* (University Park: Pennsylvania State University Press, 2000).

29. Donald Zochert, "Science and the Common Man in Ante-Bellum America," *Isis* 65 (1974): 448–473, quoting Channing on 448; Johns, *Nature of the Book*, 629–630 (Society for the Diffusion of Useful Knowledge); Bernard Lightman, "Marketing Knowledge for the General Reader: Victorian Popularizers of Science," *Endeavour* 24 (2000): 100–106, quotation on 101 (profusion). On the burgeoning religious press in America, which did much to popularize science, see Candy Gunther Brown, *The Word in the World: Evangelical Writing, Publishing, and Reading in America, 1789–1880* (Chapel Hill: University of North Carolina Press, 2004); and David Paul Nord, *Faith in Reading: Religious Publishing and the Birth of Mass Media in America* (New York: Oxford University Press, 2004).

30. Thomas Pearson, *Infidelity: Its Aspects, Causes, and Agencies*, People's ed. (London: Partridge, Oakey, 1854). I am grateful to Aileen Fyfe for bringing this work to my attention. On the religious dangers of popular literature, see Aileen Fyfe, "Expertise and Christianity: High Standards *versus* the Free Market in Popular Publishing," in *Science and Beliefs: From Natural Philosophy to Natural Sciences, 1700–1900*, ed. David M. Knight and Matthew D. Eddy (Aldershot, UK: Ashgate, 2005), 113–126.

31. Daniel Patrick Thurs, *Science Talk: Changing Notions of Science in American Popular Culture* (New Brunswick, NJ: Rutgers University Press, 2007), 55, 69–74; Aileen Fyfe, *Science and Salvation: Evangelical Popular Science Publishing in Victorian Britain* (Chicago: University of Chicago Press, 2004), 1–15, 36; William J. Astore, *Observing God: Thomas Dick, Evangelicalism, and Popular Science in Victorian Britain and America* (Aldershot, UK: Ashgate, 2002), 1–2 (aim), 8 (science), 171 (American audience). On "science and religion," see also Peter Harrison, " 'Science' and 'Religion': Constructing the Boundaries," *Journal of Religion* 86 (2006): 81–106; James Moore, "Religion and Science," in *The Modern Biological and Earth Sciences*, ed. Peter Bowler and John Pickstone, vol. 6 of *The Cambridge History of Science*, ed. David C. Lindberg and Ronald L. Numbers (Cambridge, UK: Cambridge University Press, forthcoming); and Jon H. Roberts, "Science and Religion," unpublished manuscript. On natural theology in the popular Lowell lectures in Boston, see Margaret W. Rossiter, "Benjamin Silliman and the Lowell Institute: The Popularization of Science in Nineteenth-Century America," *New England Quarterly* 44 (1971): 602–626.

32. Jonathan R. Topham, "The *Wesleyan-Methodist Magazine* and Religious Monthlies in Early Nineteenth-Century Britain," in *Science in the Nineteenth-Century Periodical: Reading the Magazine of Nature*, ed. Geoffrey Cantor et al. (Cambridge, UK: Cambridge University Press, 2004), 67–90; William Paley, *Natural Theology; or, Evidences of the Existence and Attributes of the Deity, Collected from the Appearances of Nature*, 12th ed. (1802; London: J. Faulder, 1809); Fyfe, *Science and Salvation*, 8. On Paley's influence, see D. L. LeMahieu, *The Mind of William Paley: A Philosopher and His Age* (Lincoln: University of Nebraska Press, 1976), 28. See also Jonathan R. Topham, "Periodicals and the Making of Reading Audiences for Science in Early Nineteenth-Century Britain: The *Youth's Magazine*, 1828–37," in Henson et al., *Culture and Science*, 57–69; Sally Shuttleworth and Geoffrey Cantor, "Introduction," in *Science Serialized: Representation of the Sciences in Nineteenth-Century Periodicals*, ed. Geoffrey Cantor and Sally Shuttleworth (Cambridge, MA: MIT Press, 2004), 1–15. On "Natural Theology and Amateur Botany," see Elizabeth B. Keeney, *The Botanizers: Amateur Scientists in Nineteenth-Century America* (Chapel Hill: University of North Carolina Press, 1992), 99–111.

33. Jonathan Topham, "Science and Popular Education in the 1830s: The Role of the *Bridgewater Treatises*," *British Journal for the History of Science* 25 (1992): 397–430. On popular natural theology, see also Jonathan Topham, "Science, Natural Theology, and the Practice of Christian Piety in Early-Nineteenth Religious Magazines," in Cantor and Shuttleworth, *Science Serialized*, 37–66; Bernard Lightman, "The Visual Theology of Victorian Popularizers of Science: From Reverent Eye to Chemical Retina," *Isis* 91 (2000): 651–680; and Bernard Lightman, " 'The Voices of Nature': Popularizing Victorian Science," in *Victorian Science in Context*, ed. Bernard Lightman (Chicago: University of Chicago Press, 1997), 187–211.

34. Dennis R. Dean, "The Influence of Geology on American Literature and Thought," in *Two Hundred Years of Geology in America*, ed. Cecil J. Schneer (Hanover, NH: University Press of New England, 1979), 289–303, quotation regarding "fashionable science" on 293; Rebecca Bedell, *The Anatomy of Nature: Geology and American Landscape Painting, 1825–1875* (Princeton, NJ: Princeton University Press, 2001), 3 (lectures); Ronald L. Numbers, *Creation by Natural Law: Laplace's Nebular Hypothesis in American Thought* (Seattle: University of Washington Press, 1977), 88–104. Early in the century the exhibition of mammoth skeletons generated widespread comment; see Paul Semonin, *American Monster: How the Nation's First Prehistoric Creature Became a Symbol of National Identity* (New York: New York University Press, 2000); and Claudine Cohen, *The Fate of the Mammoth: Fossils, Myth, and History*, trans. William Rodamor (Chicago: University of Chicago Press, 2002).

35. J. Wheaton Smith, *The Life of John P. Crozer* (Philadelphia: American Baptist Publication Society, 1868), 98–99 (mill owner, 1843); Benjamin Silliman, "Address before the Association of American Geologists and Naturalists, Assembled at Boston, April 24, 1842," *American Journal of Science* 43 (1842): 217–250, quotation on 243; Numbers, *Creation by Natural Law*, 89 (50 percent estimate). The two best accounts of geology and religion in this period are Nicolaas A. Rupke, *The Great Chain of History: William Buckland and the English School of Geology, 1814–1849* (Oxford: Oxford

University Press, 1983); and Rodney Lee Stiling, "The Diminishing Deluge: Noah's Flood in Nineteenth-Century American Thought," PhD diss., University of Wisconsin, Madison, 1991.

36. Perry Miller, *The Life of the Mind in America: From the Revolution to the Civil War* (New York: Harcourt, Brace & World, 1965), 278, quoting Silliman; Philip S. Shoemaker, "Stellar Impact: Ormsby MacKnight Mitchel and Astronomy in Antebellum America," PhD diss., University of Wisconsin, Madison, 1991, 201–205; Numbers, *Creation by Natural Law*, quotation on 89. Regarding Mitchel and the nebular hypothesis, see Numbers, *Creation by Natural Law*, 27, 95, 157. On Laplace, see Roger Hahn, "Laplace and the Mechanistic Universe," in Lindberg and Numbers, *God and Nature*, 256–276.

37. Schechner Genuth, "Devils' Hells and Astronomers' Heavens," 3–26; Feingold, *Newtonian Moment*, 121, quoting Voltaire.

38. Michael J. Crowe, *The Extraterrestrial Life Debate, 1750–1900: The Idea of a Plurality of Worlds from Kant to Lowell* (Cambridge, UK: Cambridge University Press, 1986), 182–188 (Chalmers), 411; Bernard Lightman, "*Knowledge* Confronts *Nature*: Richard Proctor and Popular Science Periodicals," in *Culture and Science in the Nineteenth-Century Media*, ed. Louise Henson et al. (Aldershot, UK: Ashgate, 2004), 199–210. On UFOs, see Thurs, *Science Talk*, 123–158.

39. Owsei Temkin, "Gall and the Phrenological Movement," in *"On Second Thought" and Other Essays in the History of Medicine and Science* (Baltimore: Johns Hopkins University Press, 2002), 87–130; John D. Davies, *Phrenology, Fad and Science: A 19th-Century American Crusade* (New Haven: Yale University Press, 1955), 170–171 (Parker). See also Lisle Woodruff Dalton, "Between the Enlightenment and Public Protestantism: Religion and the American Phrenological Movement," PhD diss., University of California, Santa Barbara, 1998.

40. Roger Cooter, *The Cultural Meaning of Popular Science: Phrenology and the Organization of Consent in Nineteenth-Century Britain* (Cambridge, UK: Cambridge University Press, 1984), 120–122, 120 (artisan), 169–198; John van Wyhe, *Phrenology and Origins of Victorian Scientific Naturalism* (Aldershot, UK: Ashgate, 2004), 1 (revolution).

41. David de Giustino, *Conquest of Mind: Phrenology and Victorian Social Thought* (London: Croom Helm, 1975), 108 (interests of eternity); Van Wyhe, *Phrenology*, 129 (torment).

42. Davies, *Phrenology, Fad and Science*, 21 (audiences), 60 (circulation), 153 (compatibility); Madeleine B. Stern, *Heads and Headlines: The Phrenological Fowlers* (Norman: University of Oklahoma Press, 1971), xiv (Spurzheim's visit), 195 (250,000 heads). See also Stephen Tomlinson, *Head Masters: Phrenology, Secular Education, and Nineteenth-Century Social Thought* (Tuscaloosa: University of Alabama Press, 2005); and Thurs, *Science Talk*, 22–52.

43. James A. Secord, *Victorian Sensation: The Extraordinary Publication, Reception, and Secret Authorship of* Vestiges of the Natural History of Creation (Chicago: University of Chicago Press, 2000), 6 (vision), 261 (cabbage), 511 (public street), 526 (sales); Numbers, *Creation by Natural Law*, 28–35, quotation about "atheism" on 32;

H. H. McFarland, *Report of the Trial of Willard Clark* . . . (New Haven: Thomas H. Pease, 1855), 80, 214; Thurs, *Science Talk*, 56–58. See also Ryan Cameron MacPherson, "The *Vestiges of Creation* and America's Pre-Darwinian Evolution Debates: Interpreting Theology and the Natural Sciences in Three Academic Communities," PhD diss., University of Notre Dame, 2003. In *The Politics of Evolution: Morphology, Medicine, and Reform in Radical London* (Chicago: University of Chicago Press, 1989), Adrian Desmond examines how scientific "lowlives" embraced evolution in their class struggle against Anglican Tories.

44. Robert Darnton, *Mesmerism and the End of the Enlightenment in France* (Cambridge, MA: Harvard University Press, 1968), 40 (epidemic), 71 (spiritual); Alison Winter, *Mesmerized: Powers of Mind in Victorian Britain* (Chicago: University of Chicago Press, 1998), 246–275. On electricity and the origin of life, see James A. Secord, "Extraordinary Experiment: Electricity and the Creation of Life in Victorian England," in *The Uses of Experiment: Studies in the Natural Sciences*, ed. David Gooding, Trevor Pinch, and Simon Schaffer (Cambridge, UK: Cambridge University Press, 1988), 337–383; and James E. Strick, *Sparks of Life: Darwinism and the Victorian Debates over Spontaneous Generation* (Cambridge, MA: Harvard University Press, 2000).

45. Craig James Hazen, *The Village Enlightenment in America: Popular Religion and Science in the Nineteenth Century* (Urbana: University of Illinois Press 2000), 113–149, esp. 119 regarding the number of Quimby's patients; Robert Reel, *Mary Baker Eddy: The Years of Discovery* (New York: Holt, Rinehart and Winston, 1966), 152 (200 to 300 magnetizers); Robert C. Fuller, *Mesmerism and the American Cure of Souls* (Philadelphia: University of Pennsylvania Press, 1982), 69 (audiences of two thousand), 89 (religious engine). See also Peter McCandless, "Mesmerism and Phrenology in Antebellum Charleston: 'Enough of the Marvellous,' " *Journal of Southern History* 43 (1992): 199–230; and Ann Taves, *Fits, Trances, and Visions: Experiencing Religion and Explaining Experience from Wesley to James* (Princeton, NJ: Princeton University Press, 1999), 121–165.

46. R. Laurence Moore, *In Search of White Crows: Spiritualism, Parapsychology, and American Culture* (New York: Oxford University Press, 1977), 4 (Parker); Janet Oppenheim, *The Other World: Spiritualism and Psychical Research in England, 1850–1914* (Cambridge, UK: Cambridge University Press, 1985), 59 (midway); Hazen, *Village Enlightenment in America*, 84 (spiritualism as science).

47. Ronald L. Numbers, *Prophetess of Health: A Study of Ellen G. White* (New York: Harper & Row, 1976), 48–77, Coles quotation on 60. See also Nissenbaum, *Sex, Diet, and Debility*; and James C. Whorton, *Crusaders for Fitness: The History of American Health Reformers* (Princeton, NJ: Princeton University Press, 1982).

48. Michael Sappol, *A Traffic of Dead Bodies: Anatomy and Embodied Social Identity in Nineteenth-Century America* (Princeton, NJ: Princeton University Press, 2002), 99 (traffic), 131 (Holy Writ); Ruth Richardson, *Death, Dissection and the Destitute*, 2nd ed. (Chicago: University of Chicago Press, 2000), 77 (Wakley), 90–91 (Aberdeen), 93 (resurrection), 193 (poor man's door).

49. Charles E. Rosenberg, *The Cholera Years: The United States in 1832, 1849, and 1866* (Chicago: University of Chicago Press, 1962), especially 40–54, 121–132, 220

(quotation). On the relationship between religion and insanity, see Ronald L. Numbers and Janet S. Numbers, "Millerism and Madness: A Study of 'Religious Insanity' in Nineteenth-Century America," in *The Disappointed: Millerism and Millenarianism in the Nineteenth Century*, ed. Ronald L. Numbers and Jonathan M. Butler (Bloomington: Indiana University Press, 1987), 92–117.

50. Alvar Ellegård, *Darwin and the General Reader: The Reception of Darwin's Theory of Evolution in the British Periodical Press, 1859–1872* (Göteborg, Sweden: Elanders Boktryckeri Aktiebolag, 1958), 40–41 (Huxley), 43 (human evolution), 44 (*Edinburgh Review*); W. C. Wilson, "Darwin on the Origin of Species," *Methodist Quarterly Review*, 4th ser., no. 13 (1861): 605, quoted in Jon H. Roberts, *Darwinism and the Divine in America: Protestant Intellectuals and Organic Evolution, 1859–1900* (Madison: University of Wisconsin Press, 1988), 3 (American); Charles Darwin, *The Descent of Man, and Selection in Relation to Sex*, 2 vols. (London: John Murray, 1871), 1: 152. On responses to Darwinism, see Alfred Kelly, *The Descent of Darwin: The Popularization of Darwinism in Germany, 1860–1914* (Chapel Hill: University of North Carolina Press, 1981); and Ronald L. Numbers and John Stenhouse, eds., *Disseminating Darwinism: The Role of Race, Place, Religion, and Gender* (Cambridge, UK: Cambridge University Press, 1999).

51. Ronald L. Numbers, *The Creationists: From Scientific Creationism to Intelligent Design*, expanded ed. (Cambridge, MA: Harvard University Press, 2006), 17 (crown); Anne Scott, " 'Visible Incarnations of the Unseen': Henry Drummond and the Practice of Typological Exegesis," *British Journal for the History of Science* 37 (2002): 435–454, Arnold quotation on 435–436. See also James R. Moore, "Evangelicals and Evolution: Henry Drummond, Hebert Spencer, and the Naturalisation of the Spiritual World," *Scottish Journal of Theology* 38 (1985): 383–417.

52. Numbers, *Creationists*, 51 (million-tongued press).

53. Ibid., 58–59 (Bryan); James T. Andrews, *Science for the Masses: The Bolshevik State, Public Science, and the Popular Imagination in Soviet Russia, 1917–1934* (College Station: Texas A&M University Press, 2003), 110–113. On popular depictions of evolution in the 1920s, see Constance Areson Clark, "Evolution for John Doe: Pictures, the Public, and the Scopes Trial Debate," *Journal of American History* 87 (2001): 1275–1301. The best account of the trial and its aftermath is Edward J. Larson, *Summer for the Gods: The Scopes Trial and America's Continuing Debate over Science and Religion* (New York: Basic Books, 1997).

54. Ronald L. Numbers, *Darwinism Comes to America* (Cambridge, MA: Harvard University Press, 1998), 78–79, the source of both quotations. On the radio broadcast of a creation-evolution debate in 1924, see Larry A. Witham, *Where Darwin Meets the Bible: Creationists and Evolutionists in America* (New York: Oxford University Press, 2002), 214. Regarding science, religion, and the BBC, see Peter Bowler, *Reconciling Science and Religion: The Debate in Early-Twentieth-Century Britain* (Chicago: University of Chicago Press, 2001), 45, 337–338. By the mid-1940s the Moody Institute of Science was using moving pictures to disseminate its evangelical message; see James Gilbert, *Redeeming Culture: American Religion in an Age of Science* (Chicago: University of Chicago Press, 1997), chaps. 5–6.

55. Lloyd G. Stevenson, "Religious Elements in the Background of the British Anti-Vivisection Movement," *Yale Journal of Biology and Medicine* 29 (1956): 125–157; Richard D. French, *Antivivisection and Medical Science in Victorian Society* (Princeton, NJ: Princeton University Press, 1975), 345–372; James Turner, *Reckoning with the Beast: Animals, Pain, and Humanity in the Victorian Mind* (Baltimore: Johns Hopkins University Press, 1980); Nicolaas A. Rupke, ed., *Vivisection in Historical Perspective* (London: Croom Helm, 1987). See also Rod Preece, "Darwinism, Christianity, and the Great Vivisection Debate," *Journal of the History of Ideas* 64 (2003): 399–419.

56. Allan M. Brandt, *No Magic Bullet: A Social History of Venereal Disease in the United States Since 1880* (New York: Oxford University Press, 1985), 146, 165, 180; Nancy Tomes, *The Gospel of Germs: Men, Women, and the Microbe in American Life* (Cambridge, MA: Harvard University Press, 1998), 132–134.

57. Rennie B. Schoepflin, *Christian Science on Trial: Religious Healing in America* (Baltimore: Johns Hopkins University Press, 2003); Sanford Gifford, *The Emmanuel Movement: The Origins of Group Treatment and the Assault of Lay Psychotherapy* (Boston: Francis Countway Library of Medicine, 1997); Ellen M. Umansky, *From Christian Science to Jewish Science: Spiritual Healing and American Jews* (New York: Oxford University Press, 2005).

58. Raymond J. Cunningham, "From Holiness to Healing: The Faith Cure in America, 1872–1892," *Church History* 43 (1974): 499–513; David Edwin Harrell Jr., *All Things Are Possible: The Healing and Charismatic Revivals in Modern America* (Bloomington: Indiana University Press, 1975); Grant Wacker, "The Pentecostal Tradition," in *Caring and Curing: Health and Medicine in the Western Faith Traditions*, ed. Ronald L. Numbers and Darryl W. Amundsen (New York: Macmillan, 1986), 514–538. For a superb introduction to Catholic healing, see Robert A. Orsi, *Thank You, St. Jude: Women's Devotion to the Patron Saint of Hopeless Causes* (New Haven: Yale University Press, 1996).

59. Frank M. Turner, "Rainfall, Plagues, and the Prince of Wales: A Chapter in the Conflict of Religion and Science," *Journal of British Studies* 12 (1974): 46–65; Robert Bruce Mullin, "Science, Miracles, and the Prayer-Gauge Debate," in *When Science and Christianity Meet*, ed. David C. Lindberg and Ronald L. Numbers (Chicago: University of Chicago Press, 2003), 203–224; Rick Ostrander, *The Life of Prayer in a World of Science: Protestants, Prayer, and American Culture, 1870–1930* (New York: Oxford University Press, 2000).

60. Edward J. Larson, *Sex, Race, and Science: Eugenics in the Deep South* (Baltimore: Johns Hopkins University Press, 1995); Marouf Arif Hasian Jr., *The Rhetoric of Eugenics in Anglo-American Thought* (Athens: University of Georgia Press, 1996); Leila Zenderland, "Biblical Biology: American Protestant Social Reformers and the Early Eugenics Movement," *Science in Context* 11 (1998): 511–525; Dennis Lee Durst, " 'No Legacy Annuls Heredity from God': Evangelical Social Reformers and the North American Eugenics Movement," PhD diss., St. Louis University, 2002; Christine Rosen, *Preaching Eugenics: Religious Leaders and the American Eugenics Movement* (New York: Oxford University Press, 2004).

61. Jeffrey P. Moran, *Teaching Sex: The Shaping of Adolescence in the 20th Century* (Cambridge, MA: Harvard University Press, 2000); Numbers, "Sex, Science, and Salvation," 206–226.

62. E. Brooks Holifield, A *History of Pastoral Care in America: From Salvation to Self-Realization* (Nashville: Abingdon, 1983); John C. Burnham, "The Encounter of Christian Theology with Deterministic Psychology and Psychoanalysis," *Bulletin of the Menninger Clinic* 49 (1985): 321–352; Jon H. Roberts, "Psychoanalysis and American Christianity, 1900–1945," in Lindberg and Numbers, *When Science and Christianity Meet*, 225–244. On "popular psychology and popular religion," see Taves, *Fits, Trances, and Visions*, 119–249.

63. Schoepflin, *Christian Science on Trial*; Numbers, *Creationists*. On Native American science, see, e.g., Vine Deloria Jr., *Evolution, Creationism, and Other Modern Myths: A Critical Inquiry* (Golden, CO: Fulcrum, 2002); and John Barker, "Creationism in Canada," in *The Cultures of Creationism: Anti-Evolutionism in English-Speaking Countries*, ed. Simon Coleman and Leslie Carlin (Aldershot, UK: Ashgate, 2004), 85–108, especially 101–104. For another example, see Christine Garwood, *Flat Earth: The History of an Infamous Idea* (London: Macmillan, 2007).

CHAPTER 2

This chapter first appeared in *When Science and Christianity Meet*, ed. David C. Lindberg and Ronald L. Numbers (Chicago: University of Chicago Press, 2003), 265–285, and is reprinted here with the permission of the University of Chicago Press (© 2003 by the University of Chicago. All rights reserved). I am indebted to Louise Robbins and Richard Davidson for their research assistance in the preparation of this chapter and to Edward B. Davis, Bernard Lightman, David C. Lindberg, David N. Livingstone, Robert Bruce Mullin, Margaret J. Osler, Jon H. Roberts, Michael H. Shank, and John Stenhouse for their criticisms and suggestions.

1. Opinion of Judge William R. Overton in *McLean v. Arkansas Board of Education*, in *Creationism, Science, and the Law: The Arkansas Case*, ed. Marcel C. La Follette (Cambridge, MA: MIT Press, 1983), 60. See also Michael Ruse, "Creation-Science Is Not Science," ibid., 151–154; Stephen J. Gould, "Impeaching a Self-Appointed Judge," *Scientific American*, July 1992, 118–120; *Science and Creationism: A View from the National Academy of Sciences* (Washington, DC: National Academy Press, 1984), 8; *Teaching about Evolution and the Nature of Science* (Washington, DC: National Academy Press, 1998), chap. 3.

2. Bernard Lightman, "'Fighting Even with Death': Balfour, Scientific Naturalism, and Thomas Henry Huxley's Final Battle," in *Thomas Henry Huxley's Place in Science and Letters: Centenary Essays*, ed. Alan P. Barr (Athens: University of Georgia Press, 1997), 338. Historians have also used naturalism to identify a philosophical point of view, common centuries ago but rare today, that attributes intelligence to matter. The phrase "methodological naturalism" seems to have been coined by the philosopher Paul de Vries, then at Wheaton College, who introduced it orally at a

conference in 1983 in a paper subsequently published as "Naturalism in the Natural Sciences," *Christian Scholar's Review* 15 (1986): 388–396. De Vries distinguished between what he called "methodological naturalism," a disciplinary method that says nothing about God's existence, and "metaphysical naturalism," which "denies the existence of a transcendent God."

3. G. S. Kirk and J. E. Raven, *The Presocratic Philosophers* (Cambridge, UK: Cambridge University Press, 1957), 73; G. E. R. Lloyd, *Magic, Reason and Experience: Studies in the Origin and Development of Greek Science* (Cambridge, UK: Cambridge University Press, 1979), 11, 15–29; John Clarke, *Physical Science in the Time of Nero* (London: Macmillan, 1910), 228. For a similar historical sketch of scientific naturalism, which appeared after I had written this chapter, see Edward B. Davis and Robin Collins, "Scientific Naturalism," in *The History of Science and Religion in the Western Tradition: An Encyclopedia*, ed. Gary B. Ferngren (New York: Garland, 2000), 201–207.

4. David C. Lindberg, *The Beginnings of Western Science; The European Scientific Tradition in Philosophical, Religious, and Institutional Context, 600 B.C. to A.D. 1450* (Chicago: University of Chicago Press, 1992), 198–202, 228–233; Richard C. Dales, *The Scientific Achievement of the Middle Ages* (Philadelphia: University of Pennsylvania Press, 1973), 40 (quoting Adelard). In recent years the history of medieval natural philosophy has generated heated debate. See Andrew Cunningham, "How the *Principia* Got Its Name; or, Taking Natural Philosophy Seriously," *History of Science* 29 (1991): 377–392; Roger French and Andrew Cunningham, *Before Science: The Invention of the Friars' Natural Philosophy* (Aldershot, UK: Scolar Press, 1996); Edward Grant, "God, Science, and Natural Philosophy in the Late Middle Ages," in *Between Demonstration and Imagination: Essays in the History of Science and Philosophy Presented to John D. North*, ed. Lodi Nauta and Arjo Vanderjagt (Leiden: Brill, 1999), 243–267.

5. Bert Hansen, *Nicole Oresme and the Marvels of Nature* (Toronto: Pontifical Institute of Mediaeval Studies, 1985), 59–60, 137. On Buridan's reputation, see Edward Grant, *The Foundations of Modern Science in the Middle Ages: Their Religious, Institutional, and Intellectual Contexts* (Cambridge, UK: Cambridge University Press, 1996), 144.

6. Maurice A. Finocchiaro, ed., *The Galileo Affair: A Documentary History* (Berkeley: University of California Press, 1989), 93.

7. Perez Zagorin, *Francis Bacon* (Princeton, NJ: Princeton University Press, 1998), 48–51; Paul H. Kocher, *Science and Religion in Elizabethan England* (San Marino, CA: Huntington Library, 1953), 27–28, 75.

8. Ronald L. Numbers, *Creation by Natural Law: Laplace's Nebular Hypothesis in American Thought* (Seattle: University of Washington Press, 1977), 3–4; Aram Vartanian, *Diderot and Descartes: A Study of Scientific Naturalism in the Enlightenment* (Princeton, NJ: Princeton University Press, 1953), 52 (quoting Pascal). See also Stephen Gaukroger, *Descartes: An Intellectual Biography* (Oxford: Clarendon Press, 1995), 146–292; Margaret J. Osler, *Divine Will and the Mechanical Philosophy: Gassendi and Descartes on Contingency and Necessity in the Created World* (Cambridge, UK: Cambridge University Press, 1994); and Margaret J. Osler, "Mixing Metaphors: Science and Religion or Natural Philosophy and Theology in Early Modern Europe," *History of*

Science 36 (1998): 91–113. On nature as "a law-bound system of matter in motion," see John C. Greene, *The Death of Adam: Evolution and Its Impact on Western Thought* (Ames: Iowa State University Press, 1959).

9. Robert Boyle, *A Free Enquiry into the Vulgarly Received Notion of Nature*, ed. Edward B. Davis and Michael Hunter (Cambridge, UK: Cambridge University Press, 1996), ix–x, xv, 38–39. See also Rose-Mary Sargent, *The Diffident Naturalist: Robert Boyle and the Philosophy of Experiment* (Chicago: University of Chicago Press, 1995), 93–103. On Christianity and the mechanical philosophy, see also Osler, "Mixing Metaphors," 91–113; and John Hedley Brooke, *Science and Religion: Some Historical Perspectives* (Cambridge, UK: Cambridge University Press, 1991), chap. 4, "Divine Activity in a Mechanical Universe."

10. Isaac Newton, *Mathematical Principles of Natural Philosophy and His System of the World*, trans. Andrew Motte, revised by Florian Cajori (Berkeley: University of California Press, 1960), 543–544; H. W. Turnbull, ed., *The Correspondence of Isaac Newton*, 7 vols. (Cambridge, UK: Cambridge University Press, 1959–1977), 2: 331–334. For a statement that the solar system could not have been produced by natural causes alone, see Isaac Newton, *Papers and Letters on Natural Philosophy and Related Documents*, ed. I. Bernard Cohen (Cambridge, UK: Cambridge University Press, 1958), 282. See also David Kubrin, "Newton and the Cyclical Cosmos: Providence and the Mechanical Philosophy," *Journal of the History of Ideas* 28 (1967): 325–346; Richard S. Westfall, *Never at Rest: A Biography of Isaac Newton* (Cambridge, UK: Cambridge University Press, 1980); and Cunningham, "How the *Principia* Got Its Name," 377–392.

11. Kocher, *Science and Religion in Elizabethan England*, 97; Keith Thomas, *Religion and the Decline of Magic: Studies in Popular Beliefs in Sixteenth and Seventeenth Century England* (London: Weidenfeld and Nicolson, 1971).

12. This paragraph is based largely on Ronald L. Numbers and Ronald C. Sawyer, "Medicine and Christianity in the Modern World," in *Health/Medicine and the Faith Traditions: An Inquiry into Religion and Medicine*, ed. Martin E. Marty and Kenneth L. Vaux (Philadelphia: Fortress Press, 1982), 133–160, especially 138–139. On the naturalization of mental illness, see Michael MacDonald, "Insanity and the Realities of History in Early Modern England," *Psychological Medicine* 11 (1981): 11–15; Michael MacDonald, "Religion, Social Change, and Psychological Healing in England, 1600–1800," in *The Church and Healing*, vol. 19 of *Studies in Church History*, ed. W. J. Sheils (Oxford: Basil Blackwell, 1982), 101–125; Ronald L. Numbers and Janet S. Numbers, "Millerism and Madness: A Study of 'Religious Insanity' in Nineteenth-Century America," in *The Disappointed: Millerism and Millenarianism in the Nineteenth Century*, ed. Ronald L. Numbers and Jonathan M. Butler (Bloomington: Indiana University Press, 1987), 92–117.

13. John Duffy, *Epidemics in Colonial America* (Baton Rouge: Louisiana State University Press, 1953), 30–32; Otho T. Beall Jr. and Richard H. Shryock, *Cotton Mather: First Significant Figure in American Medicine* (Baltimore: Johns Hopkins Press, 1954), 104–105 (quoting Mather); Perry Miller, *The New England Mind: From Colony to Province* (Cambridge, MA: Harvard University Press, 1953), 345–366; Maxine van de

Wetering, "A Reconsideration of the Inoculation Controversy," *New England Quarterly* 58 (1985): 46–67. On the transformation of cholera from divine punishment to public health problem, see Charles E. Rosenberg, *The Cholera Years: The United States in 1832, 1849, and 1866* (Chicago: University of Chicago Press, 1962).

14. I. Bernard Cohen, *Benjamin Franklin's Science* (Cambridge, MA: Harvard University Press, 1999), chap. 8, "Prejudice against the Introduction of Lightning Rods," quotation on 141.

15. Theodore Hornberger, "The Science of Thomas Prince," *New England Quarterly* 9 (1936): 31; William D. Andrews, "The Literature of the 1727 New England Earthquake," *Early American Literature* 7 (1973): 283.

16. Theodore Hornberger, *Scientific Thought in the American Colleges, 1638–1800* (Austin: University of Texas Press, 1945), 82.

17. Andrew Cunningham, "Getting the Game Right: Some Plain Words on the Identity and Invention of Science," *Studies in History and Philosophy of Science* 19 (1988): 365–389. See also Sydney Ross, "Scientist: The Story of a Word," *Annals of Science* 18 (1962): 65–85, which dates the earliest use of the term "scientist" to 1834.

18. Vartanian, *Diderot and Descartes*, 206 (quoting La Mettrie); Kathleen Wellman, *La Mettrie: Medicine, Philosophy, and Enlightenment* (Durham, NC: Duke University Press, 1992), 175, 186–188. See also Aram Vartanian, ed., *La Mettrie's L'Homme Machine: A Study in the Origins of an Idea* (Princeton, NJ: Princeton University Press, 1960); and Jacques Roger, *The Life Sciences in Eighteenth-Century French Thought*, ed. Keith R. Benson, trans. Robert Ellrich (Stanford: Stanford University Press, 1997).

19. Georges Louis Leclerc, comte de Buffon, *Natural History: General and Particular*, trans. William Smellie, 7 vols. (London: W. Strahan & T. Cadell, 1781), 1: 34, 63–82; Numbers, *Creation by Natural Law*, 6–8. On Buffon's religious beliefs, see Jacques Roger, *Buffon: A Life in Natural History*, trans. Sarah Lucille Bonnefoi, ed. L. Pearce Williams (Ithaca, NY: Cornell University Press, 1997), 431. On the naturalism of Buffon and his contemporaries, see Kenneth L. Taylor, "Volcanoes as Accidents: How 'Natural' Were Volcanoes to 18th-Century Naturalists?" in *Volcanoes and History*, ed. Nicoletta Morello (Genoa: Brigati, 1998), 595–618.

20. Roger Hahn, "Laplace and the Vanishing Role of God in the Physical Universe," in *The Analytic Spirit: Essays in the History of Science in Honor of Henry Guerlac*, ed. Harry Woolf (Ithaca, NY: Cornell University Press, 1981), 85–95; Roger Hahn, "Laplace and the Mechanistic Universe," in *God and Nature: Historical Essays on the Encounter between Christianity and Science*, ed. David C. Lindberg and Ronald L. Numbers (Berkeley: University of California Press, 1986), 256–276.

21. Thomas Chalmers, *On the Power, Wisdom, and Goodness of God as Manifested in the Adaptation of External Nature to the Moral and Intellectual Constitution of Man*, 2 vols. (London: William Pickering, 1835), 1: 30–32. On English attitudes toward French science, see Adrian Desmond, *The Politics of Evolution: Morphology, Medicine, and Reform in Radical London* (Chicago: University of Chicago Press, 1989), chap. 2. This and the following five paragraphs are extracted in large part from Numbers, *Creation by Natural Law*, especially 79–83, 93.

22. J. P. N[ichol], "State of Discovery and Speculation Concerning the Nebulae," *Westminster Review* 25 (1836): 406–408; J. P. Nichol, *Views of the Architecture of the Heavens*, 2nd ed. (New York: Dayton & Newman, 1842), 103–105. On Nichol, see also Simon Schaffer, "The Nebular Hypothesis and the Science of Progress," in *History, Humanity and Evolution: Essays for John C. Greene*, ed. James R. Moore (Cambridge, UK: Cambridge University Press, 1989), 131–164.

23. John LeConte, "The Nebular Hypothesis," *Popular Science Monthly* 2 (1873): 655; "The Nebular Hypothesis," *Southern Quarterly Review* 10 (1846): 228 (Great Architect). It is unclear from the transcript of his lecture whether LeConte was expressing his own view or quoting the words of someone else.

24. [Daniel Kirkwood], "The Nebular Hypothesis," *Presbyterian Quarterly Review* 2 (1854): 544.

25. "The Nebular Hypothesis," *Southern Quarterly Review*, new ser. 1 (1856): 110–111.

26. "The Nebular Hypothesis," *Southern Quarterly Review* 10 (1846): 240.

27. John Frederick William Herschel, *A Preliminary Discourse on the Study of Natural Philosophy*, new ed. (Philadelphia: Lea & Blanchard, 1839), 6, 27–28, 59, 108; Walter F. Cannon, "John Herschel and the Idea of Science," *Journal of the History of Ideas* 22 (1961): 215–239; William Minto, *Logic: Inductive and Deductive* (New York: C. Scribner's Sons, 1904), 157, quoted in Laurens Laudan, "Theories of Scientific Method from Plato to Mach: A Bibliographical Review," *History of Science* 7 (1968): 30. On the meaning of science, see also Richard Yeo, *Defining Science: William Whewell, Natural Knowledge, and Public Debate in Early Victorian Britain* (Cambridge, UK: Cambridge University Press, 1993).

28. Martin Rudwick, "Uniformity and Progression: Reflections on the Structure of Geological Theory in the Age of Lyell," in *Perspectives in the History of Science and Technology*, ed. Duane H. D. Roller (Norman: University of Oklahoma Press, 1971), 209–227; Roy Porter, *The Making of Geology: Earth Science in Britain, 1660–1815* (Cambridge, UK: Cambridge University Press, 1977), 2 (freeing the science); James R. Moore, "Charles Lyell and the Noachian Deluge," *Journal of the American Scientific Affiliation* 22 (1970): 107–115, quotation about causes on 109; Leonard G. Wilson, *Charles Lyell: The Years to 1841: The Revolution in Geology* (New Haven: Yale University Press, 1972), 256. On Lyell's indebtedness to Herschel, see Rachel Laudan, *From Mineralogy to Geology: The Foundations of a Science, 1650–1830* (Chicago: University of Chicago Press, 1987), 203–204. See also Martin J. S. Rudwick, "The Shape and Meaning of Earth History," in *God and Nature: Historical Essays on the Encounter between Christianity and Science*, ed. David C. Lindberg and Ronald L. Numbers (Berkeley: University of California Press, 1986), 296–321; and James R. Moore, "Geologists and Interpreters of Genesis in the Nineteenth Century," in Lindberg and Numbers, *God and Nature*, 322–350.

29. Charles Lyell, *Principles of Geology, Being an Attempt to Explain the Former Changes of the Earth's Surface, by Reference to Causes Now in Operation*, 3 vols. (London: John Murray, 1830–1833), 1: 75–76. On the role of Christian ministers in naturalizing earth history, see, e.g., Nicolaas A. Rupke, *The Great Chain of History: William Buckland*

and the English School of Geology (1814–1849) (Oxford: Clarendon Press, 1983); and Rodney L. Stiling, "The Diminishing Deluge: Noah's Flood in Nineteenth-Century American Geology and Theology," PhD diss., University of Wisconsin, Madison, 1992.

30. James A. Secord, introduction to *Principles of Geology*, by Charles Lyell (London: Penguin Books, 1997), xxxii–xxxiii. On the naturalization of physiology, see Alison Winter, "The Construction of Orthodoxies and Heterodoxies in the Early Victorian Life Sciences," in *Victorian Science in Context*, ed. Bernard Lightman (Chicago: University of California Press, 1997), 24–50.

31. Howard E. Gruber, *Darwin on Man: A Psychological Study of Scientific Creativity*, together with *Darwin's Early and Unpublished Notebooks*, transcribed and annotated by Paul H. Barrett (New York: E. P. Dutton, 1974), 417–418; Leonard Huxley, ed., *The Life and Letters of Thomas Henry Huxley*, 2 vols. (New York: D. Appleton, 1909), 2: 320; Mario A. di Gregorio, *T. H. Huxley's Place in Natural Science* (New Haven: Yale University Press, 1984), 51; Charles Darwin, *On the Origin of Species*, with an introduction by Ernst Mayr (Cambridge, MA: Harvard University Press, 1966), 483; Adrian Desmond, *Huxley: From Devil's Disciple to Evolution's High Priest* (Reading, MA: Addison-Wesley, 1997), 256. According to Desmond, Huxley first described atoms flashing into elephants in his "Lectures," *Medical Times and Gazette* 12 (1856): 482–483, which includes the quotation about lack of evidence for creation. For American references to atomic elephants, see Ronald L. Numbers, *Darwinism Comes to America* (Cambridge, MA: Harvard University Press, 1998), 52. As Neal C. Gillespie has shown, natural theology "had virtually ceased to be a significant part of the day-to-day practical explanatory structure of natural history" well before 1859; "Preparing for Darwin: Conchology and Natural Theology in Anglo-American Natural History," *Studies in History of Biology* 7 (1984): 95.

32. Darwin, *On the Origin of Species*, 466; S. R. Calthrop, "Religion and Evolution," *Religious Magazine and Monthly Review* 50 (1873): 205; [W. N. Rice], "The Darwinian Theory of the Origin of Species," *New Englander* 26 (1867): 608.

33. Asa Gray, *Darwiniana: Essays and Reviews Pertaining to Darwinism* (New York: D. Appleton, 1876), 78–79, from a review first published in 1860 (sufficient answer); Asa Gray, *Natural Science and Religion: Two Lectures Delivered to the Theology School of Yale College* (New York: Charles Scribner's Sons, 1880), 77 (business of science); George Frederick Wright, "Recent Works Bearing on the Relation of Science to Religion: No. II," *Bibliotheca Sacra* 33 (1876): 480.

34. The Duke of Argyll, *The Reign of Law*, 5th ed. (New York: John W. Lovell, 1868), 34; B. B. Warfield, Review of *Darwinism To-Day*, by Vernon L. Kellogg, in *Princeton Theological Review* 6 (1908): 640–650. I am indebted to David N. Livingstone for bringing the Warfield statement to my attention. For more on Warfield, see David N. Livingstone and Mark A. Noll, "B. B. Warfield (1851–1921): A Biblical Inerrantist as Evolutionist," *Isis* 91 (2000): 283–304. See also Desmond, *Huxley*, 555–556. On the scientific context of Argyll's views, see Nicolaas A. Rupke, *Richard Owen: Victorian Naturalist* (New Haven: Yale University Press, 1994).

35. Jon H. Roberts, *Darwinism and the Divine in America: Protestant Intellectuals and Organic Evolution, 1859–1900* (Madison: University of Wisconsin Press, 1988),

136; Numbers, *Darwinism Comes to America*, 40–41; Joseph LeConte, "Evolution in Relation to Materialism, *Princeton Review*, new ser. 7 (1881): 166, 174. Jon H. Roberts and James Turner, *The Sacred and the Secular University* (Princeton, NJ: Princeton University Press, 2000), 28–30, devotes a section to "the triumph of methodological naturalism." Of the eighty anthropologists, botanists, geologists, and zoologists elected to the National Academy of Sciences between its creation in 1863 and 1900, only thirteen were known agnostics or atheists; Numbers, *Darwinism Comes to America*, 41. James H. Leuba's pioneering survey of the beliefs of American scientists in 1916 turned up only 41.8 percent who affirmed belief "in a God in intellectual and affective communication with humankind, i.e. a God to whom one may pray in expectation of receiving an answer." Fifty years later the figure had declined only to 39.3 percent of respondents. See Edward J. Larson and Larry Witham, "Scientists Are Still Keeping the Faith," *Nature* 386 (1997): 435–436.

36. Frank M. Turner, *Between Science and Religion: The Reaction to Scientific Naturalism in Late Victorian England* (New Haven: Yale University Press, 1974), 16 (secularization). See also Frank M. Turner, *Contesting Cultural Authority: Essays in Victorian Intellectual Life* (Cambridge, UK: Cambridge University Press, 1993); and Bernard Lightman, *The Origins of Agnosticism: Victorian Unbelief and the Limits of Knowledge* (Baltimore: Johns Hopkins University Press, 1987).

37. Frank M. Turner, "John Tyndall and Victorian Scientific Naturalism," in *John Tyndall: Essays on a Natural Philosopher*, ed. W. H. Brock et al. (Dublin: Royal Dublin Society, 1981), 172; Turner, *Between Science and Religion*, 11–12 (quoting the devotee Beatrice Webb); Lightman, " 'Fighting Even with Death,' " 323–350. See also Ruth Barton, "John Tyndall, Pantheist: A Rereading of the Belfast Address," *Osiris*, 2nd ser., no. 3 (1987): 111–134.

38. John C. Burnham, "The Encounter of Christian Theology with Deterministic Psychology and Psychoanalysis," *Bulletin of the Menninger Clinic* 49 (1985): 321–352, quotations on 333, 337; Turner, *Between Science and Religion*, 14–16. For a comprehensive discussion of naturalism and the rise of the social sciences, see Roberts and Turner, *The Sacred and the Secular University*, 43–60. On earlier efforts to naturalize psychology, see Roger Cooter, *The Cultural Meaning of Popular Science: Phrenology and the Organization of Consent in Nineteenth-Century Britain* (Cambridge, UK: Cambridge University Press, 1984).

39. Phillip E. Johnson, "Foreword," in *The Creation Hypothesis: Scientific Evidence for an Intelligent Designer*, ed. J. P. Moreland (Downers Grove, IL: InterVarsity Press, 1994), 7–8 (naturalism rules); Larry Vardiman, "Scientific Naturalism as Science," *Impact*, no. 293 (reclaiming science), inserted in *Acts & Facts* 26 (November 1997); Paul Nelson at a conference on "Design and Its Critics," Concordia University, Mequon, Wisconsin, June 24, 2000 (rubbish). For a brief history of intelligent design, see Ronald L. Numbers, *The Creationists: From Scientific Creationism to Intelligent Design*, expanded ed. (Cambridge, MA: Harvard University Press, 2006), chap. 17. On scientific creationists and naturalism, see ibid., 107–108, 113–114, 232–233.

40. Michael J. Behe, *Darwin's Black Box: The Biochemical Challenge to Evolution* (New York: Free Press, 1996), 15, 33, 193, 232–233; "The Evolution of a Skeptic: An

Interview with Dr. Michael Behe, Biochemist and Author of Recent Best-Seller, *Darwin's Black Box,*" *The Real Issue* 15 (November/December 1996): 1, 6–8.

41. William A. Dembski, "What Every Theologian Should Know about Creation, Evolution, and Design," *Transactions* 3 (May/June 1995): 1–8. See also William A. Dembski, *Intelligent Design: The Bridge between Science and Theology* (Downers Grove, IL: InterVarsity Press, 1999). For a philosophical critique of methodological naturalism from a Christian perspective, see Alvin Plantinga, "Methodological Naturalism?" *Perspectives on Science and Christian Faith* 49 (September 1997): 143–154. For a philosophical critique of intelligent design, see Robert T. Pennock, *Tower of Babel: The Evidence against the New Creationism* (Cambridge, MA: MIT Press, 1999).

42. David K. Webb, letter to the editor, *Origins & Design* 17 (spring 1996): 5; J. W. Haas Jr., "On Intelligent Design, Irreducible Complexity, and Theistic Science," *Perspectives on Science and Christian Faith* 49 (March 1997): 1, who quotes Dawkins.

43. John Hedley Brooke has similarly challenged the common notion "that the sciences have eroded religious belief by explaining physical phenomena in terms of natural law"; see his "Natural Law in the Natural Sciences: The Origins of Modern Atheism?" *Science and Christian Belief* 4 (1992): 83.

44. Larson and Witham, "Scientists Are Still Keeping the Faith," 435–436; Frank Newport, "Almost Half of Americans Believe Humans Did Not Evolve," June 5, 2006, at www.poll.gallup.com; Claudia Wallis, "Faith and Healing," *Time*, June 24, 1996, 63.

CHAPTER 3

This chapter first appeared in Klaas van Berkel and Arjo Vanderjagt, eds., *The Book of Nature in Early Modern and Modern History* (Leuven, Belgium: Peeters, 2006), 261–274, and is reprinted with the permission of Peeters Publishers. I would like to thank Carson Burrington for his help in tracking down references to the book of nature and my friends Jon Roberts and Peter Harrison for their criticisms and suggestions.

1. James Ashton, *The Book of Nature: Containing Information for Young People Who Think of Getting Married, on the Philosophy of Procreation and Sexual Intercourse, Showing How to Prevent Conception and to Avoid Child-Bearing* (New York: Brother Jonathan, 1870); Thomas Faulkner, *Book of Nature and Marriage Guide: A Full and Explicit Explanation of the Structure and Uses of the Organs of Life and Generation, in Man and Woman* (New York: Hurst, 1891). Andrew Taylor Still, the founder of osteopathy, identified "the book of Nature" as his "chief source of study"; "How I Came to Originate Osteopathy," *Ladies' Home Journal* 25 (January 1908): 25. On the history of the book-of-nature metaphor, see Arjo Vanderjagt and Klaas van Berkel, eds., *The Book of Nature in Antiquity and the Middle Ages* (Leuven, Belgium: Peeters, 2005); and Klaas van Berkel and Arjo Vanderjagt, eds., *The Book of Nature in Early Modern and Modern History,* (Leuven, Belgium: Peeters, 2006).

2. Cotton Mather, *The Christian Philosopher*, ed. Winton U. Solberg (Urbana: University of Illinois Press, 1994), 17–18. Elsewhere (41), Mather quotes from an anonymous seventeenth-century tract titled *Theologia ruris, sive schola et scala naturae; or, The Book of Nature* (London, 1686).

3. See, e.g., John Toogood, *The Book of Nature: A Discourse on Some of Those Instances of the Power, Wisdom, and Goodness of God, Which Are within the Reach of Common Observation*, 4th ed. (Boston: Samuel Hall, 1802); *The Book of Nature: Embracing a Condensed Survey of the Animal Kingdom, as Well as Sketches of Vegetable Anatomy, Geology, Botany, Mineralogy, &c.*, ed. by an association of scientific gentlemen of Philadelphia, 2 vols. (Philadelphia: Samuel Atkinson, 1834); M. Schele de Vere, *Stray Leaves from the Book of Nature* (New York: G. P. Putnam, 1856); Worthington Hooker, *The Child's Book of Nature: For the Use of Families and Schools, Intended to Aid Mothers and Teachers in Training Children in the Observation of Nature* (New York: Harper & Brothers, 1857); and George D. Armstrong, *The Two Books of Nature and Revelation Collated* (New York: Funk & Wagnalls, 1886).

4. Daniel March, *Our Father's House; or, The Unwritten Word* (Philadelphia: Ziegler & McCurdy, 1869), 26.

5. George D. Boardman, *Studies in the Creative Week* (New York: D. Appleton, 1878), 14. On Boardman, see Joan Jacobs Brumberg, *Mission for Life: The Story of the Family of Adoniram Judson, the Dramatic Events of the First American Foreign Mission, and the Course of Evangelical Religion in the Nineteenth Century* (New York: Free Press, 1980), 151–158.

6. See, e.g., Thomas Paine, "The Existence of God," an address delivered in 1797, in Kerry S. Walters, *The American Deists: Voices of Reason and Dissent in the Early Republic* (Lawrence: University of Kansas Press, 1992), 233; Daniel Walker Howe, *The Unitarian Conscience: Harvard Moral Philosophy, 1805–1861* (Cambridge, MA: Harvard University Press, 1970), 71; Henry Ward Beecher, *Evolution and Religion* (New York: Fords, Howard & Hulbert, 1885), 44–45 (Congregationalist); Armstrong, *Two Books*, 14 (Presbyterian); Matthew Fontaine Maury to the Reverend Mr. Field, January 22, 1855, Records of the Naval Observatory, Letters Sent, vol. 11, Library of Congress, quoted in Ronald L. Numbers, *Creation by Natural Law: Laplace's Nebular Hypothesis in American Thought* (Seattle: University of Washington Press, 1977), 88 (Episcopalian); John Bachman, *The Doctrine of the Unity of the Human Race: Examined on the Principles of Science* (Charleston, SC: C. Canning, 1850), 7 (Lutheran); Boardman, *Studies in the Creative Week*, 14–17 (Baptist); Thomas Mitchell, *Cosmogony: The Geological Antiquity of the World, Evolution, Atheism, Pantheism, Deism and Infidelity Refuted, by Science, Philosophy and Scripture*, 2 vols. (New York: American Book Co., 1881), 1: xxv (Methodist); James E. Talmage, *First Book of Nature* (Salt Lake City: Contributor Co., 1888) (Mormon); Mrs. E. G. White, *Patriarchs and Prophets: The Great Conflict between Good and Evil as Illustrated in the Lives of Holy Men of Old* (Oakland, CA: Pacific Press, 1890), 599 (Adventist). See also chapter 5 of this volume on Charles Hodge's use of the metaphor.

7. White, *Patriarchs and Prophets*, 599. For a list of references, see *Comprehensive Index to the Writings of Ellen G. White*, 3 vols. (Mountain View, CA: Pacific Press,

1962), 2: 1861–1862. See also Mrs. Ellen G. White, *Principles of True Science; or, Creation in the Light of Revelation* (Takoma Park, DC: Washington College Press, 1929); and Ronald L. Numbers, *Prophetess of Health: A Study of Ellen G. White* (New York: Harper & Row, 1976).

8. Among scientists who embraced organic evolution, Joseph LeConte described the Bible and nature as "two divine, original books" in *Religion and Science: A Series of Sunday Lectures on the Relation of Natural and Revealed Religion, or the Truths Revealed in Nature and Scripture* (New York: D. Appleton, 1873), 242; James D. Dana referred to "the volume of Nature" in *The Genesis of the Heavens and the Earth: And All the Host of Them* (Hartford, CT: Student Publishing Co., 1890), 70; Asa Gray wrote of "the Author of Nature" in *Natural Science and Religion: Two Lectures Delivered to the Theological School of Yale College* (New York: Charles Scribner's Sons, 1880), 86. For references from anti-Darwinians, see, e.g., J. W. Dawson, *Archaia; or, Studies of the Cosmogony and Natural History of the Hebrew Scriptures* (Montreal: B. Dawson, 1860), 17; and Arnold Guyot, *Creation; or, The Biblical Cosmogony in the Light of Modern Science* (New York: Charles Scribner's Sons, 1884), 3. Louis Agassiz, like his colleague Gray, would sometimes refer to "the great Author" of nature; see, e.g., *The Structure of Animal Life* (New York: Scribner, Armstrong, 1865), 1. On evolution and religion in America, see James R. Moore, *The Post-Darwinian Controversies: A Study of the Protestant Struggle to Come to Terms with Darwin in Great Britain and America, 1870–1900* (Cambridge, UK: Cambridge University Press, 1979); Jon H. Roberts, *Darwinism and the Divine in America: Protestant Intellectuals and Organic Evolution, 1859–1900* (Madison: University of Wisconsin Press, 1988); and Ronald L. Numbers, *Darwinism Comes to America* (Cambridge, MA: Harvard University Press, 1998).

9. Beecher, *Evolution and Religion*, 44–45; Clifford E. Clark Jr., *Henry Ward Beecher: Spokesman for a Middle-Class America* (Urbana, IL: University of Illinois Press, 1978), 25. Jon H. Roberts has observed that Protestants such as Beecher, "who emphasized the immanence of God in His creation," were highly likely to extend "the scope of divine revelation . . . well beyond the Scriptures"; see Roberts, *Darwinism and the Divine in America*, 157–158.

10. See, e.g., [Benjamin Silliman?], Review of *A Synopsis of the Birds of North America and The Birds of America, from Drawings Made in the United States and Their Territories*, by John James Audubon, *American Journal of Science and Arts* 39 (1840): 345–348; and LeConte, *Religion and Science*, 9–10. Margaret Welch, *The Book of Nature: Natural History in the United States, 1825–1875* (Boston: Northeastern University Press, 1998), mentions but does not discuss the metaphor used as the title of her book.

11. Herbert W. Morris, *Science and the Bible; or, The Mosaic Creation and Modern Discoveries* (Philadelphia: Ziegler & McCurdy, 1871), 3–4. In a subsequent British edition of the work, published under the title *Work-Days of God; or, Science and the Bible* (London: Pickering & Inglis, n.d.), Morris noted that fifty thousand copies of the first edition has been sold in a little more than three years.

12. John Wesley Powell, *Exploration of the Colorado River of the West and Its Tributaries* (Meadville, PA: Flood & Vincent, 1875), 89, 193–194.

13. Thomas Paine, quoted in Walters, *The American Deists*, 231 (Bible); Board-man, *Studies in the Creative Week*, 5 (Archive); [Enoch Fitch Burr], *Ecce Coelum; or, Parish Astronomy* (Boston: Noyes, Holmes, 1867), 11 (missal and Natural Bible); March, *Our Father's House*, 5 (Unwritten Word); George M. Gould, *The Meaning and the Method of Life: A Search for Religion in Biology* (New York: G. P. Putnam's Sons, 1893), 290 (letter); Edward Hitchcock, *Religious Truth: Illustrated from Science, in Addresses and Sermons on Special Occasions* (Boston: Phillips, Sampson, 1857), 46 (elder Scripture).

14. Boardman, *Studies in the Creative Week*, 14, 17. Dawson, *Archaia*, 17, uses Browne epigraphically. On Browne, see Andrew Cunningham, "Sir Thomas Browne and His *Religio Medici*: Reason, Nature and Religion," in *Religio Medici: Medicine and Religion in Seventeenth-Century England*, ed. Ole Peter Grell and Andrew Cun-ningham (Aldershot, UK: Scolar Press, 1996), 12–61.

15. Sherwood Cummings, *Mark Twain and Science: Adventures of a Mind* (Baton Rouge: Louisiana State University Press, 1988), 16; Robert G. Ingersoll, "Some Mistakes of Moses," in *The Works of Robert G. Ingersoll*, 12 vols. (New York: Dresden Publishing, 1912), 2: 13–270.

16. John William Draper, *History of the Conflict between Religion and Science* (New York: D. Appleton, 1874), 226–227. The eminent German Reformed scholar Philip Schaff, who denied any *"essential"* conflict between religion and science, attributed the *"temporary* conflict" described by Draper to "our imperfect knowledge and compre-hension of the book of nature, or of the Bible, or of both." See Schaff, preface to Johann Peter Lange's *Commentary on the Holy Scriptures*, quoted in John Phin, *The Chemical History of the Six Days of Creation* (New York: American News Co., 1870), 5. Andrew Dickson White, in *The Warfare of Science* (New York: D. Appleton, 1876), 116, wrote of "God's truth as revealed in Nature."

17. Karl Barth, *The Knowledge of God and the Service of God According to the Teaching of the Reformation*, trans. J. L. M. Haire and Ian Henderson (London: Hodder and Stoughton, 1938), 6, 8–9. Useful introductions to Protestantism and science in the twentieth century include Keith E. Yandell, "Protestant Theology and Natural Science in the Twentieth Century," in *God and Nature: Historical Essays on the En-counter between Christianity and Science*, ed. David C. Lindberg and Ronald L. Numbers (Berkeley: University of California Press, 1986), 448–471; and Ian G. Barbour, *Issues in Science and Religion* (Englewood Cliffs, NJ: Prentice Hall, 1966).

18. A joint statement by W. B. Riley and Harry Rimmer in the foreword to *A Debate: Resolved, That the Creative Days in Genesis Were Aeons, Not Solar Days* [1929], 4, reprinted in *Creation–Evolution Debates*, ed. Ronald L. Numbers, vol. 2 of *Creationism in Twentieth-Century America: A Ten-Volume Anthology of Documents, 1903–1961*, ed. Ronald L. Numbers (New York: Garland, 1995), 393–325. The best introduction to American fundamentalism is still George M. Marsden, *Fundamentalism and American Culture: The Shaping of Twentieth-Century Evangelicalism, 1870–1925* (New York: Oxford University Press, 1980).

19. James Orr, "Science and Christian Faith," in *The Fundamentals: A Testimony to the Truth*, 12 vols. (Chicago: Testimony Publishing, 1910–1915), 4: 91, 104.

20. J. Gresham Machen, *Christianity and Liberalism* (New York: Macmillan, 1926), 69. On Machen, see D. G. Hart, *Defending the Faith: J. Gresham Machen and the Crisis of Conservative Protestantism in Modern America* (Baltimore: Johns Hopkins University Press, 1994).

21. William Jennings Bryan, *Orthodox Christianity* (New York: Fleming Revell, 1923), quoted in James Gilbert, *Redeeming Culture: American Religion in an Age of Science* (Chicago: University of Chicago Press, 1997), 28.

22. Riley and Rimmer, *A Debate*, 12, 15; William B. Riley, *The Finality of the Higher Criticism: The Theory of Evolution and False Theology* (Minneapolis, 1909), 94–95. On Riley, see William Vance Trollinger Jr., *God's Empire: William Bell Riley and Midwestern Fundamentalism* (Madison: University of Wisconsin Press, 1990).

23. Harry Rimmer, *Modern Science and the First Day of Creation* (Los Angeles: Research Science Bureau, 1929), 15–16 (pre-Adamic age); Harry Rimmer, *Modern Science and the Sixth Day of Creation* (Los Angeles: Research Science Bureau, 1934), 47–48 (page of nature); Harry Rimmer, *The Harmony of Science and the Scriptures* (Los Angeles: Research Science Bureau, 1927), 3 (two revelations); Harry Rimmer, *Modern Science and the First Fundamental* (Los Angeles: Research Science Bureau, 1928), 19–20 (heathen). On Rimmer, see Edward B. Davis, introduction to *The Antievolution Pamphlets of Harry Rimmer*, vol. 6 of Numbers, *Creationism in Twentieth-Century America*, ix–xxviii; and Ronald L. Numbers, *The Creationists: From Scientific Creationism to Intelligent Design*, expanded ed. (Cambridge, MA: Harvard University Press, 2006), 60–71.

24. On Price, see Numbers, *The Creationists*, 88–119 et passim, quotation from *Science* on 89.

25. George McCready Price, *If You Were the Creator: A Reasonable Credo for Modern Man* (Mountain View, CA: Pacific Press, 1942), 21; George McCready Price, *Genesis Vindicated* (Takoma Park, MD: Review and Herald Publishing Assn., 1941), 18, 39.

26. George McCready Price, *Back to the Bible; or, The New Protestantism* (Takoma Park, MD: Review and Herald Publishing Assn., 1916), 12, 18.

27. George McCready Price, *God's Two Books; or, Plain Facts about Evolution, Geology, and the Bible* (Washington, DC: Review and Herald Publishing Assn., 1911), 24–25, 168–169. In 1928 the department of education of the General Conference of Seventh-day Adventists published Marion E. Cady, *The Book of Nature: With the Creator from Season to Season* (Mountain View, CA: Pacific Press, 1928).

28. Leander S. Keyser, *The Philosophy of Christianity* (Burlington, IA: Lutheran Literary Board, 1928), 151–152. See also Leander S. Keyser, *A System of Natural Theism* (Burlington, IA: Lutheran Literary Board, 1927).

29. Frank Lewis Marsh, *Evolution, Creation, and Science* (Washington, DC: Review and Herald Publishing Assn., 1944), 25 (complementary); Frank Lewis Marsh, *Studies in Creationism* (Washington, DC: Review and Herald Publishing Assn., 1950), 188–189 (deranged by sin). Later, Marsh became suspicious of fellow Adventist Richard M. Ritland, director of the denomination's Geoscience Research Institute, for tilting too much toward the book of nature. In *A Search for Meaning in Nature: A New*

Look at Creation and Evolution (Mountain View, CA: Pacific Press, 1970), 307, Ritland argued that "the book of nature and the revelation of Scripture should . . . shed light on each other and lead to an intelligent basis for confidence about the history of life on Earth." On Marsh and Ritland, see Numbers, *The Creationists*, 129–133, 291–296. Marsh had earned a master's degree in zoology from Northwestern University in 1935 and a doctorate in botany from the University of Nebraska five years later.

30. *The Story of the American Scientific Affiliation*, an undated pamphlet announcing the formation of the ASA, 9 (creed); Peter G. Berkhout, "The Bible of Nature," *Journal of the American Scientific Affiliation* 19 (December 1967): 111–114; Edward K. Gedney, "Geology and the Bible," in *Modern Science and Christian Faith: A Symposium on the Relationship of the Bible to Modern Science* by the American Scientific Affiliation (Wheaton, IL: Van Kampen Press, 1948), 61 (Books of Works); Richard H. Bube, "Natural Revelation," in *The Encounter between Christianity and Science*, ed. Richard H. Bube (Grand Rapids, MI: Eerdmans, 1968), 69 (natural revelation); J. Frank Cassel, "The Origin of Man and the Bible," *Journal of the American Scientific Affiliation* 12 (June 1960): 15 (His revelation); William J. Tinkle, "Creation, a Finished Work," *Journal of the American Scientific Affiliation* 13 (March 1961): 16 (Author of nature). All of the above documents, except Berkhout, Bube, and DeWitt, are reprinted in Mark A. Kalthoff, ed., *Creation and Evolution in the Early American Scientific Affiliation*, vol. 10 of Numbers, *Creationism in Twentieth-Century America*. On the ASA, see also Numbers, *The Creationists*, 180–207. Berkhout attributed his use of the term "Bible of Nature" to the seventeenth-century Dutch naturalist Jan Swammerdam, who spoke of "the *Biblia Naturae*," and the Belgic Confession, which described nature as "a most elegant book."

31. Bernard Ramm, *The Christian View of Science and Scripture* (Grand Rapids, MI: Eerdmans, 1954), 23–25.

32. Gilbert, *Redeeming Culture*, 121–145.

33. L. J. Van Til, "Presuppositionalism," in *Dictionary of Christianity in America*, ed. Daniel G. Reid (Downers Grove, IL: InterVarsity Press, 1990), 937–938; Rousas John Rushdoony, *The Mythology of Science* (Nutley, NJ: Craig Press, 1967), 43. On Christian Reconstructionism, see Numbers, *The Creationists*, 346–347. On the distinction between God-given natural revelation and man-made natural theology from a presuppositionalist point of view, see Stephen R. Spencer, "Is Natural Theology Biblical?" *Grace Theological Journal* 9 (1988): 59–72.

34. John C. Whitcomb Jr. and Henry M. Morris, *The Genesis Flood: The Biblical Record and Its Scientific Implications* (Philadelphia: Presbyterian and Reformed Publishing Co., 1961), xx, 1, 214, 458.

35. John C. Whitcomb Jr., "Biblical Inerrancy and the Double-Revelation Theory," *Grace Journal* 4 (winter 1963): 3–20, reprinted as *The Origin of the Solar System: Biblical Inerrancy and the Double-Revelation Theory* (Nutley, NJ: Presbyterian and Reformed Publishing Co., 1977); John C. Whitcomb Jr., *The Early Earth* (Grand Rapids, MI: Baker Book House, 1972), 96–97 (Bible of nature).

36. John C. Whitcomb, "Creation Science and the Physical Universe," *Grace Theological Journal* 4 (1983): 289–296.

37. Henry M. Morris, *The Biblical Basis for Modern Science* (Grand Rapids, MI: Baker Book House, 1984), 46–49; Henry M. Morris, *Many Infallible Proofs: Practical and Useful Evidences of Christianity* (San Diego: Master Books, 1974), 334–335. For a brief account of the role of natural theology in the development of his own theistic beliefs, see Henry M. Morris, *The Wonder of It All: Testimony of a Scientist/Engineer* (El Cajon, CA: Institute for Creation Research, 1983). One historically challenged creationist, who credited the "double revelation theory" to Henry Ward Beecher, disliked the theory because "in practice those who promote this view put their faith in the 'revelation of God in nature' and not in the 'revelation of God in the Bible' when the two seem to conflict"; Bolton Davidheiser, Review of *The Encounter between Christianity and Science*, ed. Richard H. Bube, *Creation Research Society Quarterly* 7 (1970): 163–164.

38. William J. Tinkle and Walter E. Lammerts, "Biology and Creation," in American Scientific Affiliation, *Modern Science and Christian Faith*, 75; Tinkle, "Fitness of Earth for Life," *Creation Research Society Quarterly* 8 (June 1971): 16; N. A. Rupke, "Prolegomena to a Study of Cataclysmal Sedimentation," *Creation Research Society Quarterly* 3 (May 1966): 16. Rupke, who went on to a distinguished career in the history of science, was then an undergraduate geology student at Groningen. See also Duane T. Gish, *The Amazing Story of Creation: From Science and the Bible* (El Cajon, CA: Institute for Creation Research, 1990), 7. The statement of belief appeared on the inside cover of the *Creation Research Society Quarterly*.

39. Roland Mushat Frye, "The Two Books of God," *Theology Today* 39 (1982): 260–266, reprinted in Roland Mushat Frye, ed., *Is God a Creationist? The Religious Case against Creation-Science* (New York: Scribner's, 1983), 199–205.

40. Jeff Hardin, "What Is the Perspective from Bioscience?" *Perspectives on Science and Christian Faith* 53 (2001): 248–253.

41. C. H. Spurgeon, *Lectures to My Students* (Grand Rapids, MI: Zondervan, 1962), 406.

42. Philip Hefner, *The Human Factor: Evolution, Culture, and Religion* (Minneapolis: Fortress Press, 1993), 74.

43. John M. Templeton and Robert L. Herrmann, *The God Who Would Be Known: Revelations of the Divine in Contemporary Science* (San Francisco: Harper & Row, 1989), 15. See also Constance Holden, "Subjecting Belief to the Scientific Method," *Science* 284 (1999): 1257–1259.

44. See, e.g., Michael Novak, "John Paul II: Faith and Reason Need Each Other," *St. Louis Post-Dispatch*, January 29, 1999, B7; and Jack Hitt, "Would You Baptize an Extraterrestrial?" *New York Times*, May 29, 1994, sect. 6, p. 36. Environmentalists put the metaphor to a different use. See, e.g., Nicolas Wade, "Burning the Book of Nature," *New York Times*, November 25, 1989, sect. 1, p. 22; and Don Scheese, "'Something More Than Wood': Aldo Leopold and the Language of Landscape," *North Dakota Quarterly* 58 (1990): 72–89.

45. William A. Dembski, *Intelligent Design: The Bridge between Science and Theology* (Downers Grove, IL: InterVarsity Press, 1999), 106–107. For a historical introduction to the ID movement, see Numbers, *The Creationists*, chap. 17. John

Polkinghorne has also noted "a great revival of natural theology taking place"; see "So Finely Tuned a Universe of Atoms, Stars, Quanta and God," *Commonweal,* August 16, 1996, 16, quoted in Stephen C. Meyer, "Modern Science and the Return of the 'God Hypothesis,'" in *Science and Christianity: Four Views,* ed. Richard F. Carlson (Downers Grove, IL: InterVarsity Press, 2000), 153.

46. Patrick Henry Reardon, "The World as Text: Science, Letters, and the Recovery of Meaning," in *Signs of Intelligence: Understanding Intelligent Design,* ed. William A. Dembski and James M. Kushiner (Grand Rapids, MI: Brazos Press, 2001), 74, 78.

47. Charles B. Thaxton, Walter L. Bradley, and Roger L. Olsen, *The Mystery of Life's Origin: Reassessing Current Theories* (New York: Philosophical Library, 1984); Phillip E. Johnson, *Darwin on Trial* (Downers Grove, IL: InterVarsity Press, 1991); J. P. Moreland, ed., *The Creation Hypothesis: Scientific Evidence for an Intelligent Designer* (Downers Grove, IL: InterVarsity Press, 1994); Michael J. Behe, *Darwin's Black Box: The Biochemical Challenge to Evolution* (New York: Free Press, 1996); Michael J. Denton, *Nature's Destiny: How the Laws of Biology Reveal Purpose in the Universe* (New York: Free Press, 1998); William A. Dembski, *The Design Inference: Eliminating Chance through Small Probabilities* (Cambridge, UK: Cambridge University Press, 1998); William A. Dembski, ed., *Mere Creation: Science, Faith and Intelligent Design* (Downers Grove, IL: InterVarsity Press, 1998); Dembski, *Intelligent Design*; William A. Dembski, *No Free Lunch: Why Specified Complexity Cannot Be Purchased without Intelligence* (Lanham, MD: Rowman & Littlefield, 2002).

CHAPTER 4

This chapter first appeared in *Science, Religion, and the Human Experience,* ed. James D. Proctor (New York: Oxford University Press, 2005), 205–233, and appears here with the permission of Oxford University Press. I wish to thank Stephen Wald for his research assistance and his insightful observations and Paul Lucier, Julie Newell, Jon Roberts, and Lester Stephens for their critical reading of the manuscript.

1. Sigmund Freud, *Introductory Lectures on Psycho-Analysis: A Course of Twenty-Eight Lectures Delivered at the University of Vienna,* trans. Joan Riviere (London: George Allen & Unwin, 1922), 240–241.

2. Edward Grant, *Planets, Stars, and Orbs: The Medieval Cosmos, 1200–1687* (Cambridge, UK: Cambridge University Press, 1994), 239–243. See also Dennis R. Danielson, "The Great Copernican Cliché," *American Journal of Physics* 69 (2001): 1029–1035.

3. Charles Darwin, *The Descent of Man, and Selection in Relation to Sex,* 2 vols. (London: John Murray, 1871), 2: 389. For expressions of abhorrence, see, e.g., P. R. Russel, "Darwinism Examined," *Advent Review and Sabbath Herald,* May 18, 1876, 153; and H. L. Hastings, *Was Moses Mistaken? or, Creation and Evolution,* Anti-Infidel Library No. 36 (Boston: H. L. Hastings, 1896), 25–26.

4. A. C. Dixon, *Reconstruction: The Facts against Evolution* (n.p., n.d.), 18, from a copy in the Dixon Collection, Dargan-Carver Library of the Historical Commission

of the Southern Baptist Convention, Nashville, Tennessee; A. T. Robertson, quoted in James Moore, *The Darwin Legend* (Grand Rapids, MI: Baker Books, 1994), 119; Andrew Johnson, "The Evolution Articles," *Pentecostal Herald* 38 (September 1926): 6 (baboon boosters). See also the statement of Charles Kingsley quoted in Adrian Desmond, *Huxley: From Devil's Disciple to Evolution's High Priest* (Reading, MA: Addison-Wesley, 1997), 288.

5. James R. Moore, "Of Love and Death: Why Darwin 'Gave Up' Christianity," in *History, Humanity and Evolution: Essays for John C. Greene*, ed. James R. Moore (Cambridge, UK: Cambridge University Press, 1989), 195–230, esp. 197 (damnable doctrine). See also Adrian Desmond and James Moore, *Darwin* (London: Michael Joseph, 1991), 375–387 (Annie).

6. Susan Budd, *Varieties of Unbelief: Atheists and Agnostics in English Society, 1850–1960* (London: Heinemann, 1977), 104–107; Ronald L. Numbers, *Darwinism Comes to America* (Cambridge, MA: Harvard University Press, 1998), 40–43. Bernard Lightman, *The Origins of Agnosticism: Victorian Unbelief and the Limits of Knowledge* (Baltimore: Johns Hopkins University Press, 1987), 31, also plays down the role of science in the creation of agnosticism. Frank Miller Turner, in a superb examination of six late Victorians who lost their faith in orthodox Christianity, describes George Romanes as "one of the very few men whose loss of faith in the truth of religion can be directly ascribed to the influence of scientific naturalism"; see Turner, *Between Science and Religion: The Reaction to Scientific Naturalism in Late Victorian England* (New Haven: Yale University Press, 1974), 143–144. See also Frank Miller Turner, "The Victorian Crisis of Faith and the Faith That Was Lost," in *Victorian Faith in Crisis: Essays on Continuity and Change in Nineteenth-Century Religious Belief*, ed. Richard J. Helmstadter and Bernard Lightman (Stanford: Stanford University Press, 1990), 9–38. In his pioneering scientific study of the loss of belief among college students and scientists, James H. Leuba, *The Belief in God and Immortality* (Boston: Sherman, French, 1916), 282–288, devotes a chapter to the causes of the rejection of traditional beliefs, but evolution does not appear among them. Peter Bowler, however, has claimed that Darwinism "established a complete break between science and religion"; see his *The Eclipse of Darwinism: Anti-Darwinian Evolution Theories in the Decades around 1900* (Baltimore: Johns Hopkins University Press, 1983), 27.

In an influential analysis of the Darwinian controversies James R. Moore has drawn attention to the frequency with which evolution precipitated "spiritual crises" in the lives of those forced to contend with it. In partial confirmation of his thesis, Moore cites the alleged experiences of two Americans, James Dwight Dana and Jeffries Wyman, whom earlier scholars had described, respectively, as experiencing "a long soul-searching struggle" over evolution and as suffering from "deep distress, emotional as well as rational," over the prospect of ape-like ancestors. Moore neglects, however, to mention that his authority for Dana pointedly stated that, despite his expectations, he had found "no evidence" to support the supposition that "an inner conflict involving his religious beliefs" lay behind Dana's struggle. And a later study of Wyman, based on new evidence, concluded that Wyman experienced "very little difficulty in embracing evolution." James R. Moore, *The Post-Darwinian Controversies:*

A Study of the Protestant Struggle to Come to Terms with Darwin in Great Britain and America, 1870–1900 (Cambridge, UK: Cambridge University Press, 1979), 109; William F. Sanford Jr., "Dana and Darwinism," *Journal of the History of Ideas* 26 (1965): 531–546, quotations on 531, 543; A. Hunter Dupree, "Jeffries Wyman's Views on Evolution," *Isis* 44 (1953): 243–246, quotation on 245 (distress); Toby A. Appel, "Jeffries Wyman, Philosophical Anatomy, and the Scientific Reception of Darwin in America," *Journal of the History of Biology* 21 (1988): 69–94, quotation on 71 (little difficulty). Dana's friend Arnold Guyot did on one occasion express concern that the public debate over Dana's views on evolution was causing him emotional distress; see Arnold Guyot to Mrs. J. D. Dana, January 17, 1880, and Arnold Guyot to J. D. Dana, February 16, 1880, James Dwight Dana Correspondence, Yale University Library.

7. Mrs. Humphry Ward, *Robert Elsmere* (New York: J. S. Ogilvie, n.d.), 398; William S. Peterson, *Victorian Heretic: Mrs Humphry Ward's* Robert Elsmere (Leicester, UK: Leicester University Press, 1976), 148.

8. Basil Willey, *Darwin and Butler: Two Versions of Evolution* (New York: Harcourt, Brace, 1960), 63. On Butler in New Zealand, see John Stenhouse, "Darwinism in New Zealand, 1859–1900," in *Disseminating Darwinism: The Role of Place, Race, Religion, and Gender*, ed. Ronald L. Numbers and John Stenhouse (Cambridge, UK: Cambridge University Press, 1999), 61–90.

9. Robert J. Richards, *Darwin and the Emergence of Evolutionary Theories of Mind and Behavior* (Chicago: University of Chicago Press, 1987), 409–410. In *The Post-Darwinian Controversies*, 14–16, 111–117, Moore invokes Leon Festinger's "theory of cognitive dissonance" to help explain various responses to Darwinism, but in treating individual writers, he focuses more on intellectual than on emotional matters. The best intellectual history of Darwinism and Christianity is Jon H. Roberts, *Darwinism and the Divine in America: Protestant Intellectuals and Organic Evolution, 1859–1900* (Madison: University of Wisconsin Press, 1988), but see also Ronald L. Numbers, *The Creationists: From Scientific Creationism to Intelligent Design*, new ed. (Cambridge, MA: Harvard University Press, 2006); and David N. Livingstone, *Darwin's Forgotten Defenders: The Encounter between Evangelical Theology and Evolutionary Thought* (Grand Rapids, MI: Eerdmans, 1987). On the history of science and Christianity generally, see David C. Lindberg and Ronald L. Numbers, eds., *God and Nature: Historical Essays on the Encounter between Christianity and Science* (Berkeley: University of California Press, 1986); David C. Lindberg and Ronald L. Numbers, eds., *When Science and Christianity Meet* (Chicago: University of Chicago Press, 2003); and John Hedley Brooke, *Science and Religion: Some Historical Perspectives* (Cambridge, UK: Cambridge University Press, 1991).

10. All four of these men were Protestants. For parallels in the Catholic community, see, e.g., Jacob W. Gruber, *A Conscience in Conflict: The Life of St. George Jackson Mivart* (New York: Columbia University Press, 1960); and Ralph E. Weber, *Notre Dame's John Zahm: American Catholic Apologist and Educator* (Notre Dame, IN: University of Notre Dame Press, 1961). Regarding Zahm, see also R. Scott Appleby, "Exposing Darwin's 'Hidden Agenda': Roman Catholic Responses to Evolution, 1875–1925," in Numbers and Stenhouse, *Disseminating Darwinism*, 173–208.

11. Joseph LeConte, *Evolution and Its Relation to Religious Thought* (New York: D. Appleton, 1888), 8 (definition); Joseph LeConte, *The Autobiography of Joseph LeConte*, ed. William Dallam Armes (New York: D. Appleton, 1903), 335 (rational theism); Joseph LeConte, *Religion and Science: A Series of Sunday Lectures on the Relation of Natural and Revealed Religion, or the Truths Revealed in Nature and Scripture* (New York: D. Appleton, 1873), 276 (demon). For a typical reference to LeConte's definition of evolution, see Andrew Johnson, "Evolution Outlawed by Science [No. 3]," *Pentecostal Herald* 37 (December 1925): 9.

12. LeConte, *Autobiography*, 16–17, 41–44. See also Lester D. Stephens, *Joseph LeConte: Gentle Prophet of Evolution* (Baton Rouge: Louisiana State University Press, 1982); and Timothy Odom Brown, "Joseph LeConte: Prophet of Nature and Child of Religion," MA thesis, University of North Carolina, Chapel Hill, 1977.

13. Joseph LeConte, *Inaugural Address: Delivered in the State House, Dec. 8, 1857, by Order of the Board of Trustees of the South Carolina College* (Columbia, SC: R. W. Gibbes, 1858), 27. See also Joseph LeConte, "The Relation of Organic Science to Sociology," *Southern Presbyterian Review* 13 (1861): 39–77; LeConte, *Autobiography*, 290; and Brown, "Joseph LeConte," 72. On positivism, see Charles D. Cashdollar, *The Transformation of Theology, 1830–1890: Positivism and Protestant Thought in Britain and America* (Princeton, NJ: Princeton University Press, 1989).

14. LeConte, *Autobiography*, 177; Stephens, *Joseph LeConte*, 77–78.

15. LeConte, *Religion and Science*, 3, 9–10, 22–24, 28–29, 230–233, 276–277. LeConte recycled the comment about standing "where the current runs swiftest" in "Evolution in Relation to Materialism," *Princeton Review*, 4th ser., no. 7 (1881): 149–174. The reference to being "a reluctant evolutionist" at the time appeared in LeConte, *Autobiography*, 336. See also chapter 3 in this volume.

16. Joseph LeConte, "On Critical Periods in the History of the Earth and Their Relation to Evolution," *American Journal of Science* 114 (1877): 99–114, quotation on 101; LeConte, *Autobiography*, 266 (most important), 336 (thorough and enthusiastic; woe is me): Joseph LeConte, "Evolution in Relation to Religion," *Proceedings at the Annual Dinner of the Chit-Chat Club* [San Francisco, 1877], 1–12, quoted in Stephens, *Joseph LeConte*, 165; Joseph LeConte, *Evolution and Its Relation to Religious Thought*, a second edition of which appeared under the title *Evolution: Its Nature, Evidences, and Relation to Religious Thought* (New York: D. Appleton, 1896). See also LeConte's pamphlet, *The Relation of Evolution to Religious Thought* (San Francisco: Pacific Coast Conference of Unitarian and Other Christian Churches, [1887]).

17. LeConte, *Religion and Science*, 233 (difficulty and distress); Joseph LeConte, "Man's Place in Nature," *Princeton Review*, 4th ser., no. 2 (1878): 789 (dearly cherished); LeConte, "Evolution in Relation to Materialism," 159–160 (distinct); Joseph LeConte, "A Brief Confession of Faith, Written in 1890, Slightly Revised and Added to in 1897," LeConte Family Papers, Box 1, Bancroft Library, University of California, Berkeley. In "Man's Place in Nature," 794, LeConte insisted that "Christian pantheism is the only true philosophic view." On the innocuous effects of evolution on religion, see also LeConte, *The Relation of Evolution to Religious Thought*, 2. For LeConte's later views on the harmony of Genesis and geology, see [Joseph LeConte],

Review of *Creation; or, The Biblical Cosmogony in the Light of Modern Science*, by Arnold Guyot, *Science* 3 (1884): 599–601.

18. Joseph LeConte, "Immortality in Modern Thought," *Science* 6 (1885): 126–127 (science says nothing); Josiah Royce, *The Conception of God*, with comments by Sidney Edward Mezes, Joseph LeConte, and G. H. Howison (Berkeley: Philosophical Union of the University of California, 1895), 49–50 (whole purpose balked); Bessie LeConte to Joseph LeConte, March [?], 1903, LeConte Family Papers, Box 1, Bancroft Library. On LeConte's "preoccupation" with immortality, see Brown, "Joseph LeConte," 130, 168. On immortality, see also Joseph LeConte, "The Natural Grounds of Belief in a Personal Immortality," *Andover Review* 14 (1890): 1–13; and Stephen E. Wald, "Revelations of Consciousness: Joseph LeConte, the Soul, and the Challenge of Scientific Naturalism," unpublished manuscript, Duke University, 1998. I am especially indebted to Timothy Odom Brown, "Joseph LeConte," for his insights into LeConte's changing views on immortality.

19. Mary Lesley Ames, ed., *Life and Letters of Peter and Susan Lesley*, 2 vols. (New York: G. P. Putnam's Sons, 1909), 1: 22–23, 39, 114–116, 134; Benjamin Smith Lyman, "Biographical Notice of J. Peter Lesley," *Transactions of the American Institute of Mining Engineers*, reprinted in ibid., 2: 452–483; see especially 2: 455–458. Ames was Lesley's daughter; Lyman, his nephew. There is no scholarly biography of Lesley, but on his career as a consulting geologist, see Paul Lucier, "Commercial Interests and Scientific Disinterestedness: Consulting Geologists in Antebellum America," *Isis* 86 (1995): 245–267.

20. M. L. Ames, *Life and Letters*, 1: 162–166; Lyman, "Biographical Notice," 2: 458–461; Patsy Gerstner, *Henry Darwin Rogers, 1808–1866: American Geologist* (Tuscaloosa: University of Alabama Press, 1994), 184; W. M. Davis, "Biographical Memoir of Peter Lesley, 1819–1903," National Academy of Sciences, *Biographical Memoirs* 8 (1919): 174, 192–193. For Lesley's perspective, see his *Address to the Suffolk North Association of Congregational Ministers* (Boston: Wm. Crosby and H. P. Nichols, 1849). The British geologist Charles Lyell, who had recently visited the United States, reported in his published memoir that a young ministerial candidate (whom Lyell does not name) in America had failed to receive ordination because he believed that the first book of Genesis was "inconsistent with discoveries now universally admitted, respecting the high antiquity of the earth and the existence of living beings on the globe long anterior to man." Charles Lyell, *A Second Visit to the United States*, 2 vols. (London, 1849), 1: 218, quoted in Lyman, "Biographical Notice," 2: 461–462. Lesley insisted that "Lyell was quite wrong," but something of the sort seems to have happened; see Davis, "Biographical Memoir," 174–175.

21. Davis, "Biographical Memoir," 176–197.

22. M. L. Ames, *Life and Letters*, 1: 504–515; J. P. Lesley, *Man's Origin and Destiny* (Philadelphia: J. B. Lippincott, 1868), 19, 43, 45, 50.

23. Lesley, *Man's Origin and Destiny*, 76–82. On the response of American scientists to evolution, see Numbers, *Darwinism Comes to America*, 24–48.

24. Lesley, *Man's Origin and Destiny*, 18, 117, 119; J. P. Lesley to Susan Lesley, January 11, 1866, quoted in M. L. Ames, *Life and Letters*, 1: 512. Regarding Gray, see

Numbers, *Darwinism Comes to America*, 27. On the history of polygenism in America, see William Stanton, *The Leopard's Spots: Scientific Attitudes toward Race in America, 1815–59* (Chicago: University of Chicago Press, 1960); David N. Livingstone, *The Preadamite Theory and the Marriage of Science and Religion* (Philadelphia: American Philosophical Society, 1992); and G. Blair Nelson, "'Men before Adam!' American Debates over the Unity and Antiquity of Humanity," in Lindberg and Numbers, *When Science and Christianity Meet*, 161–181. In the early 1880s Lesley returned briefly to the subject of evolution, adding six new chapters to *Man's Origin and Destiny* (Boston: Geo. H. Ellis, 1881).

25. Lyman, "Biographical Notice," 2: 471–475, 482; Charles Gordon Ames, "A Memorial Discourse, Preached in the Church of the Disciples, Boston, January 24, 1904," in M. L. Ames, *Life and Letters*, 2: 530–531. Charles Gordon Ames, a Unitarian minister, was not only a close friend of the Lesleys but the father-in-law of their daughter.

26. Lyman, "Biographical Notice," 2: 473–475, 482. Since 1859 he had held a nominal position as professor of mining at the University of Pennsylvania.

27. J. P. Lesley to Allen Lesley, February 15, 1867, in M. L. Ames, *Life and Letters*, 2: 17 (pantheist); J. P. Lesley to his son-in-law Charles, March 11, 1888, in ibid., 2: 350–351 (God is Nature). On Lesley's connection to Unitarianism, see C. G. Ames, "A Memorial Discourse," 2: 524; and Davis, "Biographical Memoir," 166. On his belief in immortality, see Lesley to Susan Lesley, June 18, 1888, and June 24, 1890, in M. L. Ames, *Life and Letters*, 2: 359, 393; and J. P. Lesley, "The Idea of Life after Death," *The Forum* 10 (1890–1891): 207–215.

28. J. P. Lesley to Susan Lesley, July 8 and 9, 1880, quoted in M. L. Ames, *Life and Letters*, 2: 253–255; J. P. Lesley, letter to the editor, *Science* 10 (1887): 308–309; Lyman, "Biographical Notice," 2: 472–473. Davis paraphrased Lyman in his "Biographical Memoir," 215. Regarding Darwinism, see also Lesley's essay in the *United States Railroad and Mining Register*, December 13, 1873, quoted in Lyman, "Biographical Notice," 472.

29. George Frederick Wright, *Story of My Life and Work* (Oberlin, OH: Bibliotheca Sacra, 1916), 116, 123, 132. See also George Frederick Wright, "Recent Works on Prehistoric Archaeology," *Bibliotheca Sacra* 30 (1873): 381–384; and George Frederick Wright, *Studies in Science and Religion* (Andover, MA: Warren F. Draper, 1882), 352–354. For Asa Gray's views, see his *Darwiniana: Essays and Reviews Pertaining to Darwinism*, ed. A. Hunter Dupree (Cambridge, MA: Harvard University Press, 1963); and [George Frederick Wright], Reviews of *Letters of Asa Gray*, ed. Jane Loring Gray, *Bibliotheca Sacra* 51 (1894): 182. For Gray's influence on Wright, see George Frederick Wright to Asa Gray, June 26, 1875, Archives, Gray Herbarium, Harvard University. This discussion of Wright is taken from Ronald L. Numbers, "George Frederick Wright: From Christian Darwinist to Fundamentalist," *Isis* 79 (1988): 624–645; and Numbers, *The Creationists*, 33–50.

30. Gray, *Darwiniana*, 130; George Frederick Wright, "The Debt of the Church to Asa Gray," *Bibliotheca Sacra* 45 (1888): 527.

31. George Frederick Wright, "Recent Works Bearing of the Relation of Science to Religion: No. II—The Divine Method of Producing Living Species," *Bibliotheca Sacra* 33 (1876): 455, 466, 474, 487, 492–494. Wright stopped short of identifying himself as "a disciple of Mr. Darwin or as a champion of his theory."

32. Wright, *Studies in Science and Religion*, 347–350, 368–370.

33. George Frederick Wright, "Some Will-o'-the-Wisps of Higher Criticism," *Congregationalist*, March 12, 1891, 84. See also [George Frederick Wright], "Professor Wright and Some of His Critics," *Bibliotheca Sacra* 42 (1885): 352. About this time Green turned to B. B. Warfield and W. H. Green for help in accommodating estimates of human life on earth that exceeded the six thousand years commonly attributed to the Old Testament genealogies. See George Frederick Wright, "How Old Is Mankind?" *Sunday School Times* 55 (January 1913): 52; George Frederick Wright, "Recent Discoveries Bearing on the Antiquity of Man," *Bibliotheca Sacra* 48 (1891): 309. On Warfield, see David N. Livingstone and Mark A. Noll, "B. B. Warfield (1851–1921): A Biblical Inerrantist As Evolutionist," *Isis* 91 (2000): 283–304. On Green, see chapter 6 of this volume.

34. George Frederick Wright, "The First Chapter of Genesis and Modern Science," *Homiletic Review* 35 (1898): 392–393. See also George Frederick Wright, "Editorial Note on Genesis and Geology," *Bibliotheca Sacra* 54 (1897): 570–572; and George Frederick Wright, *Scientific Confirmations of Old Testament History* (Oberlin, OH: Bibliotheca Sacra, 1906), 368–386. On Guyot, see Ronald L. Numbers, *Creation by Natural Law: Laplace's Nebular Hypothesis in American Thought* (Seattle: University of Washington Press, 1977), 91–100. The Princeton theologian Charles Hodge also endorsed Guyot's interpretation; see chapter 5 of this volume.

35. [George Frederick Wright], Review of *Darwinism and Other Essays*, by John Fiske, *Bibliotheca Sacra* 36 (1879); 784; [George Frederick Wright], "Transcendental Science," *Independent* 41 (October 1889): 10. See also George Frederick Wright, "Darwin on Herbert Spencer," *Bibliotheca Sacra* 46 (1889): 181–184.

36. George Frederick Wright, "Present Aspects of the Questions concerning the Origin and Antiquity of the Human Race," *Protestant Episcopal Review* 11 (1898): 319–323; George Frederick Wright, "The Revision of Geological Time," *Bibliotheca Sacra* 60 (1903): 580; George Frederick Wright, "The Uncertainties of Science," *Advance* 43 (1902): 624–625.

37. George Frederick Wright, "The Passing of Evolution," in *The Fundamentals*, 12 vols. (Chicago: Testimony Publishing Co., n.d.), 7: 5–20, emphasis added. For a fuller discussion of Wright's somewhat ambiguous views on the origin of humans, see Numbers, *The Creationists*, 46–49.

38. Ellen G. White, *Spiritual Gifts: Important Facts of Faith, in Connection with the History of Holy Men of Old* (Battle Creek, MI: Seventh-day Adventist Publishing Assn., 1864), 77–79, 90–91. On White and Adventism, see Ronald L. Numbers, *Prophetess of Health: A Study of Ellen G. White* (New York: Harper & Row, 1976).

39. G. M. Price to H. W. Clark, June 15, 1941, Price Papers, Adventist Heritage Center, Andrews University Library, Berrien Springs, MI; G. M. Price, *Genesis Vindicated* (Washington, DC: Review and Herald Publishing Assn., 1941), 300. See also

G. M. Price, "Some Early Experiences with Evolutionary Geology," *Bulletin of Deluge Geology* 1 (November 1941): 77–92. This discussion of Price is taken from Numbers, *The Creationists*, 72–101.

40. Price, "Some Early Experiences," 79–80; G. M. Price, "If I Were Twenty-One Again," *These Times* 69 (September 1960): 22.

41. Geo. E. McCready Price, *Outlines of Modern Christianity and Modern Science* (Oakland, CA: Pacific Press, 1902); G. M. Price to William Guthrie, August 26, 1904; G. M. Price to W. H. Thurston, August 28, 1904; W. H. Thurston to A. G. Daniells, January 19, 1905; William Guthrie to A. G. Daniells, January 23, 2905; all in RG 11 of the Archives of the General Conference of Seventh-day Adventists, Silver Spring, Maryland, hereinafter cited as SDA Archives. I am indebted to Bert Haloviak for bringing these and related documents to my attention.

42. George E. Price to William Guthrie, December 28, 1904; A. G. Daniells to Mrs. G. E. Price, January 16, 1905; A. G. Daniells to C. H. Edwards, January 16, 1905; A. G. Daniells to George E. Price, January 17 and 31, 1905; George E. Price to A. G. Daniells, January 25 and March 19, 1905; all in RG 11, SDA Archives.

43. George McCready Price, "I'd Have an Aim," *Advent Review and Sabbath Herald* 138 (February 1961): 14–15; George McCready Price, *Illogical Geology: The Weakest Point in the Evolution Theory* (Los Angeles: Modern Heretic Co., 1906), 9; G. M. Price to Martin Gardner, May 13, 1952, courtesy of Martin Gardner.

44. George McCready Price, *The New Geology* (Mountain View, CA: Pacific Press, 1923), 637–638.

45. *Science*, March 5, 1926, 259; G. M. Price to Molleurus Couperus, November 1946, courtesy of the late Molleurus Couperus. On Price's reputation, see also Martin Gardner, *Fads and Fallacies in the Name of Science* (New York: Dover, 1957), 127. For a typically negative review by a prominent geologist, see Charles Schuchert, Review of *The New Geology*, by George McCready Price, *Science*, May 30, 1924, 486–487.

46. G. M. Price to E. T. Brewster, May 2, 1930, Price Papers; G. M. Price, "A Brief History of the Flood Theory," *Signs of the Times* 61 (October 1934): 15; J. C. Whitcomb to D. J. Whitney, August 31, 1957, Whitcomb Papers, private collection, courtesy of John C. Whitcomb Jr.; Roy M. Allen, letter to the editor, *Journal of the American Scientific Affiliation* 17 (June 1965): 62. Price's reaction to *The Genesis Flood* appeared in an undated brochure advertising the book, in Price Papers. On Price's seminal influence on the creationist revival of the late twentieth century, see Numbers, *The Creationists*.

47. Martin Gardner, *The Flight of Peter Fromm* (Los Altos, CA: William Kaufmann, 1973), especially 48–51. On Gardner's own brand of theism, see *The Whys of a Philosophical Scrivener* (New York: Quill, 1983). The Quaker animal ecologist Warder Clyde Allee found his faith challenged in a course on evolution at the University of Chicago; see Gregg Mitman, *The State of Nature: Ecology, Community, and American Social Thought, 1900–1950* (Chicago: University of Chicago Press, 1992), 52–53.

48. Accepting the geological timescale, or a piece of it, was only the beginning of my loss of faith; for the rest of the story, see Jonathan M. Butler, "The Historian as Heretic," in *Prophetess of Health: Ellen G. White and the Origins of Seventh-day*

Adventist Health Reform, by Ronald L. Numbers (Knoxville: University of Tennessee Press, 1992), xxv–lxviii.

49. J. Frank Cassel, "Evolution of Evangelical Thinking on Evolution," *Journal of the American Scientific Affiliation* 11 (December 1959): 27; Philip B. Marquart, letter to the editor, *Journal of the American Scientific Affiliation* 14 (September 1963): 100; Henry M. Morris, *The Twilight of Evolution* (Grand Rapids, MI: Baker Book House, 1963), 93. One of the most poignant cases of conflict with evolution was that of the Missouri Lutheran Alfred H. Meyer; see Numbers, *The Creationists*, 302–304.

50. Richards, *Darwin and the Emergence of Evolutionary Theories*, 409–450. Richard Dawkins, *The Blind Watchmaker* (New York: Norton, 1986), 6, has famously thanked Darwin for making "it possible to be an intellectually fulfilled atheist."

51. Deborah Jordan Brooks, "Substantial Numbers of Americans Continue to Doubt Evolution as Explanation for Origin of Humans," Gallup Poll Releases, March 5, 2001.

CHAPTER 5

This chapter initially appeared in *Charles Hodge Revisited: A Critical Appraisal of His Life and Work*, ed. John W. Stewart and James H. Moorhead (Grand Rapids, MI: Eerdmans, 2002), 77–101, and is reprinted with the permission of the Eerdmans Publishing Company. I thank Tomomi Kunakawa for her research assistance and William O. Harris and Raymond D. Cannata of the office of Archives and Special Collections, Princeton Theological Seminary, for providing me with much-needed sources. I am especially grateful to Jon H. Roberts for his suggestions, criticisms, and encouragement. My title was inspired by Larkin B. Coles's *The Beauties and Deformities of Tobacco-Using* (Boston: Ticknor, Reed, and Fields, 1851).

1. Theodore Dwight Bozeman, *Protestants in an Age of Science: The Baconian Ideal and Antebellum American Religious Thought* (Chapel Hill: University of North Carolina press, 1977), 35 (strongest journal); Alexander A. Hodge, *The Life of Charles Hodge, D.D., LL.D.* (London: T. Nelson and Sons, 1881), 521 (no new idea). In the absence of a recent biography, the best introduction to Hodge's life and work is John W. Stewart and James H. Moorhead, eds., *Charles Hodge Revisited: A Critical Appraisal of His Life and Work* (Grand Rapids, MI: Eerdmans, 2002).

2. A. A. Hodge, *Life of Charles Hodge*, 46, 68, 98; John W. Stewart, "Mediating the Center: Charles Hodge on American Science, Language, Literature, and Politics," *Studies in Reformed Theology and History* 3 (winter 1995): 1–114, especially 7; Bozeman, *Protestants in an Age of Science*, 40. Samuel Miller included scientific developments in his pioneering *A Brief Retrospect of the Eighteenth Century* (New York: T. & J. Swords, 1803).

3. Stewart, "Mediating the Center," 17; A. A. Hodge, *Life of Charles Hodge*, 112–114, 162, 170, 190–191.

4. A. A. Hodge, *Life of Charles Hodge*, 236–240, 364; Bozeman, *Protestants in an Age of Science*, 35; Review of *The Annual of Scientific Discovery*, ed. David A. Wells,

Biblical Repertory and Princeton Review (hereafter cited as *BRPR*) 22 (1850): 492–493; [Samuel Tyler], "Agricultural Chemistry," *BRPR* 16 (1844): 508–517; [Albert Baldwin Dod], "Analytical Geometry," *BRPR* 13 (1841): 523–538; "Survey of the Valley of the Great Salt Lake of Utah," *BRPR* 24 (1852): 687–696; [John Stillwell Schank], "What's the Use of Breathing?" *BRPR* 37 (1865): 135–147; [Joseph Henry], "The British Scientific Association," *BRPR* 13 (1841): 132–149; [Joseph Henry], "Coast Survey," *BRPR* 17 (1845): 321–344; Hugh Richard Slotten, *Patronage, Practice, and the Culture of American Science: Alexander Dallas Bache and the U.S. Coast Survey* (Cambridge, UK: Cambridge University Press, 1994), 83; Stewart, "Mediating the Center," 25 (twin daughters); Charles Hodge, *What Is Darwinism?* (New York: Scribner, Armstrong, 1874), 131. The sections on "Quarterly Scientific Intelligence" appeared in *BRPR* 24 (1852): 350–356, 526–531. On Hodge's meteorological activities, see also Joseph Henry to James Henry Coffin, September 9, 1842, in *The Papers of Joseph Henry*, ed. Nathan Reingold and Marc Rothenberg, 6 vols. to date (Washington, DC: Smithsonian Institution Press, 1972), 5: 266–267.

5. Hodge, *What Is Darwinism?* 132, 134–135, 140–142; [Charles Hodge], "The Unity of Mankind," *BRPR* 31 (1859): 103–149, quotations on 104–105; Charles Hodge, "Address at the Inauguration of James McCosh," 1866, Hodge Papers, Princeton University Library, quoted in Stewart, "Mediating the Center," 25 (satanic). Unfortunately, Hodge's correspondence in the Hodge Papers contains few references to science.

6. Herbert Hovenkamp, *Science and Religion in America, 1800–1860* (Philadelphia: University of Pennsylvania Press, 1978), 216 (paranoid); Joseph E. Illick III, "The Reception of Darwinism at the Theological Seminary and the College at Princeton, New Jersey," *Journal of Presbyterian History* 38 (1960): 152–165, 234–243, quotation on 157 (immature hostility, which describes some articles in *BRPR*, some of which were written by Hodge); Hugh Foster, *The Modern Movement in American Theology: Sketches in the History of American Protestant Thought from the Civil War to the World War* (New York: Fleming H. Revell, 1939), 49 (understanding); Walter J. Wilkins, *Science and Religious Thought: A Darwinism Case Study* (Ann Arbor, MI: UMI Press, 1987), 37 (forerunner); Neal C. Gillespie, *Charles Darwin and the Problem of Creation* (Chicago: University of Chicago Press, 1979), 112 (astute); James R. Moore, *The Post-Darwinian Controversies: A Study of the Protestant Struggle to Come to Terms with Darwin in Great Britain and America, 1870–1900* (Cambridge, UK: Cambridge University Press 1979), 204 (perceptive); Stewart, "Mediating the Center." For an additional positive assessment, see Mark A. Noll and David N. Livingstone, introduction to *What Is Darwinism?* by Charles Hodge (Grand Rapids, MI: Baker Books, 1994), 22.

7. [Julius H. Seelye], "Dr. Hickok's Philosophy," *BRPR* 34 (1862): 369–406, editorial note on 369; *The Biblical Repertory and Princeton Review: Index Volume from 1825–1868* (Philadelphia: Peter Walker, 1871).

8. [Joseph Clark], "The Scepticism of Science," *BRPR* 35 (1863): 43–75, quotations on 43, 47, 63, 65, 68. On Clark's identity, see Noll and Livingstone, introduction, 51.

9. "Scripture and Science," *New York Observer*, March 12, 1863, 82.

10. Charles Hodge, "The Bible in Science," *New York Observer*, March 26, 1863, 98–99.

11. Walter H. Conser Jr., *God and the Natural World: Religion and Science in Antebellum America* (Columbia: University of South Carolina Press, 1993), 69; "Advancement of Society," *BRPR* 3 (1831): 306–319, quotation on 315; "Rauch's Psychology," *BRPR* 12 (1840): 394–410, quotation regarding demarcation on 396. As Peter Hicks has perceptively noted, Hodge adopted the language of Baconianism and commonsense philosophy "because they gave adequate expression to his theological and philosophical ideas, rather than because they controlled those ideas"; Hicks, *The Philosophy of Charles Hodge: A 19th Century Evangelical Approach to Reason, Knowledge and Truth* (Lewiston, ME: Edwin Mellen Press, 1997), 79.

12. On phrenology in America, see John D. Davies, *Phrenology, Fad and Science: A 19th-Century American Crusade* (New Haven: Yale University Press, 1955); on mesmerism, see Robert C. Fuller, *Mesmerism and the American Cure of Souls* (Philadelphia: University of Pennsylvania Press, 1982).

13. "Phrenology," *BRPR* 10 (1838): 279–320, quotations on 319–320 (quackery, signatures); Review of *Phrenology Examined*, by P. Flourens, *BRPR* 18 (1846): 354–358, quotation on 355 (hoaxed); Review of *Phrenology Examined, and Shown to Be Inconsistent with the Principles of Physiology, Mental and Moral Science, and the Doctrines of Christianity*, by N. L. Rice, *BRPR* 21 (1849): 298–300 (folly, absurd).

14. Amariah Brigham, *Observations on the Influence of Religion upon the Health and Physical Welfare of Mankind* (Boston, 1835), 260, 284–285, 291, 312; [Frederick A. Packard], "The Relations of Religion to What Are Called Diseases of the Mind," *BRPR* 22 (1850): 1–41; [Matthew Boyd Hope], "Religious Melancholy," *BRPR* 16 (1844): 352–379, quotation on 353. On Millerism and insanity, see Ronald L. Numbers and Janet S. Numbers, "Millerism and Madness: A Study of 'Religious Insanity' in Nineteenth-Century America," in *The Disappointed: Millerism and Millenarianism in the Nineteenth Century*, ed. Ronald L. Numbers and Jonathan M. Butler (Bloomington: Indiana University Press, 1987), 92–117.

15. Charles Hodge to Hugh Hodge, August 15, 1839, quoted in A. A. Hodge, *Life of Charles Hodge*, 244–245.

16. [Packard], "Relations of Religion," 40; [Lyman H. Atwater], "Moral Insanity," *BRPR* 29 (1857): 345–375, quotation on 354.

17. "Materialism—Physiological Psychology," *BRPR* 41 (1869): 615–625, quotations on 623–624. See also [Hope], "Religious Melancholy," 377.

18. Review of *The Indications of the Creator; or, The Natural Evidences of Final Cause*, by George Taylor, *BRPR* 24 (1852): 141–146, quotation on 145; Charles Hodge, *Systematic Theology*, 3 vols. (New York: Scribner, 1871–1873), 1: 292–293. See also Review of *Essays on Life, Sleep, Pain, &c.*, by Samuel Henry Dickson, *BRPR* 24 (18562): 507; and Review of *A Treatise on the Forces Which Produce the Organization of Plants*, by John William Draper, *BRPR* 17 (1845): 345–347.

19. See Martin J. S. Rudwick, "The Shape and Meaning of Earth History," in *God and Nature: Historical Essays on the Encounter between Christianity and Science*, ed. David

C. Lindberg and Ronald L. Numbers (Berkeley: University of California Press, 1986), 296–321; James R. Moore, "Geologists and Interpreters of Genesis in the Nineteenth Century," in Lindberg and Numbers, *God and Nature*, 322–350; Rodney L. Stiling, "The Diminishing Deluge: Noah's Flood in Nineteenth-Century American Geology and Theology," PhD diss., University of Wisconsin, Madison, 1992.

20. Ronald L. Numbers, *Creation by Natural Law: Laplace's Nebular Hypothesis in American Thought* (Seattle: University of Washington Press, 1977), 89–90.

21. Ibid., 90–91.

22. Ibid., 91–100.

23. Ibid., 25–26, 60–63, 87.

24. [Matthew Boyd Hope], "Relation between Scripture and Geology," *BRPR* 13 (1841): 368–393, quotations on 379, 389, 390; Review of *The Principles of Geology Explained and Reviewed in Their Relations to Revealed and Natural Religion*, by David King, *BRPR* 23 (1851): 164–165 (human race). For optimistic assessments about reconciling Genesis and geology, see also Review of *Geognosy; or, The Facts and Principles of Geology against Theories*, by David N. Lord, *BRPR* 28 (1856): 161–163; and "Primeval Period of Sacred History," *BRPR* 32 (1860): 90–100.

25. [Hope] "Relation between Scripture and Geology," 391 (zealous friends); [Joseph Henry], Review of *The Epoch of Creation*, by Eleazar Lord, *BRPR* 23 (1851): 696–698; "The Logical Relations of Religion and Natural Science," *BRPR* 32 (1860): 579 (any old-fashioned Christian). Hodge invited Henry to review Lord's little work on geology in an undated latter, Box 12, Folder 21, Joseph Henry Collection, Record Unit 7001, Smithsonian Institution Archives.

26. Hodge, *Systematic Theology*, 1: 224–225, 550, 552, 556–558.

27. Ibid., 1: 573. Much of this section on "The Mosaic Account of the Creation," though not the comments about Guyot and Dana, comes from a manuscript titled "Creation," ca. December 1846, Item 22, Box 1, Charles Hodge MS Collection, Princeton Theological Seminary Library. On Hodge and Dawson, see Charles F. O'Brien, *Sir William Dawson: A Life in Science and Religion* (Philadelphia: American Philosophical Society, 1971), 19–22.

28. [Charles Hodge], "The Inspiration of the Holy Scripture: Its Nature and Proof," *BRPR* 29 (1857): 660–698, quotation on 683 (astronomy and geology); Review of *The Races of Men*, by Robert Knox, *BRPR* 23 (1851): 168–171, quotation on 171 (anthropology). I am indebted to Jon Roberts for bringing the former article to my attention.

29. J. C. Nott and Geo. R. Gliddon, *Types of Mankind* (Philadelphia: Lippincott, Grambo, 1854). For historical accounts of the American school of anthropology, see William Stanton, *The Leopard's Spots: Scientific Attitudes toward Race in America, 1815–59* (Chicago: University of Chicago Press, 1960); Lester G. Stephens, *Science, Race, and Religion in the Nineteenth-Century American South: John Bachman and the Charleston Circle of Naturalists* (Chapel Hill: University of North Carolina Press, 1999); and G. Blair Nelwon, "'Men before Adam!' American Debates over the Unity and Antiquity of Humans," in *When Science and Christianity Meet*, ed. David C. Lindberg and Ronald L. Numbers (Chicago: University of Chicago Press, 2003), 161–181. On

Smith's views, see Mark A. Noll, *Princeton and the Republic, 1768–1822: The Search for a Christian Enlightenment in the Era of Samuel Stanhope Smith* (Princeton, NJ: Princeton University Press, 1989), 115–124.

30. [Charles Hodge], "The Unity of Mankind," *BRPR* 31 (1859): 103–149, quotations on 112, 144; [Charles Hodge], "Examination of Some Reasonings against the Unity of Mankind," *BRPR* 34 (1862): 435–464, quotation on 446. Hodge recycled some of the material from "The Unity of Mankind" in his *Systematic Theology*, 2: 77–80. Stephen Jay Gould has criticized Morton for the same methodological shortcomings; see Gould, *The Mismeasure of Man* (New York: Norton, 1981), chap. 2.

31. Hodge, *Systematic Theology*, 2: 39–40, 86.

32. [Hodge], "Unity of Mankind," 107; [Matthew Boyd Hope], "Professor Bachman on the Unity of the Human Races," *BRPR* 22 (1850): 313–320, quotation on 315; [James Read Eckard],"The Logical Relations of Religion and Natural Science," *BRPR* 32 (1860): 577–608, quotation on 605.

33. Hodge, *Systematic Theology*, 2: 91; [Hodge], "Unity of Mankind," 104–105, 148. For similar complaints about the arrogance of naturalists in this debate, see [Hope], "Professor Bachman on the Unity of the Human Races," 316.

34. [Charles Hodge], "Examination of Some Reasonings against the Unity of Mankind," *BRPR* 34 (1862): 435–464, quotation on 461 (Darwin); Hodge, *Systematic Theology*, 2: 10 (Tyndall). For a sampling of opinion on the development hypothesis in the *Princeton Review* before 1859, see [Albert Baldwin Dod], Review of *Vestiges of the Natural History of Creation*, *BRPR* 17 (1845): 505–557; Review of *The Course of Creation*, by John Anderson, *BRPR* 24 (1852): 146–151, especially 149–150; "Lectures at the University of Virginia," *BRPR* 24 (1852): 250–294, especially 280–281. On Darwin's goals, see, e.g., Ronald L. Numbers, *Darwinism Comes to America* (Cambridge, MA: Harvard University Press, 1998), 26.

35. Hodge, *Systematic Theology*, 2: 12, 16, 18–19, 26–27.

36. Asa Gray, "Evolution and Theology," *The Nation*, January 15, 1874, 44–46, reprinted in Asa Gray, *Darwiniana: Essays and Reviews Pertaining to Darwinism* (New York: Appleton, 1876). For additional negative commentary on Hodge's discussion of development in his *Systematic Theology*, see "Lyell's Principles of Geology," *Bibliotheca Sacra* 31 (1874): 785–790. On Gray, see A. Hunter Dupree, *Asa Gray, 1810–1888* (Cambridge, MA: Harvard University Press, 1959).

37. "Discussion on Darwinism and the Doctrine of Development," in *History, Essays, Orations, and Other Documents of the Sixth General Conference of the Evangelical Alliance, Held in New York, October 2–12, 1873*, ed. Philip Schaff and S. Irenaeus Prime (New York: Harper & Brothers, 1974), 318, 320.

38. Hodge, *What Is Darwinism?* 26, 40–41, 52, 141, 168, 177. For Hodge's assessment of natural theology, see *Systematic Theology*, 1: 25. See also Jonathan Wells, *Charles Hodge's Critique of Darwinism: An Historical-Critical Analysis of Concepts Basic to the 19th Century Debate* (Lewiston, ME: Edwin Mellen Press, 1988). On the writing of *What Is Darwinism?* see Noll and Livingstone, introduction, 28. For a contrasting view, which highlights Hodge's philosophical as opposed to biblical concerns,

see David N. Livingstone, *Darwin's Forgotten Defenders: The Encounter between Evangelical Theology and Evolutionary Thought* (Grand Rapids, MI: Eerdmans, 1987), 102–103.

39. "Philosophy, Metaphysics, and General Science," *Methodist Quarterly Review* 64 (1882): 586–592, quotation on 592; [Asa Gray], "What Is Darwinism?" *The Nation*, May 28, 1874, 348–351, reprinted in *Darwiniana*; Asa Gray to Charles Darwin, June 16, 1874, quoted in Noll and Livingstone, introduction, 33; William Berryman Scott, *Some Memories of a Paleontologist* (Princeton, NJ: Princeton University Press, 1939), 49 (grandson). Positive reviews of *What Is Darwinism?* appeared in the following journals: *Catholic World* 19 (1874): 429–430; *American Church Review* 26 (1874): 316–319; *Unitarian Review and Religious Magazine* 3 (1875): 237–250; *Methodist Quarterly Review* 41 (1874): 514–516; *Presbyterian Quarterly and Princeton Review*, new ser., vol. 3 (1874): 558–559; *Baptist Quarterly* 8 (1874): 374–375.

40. Hodge, *What Is Darwinism?* 2, 39–40.

41. Ibid., 126–128, 134–135, 140–142.

CHAPTER 6

This chapter, based on my 2000 presidential address to the American Society of Church History, was published in *Church History* 69 (2000): 257–276, and appears here with the permission of the American Society of Church History. I am indebted to Richard Davidson, Libbie Freed, Spencer Fluhman, and Craig McConnell for their research assistance; to William O. Harris and Wesley W. Smith, Office of Archives and Special Collections, Princeton Theological Seminary Libraries, for providing needed sources; to Marc Rothenberg, editor of the Joseph Henry Papers, Smithsonian Institution, for supplying copies of Green's correspondence with Henry; to Mark A. Noll for early advice; and to Jon H. Roberts for critically reading the manuscript.

1. Jacobo Usserio, *Annales Veteris Testamenti* (London, 1650), 1, translated as James Ussher, *The Annals of the World* (London, 1658), 1; George Macloskie to George Frederick Wright, November 23, 1904, G. F. Wright Papers, Oberlin College Archives. As William R. Brice points out in "Bishop Ussher, John Lightfoot, and the Age of Creation," *Journal of Geological Education* 30 (1982): 18–24, it was John Lightfoot, writing eight years before Ussher, who claimed that the creation had begun at 9 A.M.—in 3928 B.C. See also R. Buick Knox, *James Ussher: Archbishop of Armagh* (Cardiff: University of Wales Press, 1967), 105–107.

2. John William Colenso, *The Pentateuch and the Book of Joshua Critically Examined, Part 1: The Pentateuch Examined As an Historical Narrative* (London: Longman, Green, Longman, Roberts & Green, 1862); Charles Augustus Briggs, *General Introduction to the Study of Holy Scripture* (New York: Charles Scribner's Sons, 1899), 284–285.

3. Colenso, *The Pentateuch*, vii–viii.

4. Ibid., 10 (self-contradictions), xiv (unhistorical), 34 (Lev. 8:14), 37 (Deut. 1:1), 46 (Ex. 16:16).

5. Green's marginalia, found in his personal copy of Colenso's book in the Speer Library at Princeton Theological Seminary, are quoted in Marion Ann Taylor, *The Old Testament in the Old Princeton School (1812–1929)* (San Francisco: Mellen Research University Press, 1992), 218. American editions of Colenso included *The Pentateuch and Book of Joshua Critically Examined* (New York: D. Appleton, 1863); *Abstract of Colenso on the Pentateuch: Showing Who Wrote the Five Books of Moses, and When They Were Written* (New York: American News Co., [1871]); and *The Pentateuch and Book of Joshua Critically Examined*, new ed. (New York: Longmans, Green, 1888).

6. William Henry Green, *The Pentateuch Vindicated from the Aspersions of Bishop Colenso* (New York: John Wiley, 1863), 69 (childish), 15 (arithmetic), 11 (superficial), 32 (caviller), 193 (brain), 194 (incapacity), 24 (astronomical error), 29 (confession), 33 (punctilious), 104 (dishonest), 111 (absurd), 174 (clumsy), 137 (pedantry), 161 (misrepresentation), 193 (sophisms), 194 (epithets).

7. Ibid., 194 (infallible), 19 (want of confidence), 195 (life or death).

8. Ibid., 122–224.

9. Ibid., 128.

10. "The Antiquity of Man," *Westminster Review* 79 (1863): 518, quoted in Donald K. Grayson, *The Establishment of Human Antiquity* (New York: Academic Press, 1983), 202; Thomas R. Trautmann, *Lewis Henry Morgan and the Invention of Kinship* (Berkeley: University of California Press, 1987), 32; J. C. Nott and Geo. R. Gliddon, *Types of Mankind* (Philadelphia: Lippincott, 1854), 60, from a section written by Nott. On the midcentury debates over human antiquity, see especially Grayson, *Establishment*, 179–186; and A. Bowdoin Van Riper, *Man among the Mammoths: Victorian Science and the Discovery of Human Prehistory* (Chicago: University of Chicago Press, 1993). On Genesis and geology in America, see Rodney L. Stiling, "Scriptural Geology in America," in *Evangelicals and Science in Historical Perspective*, ed. David N. Livingstone, D. G. Hart, and Mark A. Noll (New York: Oxford University Press, 1999), 177–192; and Rodney L. Stiling, "The Genesis Flood in Nineteenth-Century American Thought," PhD diss., University of Wisconsin, Madison, 1991.

11. Mark A. Noll, *Between Faith and Criticism: Evangelicals, Scholarship, and the Bible in America* (San Francisco: Harper & Row, 1986), 24. The most extensive treatment of Green in print, Taylor's *The Old Testament in the Old Princeton School*, 167–251, neither mentions Green's primeval chronology nor cites his article on that subject in her extensive bibliography of his writings. The same is true of Dwayne Cox's unpublished manuscript, "William Henry Green: Princeton Theologian," MA thesis, University of Louisville, 1976. Peter J. Wallace, "The Foundations of Reformed Biblical Theology: The Development of Old Testament Theology at Old Princeton, 1812–1932," *Westminster Theological Journal* 59 (1997): 41–69, also discusses Green at length without mentioning his chronological work.

12. Francis A. Schaeffer, *Genesis in Space and Time: The Flow of Biblical History* (Downers Grove, IL: InterVarsity Press, 1972), 122, refers to "Professor William Greene." In his introduction to the reprint of Green's *Higher Criticism of the Pentateuch* (Grand Rapids, MI: Baker Book House, 1978), v, Ronald F. Youngblood places Green's death in 1896, four years too early. Hugh Ross, *Creation and Time: A Biblical*

and Scientific Perspective on the Creation-Date Controversy (Colorado Springs: NavPress, 1994), 151, erroneously claims that Green possessed an advanced degree and implies that Green was writing in the 1970s. Pattle P. T. Pun, *Evolution: Nature and Scripture in Conflict?* (Grand Rapids, MI: Zondervan, 1982), 256, identifies Green as a contributor to *The Fundamentals*, which began appearing a decade after Green's death. Ernest Nicholson, *The Pentateuch in the Twentieth Century: The Legacy of Julius Wellhausen* (Oxford: Clarendon Press, 1998), says nothing about Green's influence.

13. This biographical sketch is based on the documents in *Celebration of the Fiftieth Anniversary of the Appointment of Professor William Henry Green as an Instructor in Princeton Theology Seminary, May 5, 1896* (New York: Charles Scribner's Sons, 1896), 69 (Greek and Hebrew), 82 (Rabbi), et passim. Green describes his visit to Berlin in a letter to Charles Hodge, August 17, 1858, in the Charles Hodge Collection, Firestone Library, Princeton University, Box 16, Folder 19, copy courtesy of William O. Harris. Warner M. Bailey, "William Robertson Smith and American Biblical Studies," *Journal of Presbyterian History* 51 (1973): 303–304, describes Green as "a protégé of Hengstenberg"; Cox, "William Henry Green," 15, claims that Green "traveled to Germany to study under the Old Testament exegete Ernst Wilhelm Hengstenberg."

14. W. H. Green, manuscript, sermon on Genesis 1:1, delivered at Central Church, May 20, 1849, William Henry Green Papers, Box 1, File 2, Office of Archives and Special Collections, Princeton Theological Seminary Libraries; W. H. Green, *An Inaugural Discourse*, 39, 66, 67, an undated booklet based on a September 30, 1851, lecture, copy in the Brown University Library. Regarding Green's early willingness to accept the nebular hypothesis and geological ages, see also W. H. Green, manuscript, sermon on Gen. 12:1, at the Central Church, February 9, 1851, Green Papers, Box 1, File 3.

15. W. Henry Green, *The Value of Physical Science in the Work of Education* (Easton, PA: Lafayette College, 1865), 27. Regarding the two accounts of creation, see W. Henry Green, Review of *An Introduction to the Literature of the Old Testament*, by S. R. Driver, *Presbyterian and Reformed Review* 3 (1892): 340; and W. Henry Green, *The Unity of the Book of Genesis* (New York: Charles Scribner's Sons, 1895), 17 (successive periods), 22, 25 (days), 29, 33. On Guyot's and Dawson's interpretation of Genesis 1, see Ronald L. Numbers, *Creation by Natural Law: Laplace's Nebular Hypothesis in American Thought* (Seattle: University of Washington Press, 1977), 91–94, 100. On Green's relationship with Dawson, see Susan Sheets-Pyenson, *John William Dawson: Faith, Hope, and Science* (Montreal: McGill-Queen's University Press, 1996), 87–88.

16. Review of *The Pentateuch Vindicated from the Aspersions of Bishop Colenso*, by William Henry Green, *Methodist Quarterly Review* 23 (1863): 518–519. On Green's use of ridicule and humor, see, respectively, "Prof. Green on Colenso," *New-York Observer*, March 26, 1863; and Review of *The Pentateuch Vindicated from the Aspersions of Bishop Colenso*, by William Henry Green, *Christian Advocate and Journal*, April 9, 1863, 119. On Colenso, see George W. Cox, *The Life of John William Colenso, D.D., Bishop of Natal*, 2 vols. (London: W. Ridgway, 1888); Peter Hinchliff, *John William Colenso: Bishop of Natal* (London: Nelson, 1964); and Jeff Guy, *The Heretic: Study of the Life of John William Colenso, 1814–1883* (Pietermaritzburg: University of Natal Press,

1983). For a positive assessment of Colenso's *Pentateuch*, which appeared in seven parts between 1862 and 1879, see John Rogerson, *Old Testament Criticism in the Nineteenth Century: England and Germany* (London: Society for Promoting Christian Knowledge, 1984), 220–237. According to Rogerson, 220, "Colenso's *Pentateuch* was one of the most original British contributions to biblical criticism in the nineteenth century."

17. Charles Hodge, *Systematic Theology*, 3 vols. (New York: Scribner, 1871–1873), 2: 40–41. Alexander Hodge's recollection is quoted in Arthur C. Custance, *Two Men Called Adam* (Brockville, Ontario: Doorway Publications, 1983), 5. On Charles Hodge's attitudes toward science, see chapter 5 of this volume.

18. W. H. Green, *The Hebrew Feasts: In Their Relation to Recent Critical Hypotheses Concerning the Pentateuch* (New York: Robert Carter, 1885), 13 (compilation); W. H. Green, "Prof. Robertson Smith on the Pentateuch," *Presbyterian Review* 3 (1882): 109 (fancy); W. H. Green, "The Perpetual Authority of the Old Testament," *Presbyterian Quarterly and Princeton Review*, new ser. 6 (1877): 221 (no errors); W. H. Green to C. A. Briggs, July 8, 1881, Letter 1535, Transcripts of C. A. Briggs's Correspondence, Union Theological Seminary Archives (locked up); W. H. Green, *Moses and the Prophets* (New York: Robert Carter, 1883), 9–10 (unbelievers, radicals, and cowards). Regarding Wellhausen, see also W. H. Green, "Pentateuchal Analysis a Failure," *Independent*, May 3, 1894, 1. On Smith, see Bailey, "William Robertson Smith," 285–308.

19. David Hoeveler Jr., *James McCosh and the Scottish Intellectual Tradition: From Glasgow to Princeton* (Princeton, NJ: Princeton University Press, 1981), 227 (presidency); W. R. Smith to C. A. Briggs, February 8, 1883, Letter 2089, Briggs's Correspondence; *Sunday School Times*, June 18, 1887, 385. Green's "Critical Notes" appeared in the *Sunday School Times* from January 1, 1887, through June 11, 1887. The Harper–Green exchange, titled "The Pentateuchal Question," appeared in *Hebraica* between 1888 and 1892. For a critical appraisal of Harper's role in this exchange, see Robert Lee Carter, "The 'Message of the Higher Criticism': The Bible Renaissance and Popular Education in America, 1880–1925," PhD diss., University of North Carolina, Chapel Hill, 1995, 204. On Harper, see James P. Wind, *The Bible and the University: The Messianic Vision of William Rainey Harper* (Atlanta: Scholars Press, 1987), which mentions Green only in passing. On Green and the American Bible Revision Committee, see Peter J. Thuesen, *In Discordance with the Scriptures: American Protestant Battles over Translating the Bible* (New York: Oxford University Press, 1999), 43–44, 49, 58–59. In the mid-1860s Joseph Henry, secretary of the Smithsonian Institution, consulted Green about a manuscript on "Systems of Consanguinity and Affinity of the Human Family," submitted by the anthropologist Lewis Henry Morgan for publication to the *Smithsonian Contributions to Knowledge*. Henry could think of no one "better qualified to judge" the work; Joseph Henry to W. H. Green, December 6, 1865, Record Unit 33, Outgoing Correspondence, Office of the Secretary, Smithsonian Institution Archives, a copy of which was provided by Marc Rothenberg. For Green's assessment of this landmark study, see W. H. Green to Joseph Henry, March 14, 1866, Record Unit 26, Incoming Correspondence, Office of the Secretary, Smithsonian Institution Archives.

20. Review of *The Higher Criticism of the Pentateuch*, by W. H. Green, *Expository Times* 7 (1895–1896): 227 (battle-flag); W. H. Green, "Heresy Hunters," *Presbyterian*, February 15, 1893, 12; Charles Augustus Briggs, *General Introduction to the Study of Holy Scripture* (New York: Charles Scribner's Sons, 1899), 289 (Hengstenberg); Charles Augustus Briggs, *The Higher Criticism of the Hexateuch* (New York: Charles Scribner's Sons, 1893), 143; Edward L. Curtis, Review of *General Introduction to the Old Testament: The Canon*, by W. H. Green, *Biblical World* 14 (1899): 459. Regarding the Briggs affair, see Mark Stephen Massa, *Charles Augustus Briggs and the Critics of Historical Criticism* (Philadelphia: Fortress Press, 1990). For British and German criticism of Green, see J. A. Selbie, "Critics and Apologists," *Expository Times* 10 (1898–1899): 221–223; and C. Steuernagel, "Dr. W. H. Green of Princeton: A Reply to Dr. Dunlop Moore," *Expository Times* 10 (1898–1899): 476–480. For criticism of Green's critics, see Dunlop Moore, "Critics and Apologists," *Presbyterian and Reformed Review* 10 (1899): 533–542.

21. George Frederick Wright, *Studies in Science and Religion* (Andover, MA: Warren F. Draper, 1882), 376–379; George Frederick Wright, "How Old Is Mankind?" *Sunday School Times*, January 25, 1913, 52 (visit with Green). For a second account of Wright's visit with Green, see George Frederick Wright, "The Flood and Genesis," *Independent*, August 8, 1901, 1858–1859. On Wright, see Ronald L. Numbers, "George Frederick Wright: From Christian Darwinism to Fundamentalist," *Isis* 79 (1988): 624–645; and Ronald L. Numbers, *The Creationists: From Scientific Creationism to Intelligent Design*, expanded ed. (Cambridge, MA: Harvard University Press, 2006), 33–50.

22. W. H. Green, "Primeval Chronology," *Bibliotheca Sacra* 47 (1890): 285–303, quotations on 300 (needed relief) and 303 (precise date); W. H. Green, "Pre-Abrahamic Chronology," *Independent*, June 18, 1891, 1–2; John William Draper, *History of the Conflict between Religion and Science* (New York: Appleton, 1874).

23. Frank Cramer, "The Theological and Scientific Theories of the Origin of Man," *Bibliotheca Sacra* 48 (1891): 511 (margin); George Frederick Wright, "The Harmony of Science and Revelation," *Homiletic Monthly* 33 (1897): 210; George Frederick Wright, *Scientific Confirmations of Old Testament History* (Oberlin, OH: Bibliotheca Sacra Co., 1906), 190–197; George Frederick Wright, *Origin and Antiquity of Man* (Oberlin, OH: Bibliotheca Sacra Co., 1912), 443–444. For additional tributes to Green by Wright, see, e.g., George Frederick Wright, "Recent Discoveries Bearing on the Antiquity of Man," *Bibliotheca Sarca* 48 (1891): 298–309; George Frederick Wright, "Adjustments between the Bible and Science," *Bibliotheca Sarca* 49 (1992): 153–156; and George Frederick Wright, "Present Aspects of the Questions Concerning the Origin and Antiquity of the Human Race," *Protestant Episcopal Review* 11 (1989): 301–303.

24. *Celebration of the Fiftieth Anniversary*; Macloskie to Wright, November 23, 1904, and Macloskie to Wright, November 4, 1911, G. F. Wright Papers (theologians). Charles Hodge's famous quip appears in Alexander A. Hodge, *The Life of Charles Hodge, D.D., LL.D.* (London: T. Nelson and Sons, 1881), 521. A number of obituaries can be found in the William Henry Green Papers. Macloskie drew attention to

Green's discovery in "The Outlook of Science and Faith," *Princeton Theological Review* 1 (1903): 603; and "Monism and Darwinism," *Princeton Theological Review* 2 (1904): 434–435. The fullest account of Macloskie appears in David N. Livingstone and Ronald A. Wells, *Ulster-American Religion: Episodes in the History of a Cultural Connection* (Notre Dame, IN: University of Notre Dame Press, 1999), 40–48.

25. B. B. W[arfield], editorial notes, *Bible Student*, new ser. 8 (1903): 241–252. Warfield expressed similar sentiments in "On the Antiquity and the Unity of the Human Race," *Princeton Theological Review* 9 (1911): 1–25. On Warfield and science, see David N. Livingstone and Mark A. Noll, "B. B. Warfield (1851–1921): A Biblical Inerrantist as Evolutionist," *Isis* 91 (2000): 283–304.

26. Dyson Hague, "The History of Higher Criticism," in *The Fundamentals*, 12 vols. (Chicago: Testimony Publishing Co., [1910–1915]), 1: 120; M. G. Kyle, "The Antiquity of Man According to the Genesis Account," *Journal of the Transactions of the Victoria Institute* 57 (1925): 134–135. The Scottish theologian James Orr, *The Problem of the Old Testament: Considered with Reference to Recent Criticism* (New York: Charles Scribner's Sons, 1923), and the American Old Testament scholar Oswald T. Allis, *The Five Books of Moses* (Philadelphia: Presbyterian and Reformed Publishing Co., 1943), mentioned Green repeatedly. See also Alexander Hardie, *Evolution: Is It Philosophical, Scientific or Scriptural?* (Los Angeles: Times-Mirror Press, 1924), 185, 198; and A. Rendle Short, *Modern Discovery and the Bible* (1942; Chicago: InterVarsity Press, 1955), 97–98.

27. For an example of scholars struggling over Green's authority, see Stephen R. Schrader and Davis A. Young, "Was the Earth Created a Few Thousand Years Ago?" in *The Genesis Debate: Persistent Questions about Creation and the Flood*, ed. Ronald Youngblood (Nashville: Thomas Nelson, 1986), 56–85.

28. Paul Nelson, introduction to *The Creationist Writings of Byron C. Nelson*, vol. 5 of *Creationism in Twentieth-Century America*, ed. Ronald L. Numbers, 10 vols. (New York: Garland, 1995), 1: xiv (late 1930s); Numbers, *The Creationists*, 105–116; Byron C. Nelson, *Before Abraham: Prehistoric Man in Biblical Light* (Minneapolis: Augsburg Publishing House, 1948), 1, 5–6, 16.

29. Bernard Ramm, *The Christian View of Science and Scripture* (Grand Rapids, MI: Eerdmans, 1954), 313–314; Donald R. Wilson, "How Early Is Man?" *Christianity Today*, September 14, 1962, 1175–1176.

30. [Carl F. H. Henry], "American Evangelicals and Theological Dialogue," *Christianity Today*, January 15, 1965, 395–397; James O. Buswell III, letter to the editor, *Christianity Today*, March 12, 1965, 618; James O. Buswell III, "Homo Habilis: Implications for the Creationist," *Journal of the American Scientific Affiliation* 17 (1965): 74–78. For later invocations of Green, see, e.g., William J. Kornfield, "The Early-Date Genesis Man," *Christianity Today*, June 8, 1973, 931–934; and James O. Buswell III, "Creationist Views on Human Origin," *Christianity Today*, August 8, 1975, 1046–1048. In "A Creationist Interpretation of Prehistoric Man," in *Evolution and Christian Thought Today*, ed. Russell L. Mixter (Grand Rapids, MI: Eerdmans, 1959), 165–189, Buswell mentioned Green in a note (168), but not in connection with his chronology. Both Buswell and Kornfield, who also taught anthropology at Wheaton, cited Wheaton's Samuel J. Schultz, who in *The Old Testament Speaks*, 2nd

ed. (New York: Harper & Row, 1970), 12–13, rejected Ussher in favor of Green. Robert Brow, "The Late-Date Genesis Man," *Christianity Today*, September 15, 1972, 1128–1129, argued that Adam was created about 3900 B.C.

31. Walter C. Kaiser Jr., ed., *Classical Evangelical Essays in Old Testament Interpretation* (Grand Rapids, MI: Baker Book House, 1972), unpaginated introduction; Robert C. Newman and Herman J. Eckelmann Jr., *Genesis One and the Origin of the Earth* (Downers Grove, IL: InterVarsity Press, 1977), 59–60, 105–123; Schaeffer, *Genesis in Space and Time*, 122, 134; Ronald Youngblood, *How It All Began: A Biblical Commentary for Laymen: Genesis 1–11* (Ventura, CA: Regal Books, 1980), 89–91; Youngblood, introduction to *The Higher Criticism of the Pentateuch*, vi (quotation); Davis A. Young, *Christianity and the Age of the Earth* (Grand Rapids, MI: Zondervan, 1982), 59, 152. Buswell had anointed Green's "Primeval Chronology" a "classic" as early as 1965; Buswell, letter to the editor, 22.

32. John C. Whitcomb Jr. and Henry M. Morris, *The Genesis Flood: The Biblical Record and Its Scientific Implications* (Philadelphia: Presbyterian and Reformed Publishing Co., 1961), 476; Henry M. Morris, *The Genesis Record: A Scientific and Devotional Commentary on the Book of Beginnings* (Grand Rapids, MI: Baker Book House, 1976), 45–46, 285, 309 (modified); John C. Whitcomb Jr., *The Early Earth* (Grand Rapids, MI: Baker Book House, 1972), 107–110 (absurdity); Henry M. Morris, *Many Infallible Proofs: Practical and Useful Evidences of Christianity* (San Diego: Creation-Life Publishers, 1974), 290 (much-maligned). See also Henry M. Morris, *Biblical Cosmology and Modern Science* (Nutley, NJ: Craig Press, 1970), 66–67. On Whitcomb and Morris, see Numbers, *The Creationists*, 184–213. On the "impropriety" and "absurdity" of using Green to justify a great antiquity of humans, see Marvin L. Ludenow, *Bones of Contention: A Creationist Assessment of Human Fossils* (Grand Rapids, MI: Baker Books, 1992), 227–229.

33. Arthur C. Custance, *Hidden Things of God's Revelation*, vol. 7 of *The Doorway Papers* (Grand Rapids, MI: Zondervan, 1977), 222 (no gaps, small details), from an essay titled "The Genealogies of the Bible: A Neglected Subject," first published in 1967; Custance, *Two Men Called Adam*, 4–6 (thin edge). On Custance, see Numbers, *The Creationists*, 170–171, 175–176, 255–256, 271–272.

CHAPTER 7

This conclusion is extracted from a longer essay, "What Hath Science Wrought? Science and Secularization Revisited," to appear in *The Future of Christianity in the West*, ed. John Stenhouse and Brett Knowles (Adelaide, Australia: ATF Press, forthcoming). It also appears in Nicolaas A. Rupke, ed., *Eminent Lives in Twentieth-Century Science and Religion* (Göttingen, Germany: Universitätsverlag Göttingen, 2006). I would like to thank my friends Jon Roberts and John Stenhouse for their encouragement and suggestions.

1. Rodney Stark, "Secularization: The Myth of Religious Decline," *Fides et Historia* 30 (summer/fall 1998): 1–19, quotation on 5, a statement subsequently

incorporated into "Secularization, R.I.P.," *Sociology of Religion* 60 (1999): 249–273; Keith Thomas, *Religion and the Decline of Magic: Studies in Popular Beliefs in Sixteenth and Seventeenth Century England* (London: Weidenfeld and Nicolson, 1971), 643; Anthony F. C. Wallace, *Religion: An Anthropological View* (New York: Random House, 1966), 264–265. On the early modern period, see also C. John Sommerville, *The Secularization of Early Modern England: From Religious Culture to Religious Faith* (New York: Oxford University Press, 1992), especially 153–158.

2. Gabriel A. Almond, R. Scott Appleby, and Emmanuel Sivan, *Strong Religion: The Rise of Fundamentalisms around the World* (Chicago: University of Chicago Press, 2003); David B. Barrett, George T. Kurian, and Todd M. Johnson, *World Christian Encyclopedia: A Comparative Survey of Churches and Religions in the Modern World*, 2nd ed., 2 vols. (New York: Oxford University Press, 2001), 1: 12 (Pentecostalism); John Mbiti, quoted in Philip Jenkins, *The Next Christendom: The Coming of Global Christianity* (New York: Oxford University Press, 2002), 2.

3. Hugh McLeod, *Secularisation in Western Europe, 1848–1914* (New York: St. Martin's Press, 2000), 287; Adam Sage, "The Miracle Hunters," *The Times* (London), February 19, 2002, 2. See also Ruth Harris, *Lourdes: Body and Spirit in the Secular Age* (New York: Viking, 1999); and Willem B. Drees, "Where Are We? Who Are We? What Are We Doing?" *ESSSAT (European Society for the Study of Science and Theology) News* 14 (June 2004): 4. For an excellent microhistory of secularization in Great Britain that does not implicate science in the process, see S. J. D. Green, *Religion in the Age of Decline: Organisation and Experience in Industrial Yorkshire, 1870–1920* (Cambridge, UK: Cambridge University Press, 1996). Callum G. Brown's revisionist *The Death of Christian Britain: Understanding Secularisation, 1800–2000* (London: Routledge, 2001) sees secularization taking off not during the industrial revolution of the late nineteenth century but during the cultural revolution of the 1960s. Popular media and changing gender roles totally eclipse science in his narrative.

4. Peter L. Berger, "The Desecularization of the World: A Global Overview," in *The Desecularization of the World: Resurgent Religion and World Politics*, ed. Peter L. Berger (Grand Rapids, MI: Eerdmans, 1999), 9, from an essay that first appeared in *The National Interest*, no. 46 (winter 1996–1997); Steve Bruce, *God Is Dead: Secularization in the West* (Oxford: Blackwell, 2002), 88 (status of science) and chap. 5, "Science and Secularization," 106–117. Bruce, who emphasizes the growth of indifference to religion, identifies "the lack of religious socialization and the lack of constant background affirmation of beliefs" as "the primary cause of indifference" (140). For similar sentiments expressed earlier, see Steve Bruce, *Religion in the Modern World: From Cathedrals to Cults* (New York: Oxford University Press, 1996), 48–52; and Steve Bruce, *Choice and Religion: A Critique of Rational Choice* (Oxford: Oxford University Press, 1999), 15–17. For Berger's earlier views on secularization, which say little about the role of science, see *The Sacred Canopy: Elements of a Sociological Theory of Religion* (Garden City, NY: Doubleday, 1967). On the alleged devaluation of science as a continuing agent of secularization, see also Wilfred M. McClay, "Two Concepts of Secularism," in *Religion Returns to the Public Square: Faith and Policy in America*, ed. Hugh Heclo and Wilfred M. McClay (Baltimore: Johns Hopkins University Press,

2003), 31–61, especially 37–38. For historically sensitive treatments of secularization by sociologists of religion, see Philip S. Gorski, "Historicizing the Secularization Debate: Church, State, and Society in Late Medieval and Early Modern Europe, ca. 1300 to 1700," *American Sociological Review* 65 (2000): 138–167; John H. Evans, *Playing God? Human Genetic Engineering and the Rationalization of Public Bioethical Debate* (Chicago: University of Chicago Press, 2002); and Christian Smith, ed., *The Secular Revolution: Power, Interests, and Conflict in the Secularization of American Public Life* (Berkeley: University of California Press, 2003). Unfortunately, the essay in *The Secular Revolution* that focuses explicitly on the secularization of American science (Eva Marie Garroutte, "The Positivist Attack on Baconian Science and Religious Knowledge in the 1870s," 197–215) is badly flawed. For a nuanced assessment of science and secularization by a sociologist of religion, see Robert Wuthnow, *The Struggle for America's Soul: Evangelicals, Liberals, and Secularism* (Grand Rapids, MI: Eerdmans, 1989), 142–157.

5. John Hedley Brooke, *Science and Religion: Some Historical Perspectives* (Cambridge, UK: Cambridge University Press, 1991), 11; George M. Marsden, *The Soul of the American University: From Protestant Establishment to Established Nonbelief* (New York: Oxford University Press, 1994), 286, 430; George M. Marsden, "The Soul of the American University: A Historical Overview," in *The Secularization of the Academy*, ed. George M. Marsden and Bradley J. Longfield (New York: Oxford University Press, 1992), 9–45, quotation regarding "irrelevance" on 15; Jon H. Roberts and James Turner, *The Sacred and the Secular University* (Princeton, NJ: Princeton University Press, 2000). See also John Hedley Brooke, "Science and Secularization," in *Reinventing Christianity: Nineteenth-Century Contexts*, ed. Linda Woodhead (Aldershot, UK: Ashgate, 2001), 229–238; and John Hedley Brooke, "Science and Religion," in *Eighteenth-Century Science*, vol. 4 of *The Cambridge History of Science*, ed. Roy Porter (Cambridge, UK: Cambridge University Press, 2003), 741–761. For dissenting views on the alleged secularization of the American university, see D. G. Hart, *The University Gets Religion: Religious Studies in American Higher Education* (Baltimore: Johns Hopkins University Press, 1999); and Conrad Cherry, Betty A. De Berg, and Amanda Porterfield, *Religion on Campus* (Chapel Hill: University of North Carolina Press, 2001). See also Julie A. Reuben, *The Making of the Modern University: Intellectual Transformation and the Marginalization of Morality* (Chicago: University of Chicago Press, 1996).

6. Jon H. Roberts, "Religion, Secularization, and Cultural Spaces in America," in *American Catholic Traditions: Resources for Renewal*, ed. Sandra Yocum Mize and William Portier (Maryknoll, NY: Orbis, 1997), 185–205, quotations on 193, 198; David A. Hollinger, "Jewish Intellectuals and the De-Christianization of American Public Culture in the Twentieth Century," in *Science, Jews, and Secular Culture: Studies in Mid-Twentieth-Century American Intellectual History* (Princeton, NJ: Princeton University Press, 1996), 17–41; James Gilbert, *Redeeming Culture: American Religion in an Age of Science* (Chicago: University of Chicago Press, 1997), 13; R. Laurence Moore, "Secularization: Religion and Social Sciences," in *Between the Times: The Travail of the Protestant Establishment in America, 1900–1960*, ed. William R. Hutchison (Cambridge,

UK: Cambridge University Press, 1989), 233–252, quotation on 250. Michael Heyd edited an issue of *Science in Context* (vol. 15, 2002) devoted to "Science and Secularization."

7. Owen Chadwick, *The Secularization of the European Mind in the Nineteenth Century* (Cambridge, UK: Cambridge University Press, 1975), 17; Hollinger, "Jewish Intellectuals," 17–41; Hans Blumenberg, *The Legitimacy of the Modern Age*, trans. Robert M. Wallace (Cambridge, MA: MIT Press, 1985), 3. See also David A. Hollinger, "The 'Secularization' Question and the United States in the Twentieth Century," *Church History* 70 (2001): 132–143; and the subsequent exchange with C. John Sommerville in Sommerville, "Post-secularism Marginalizes the University: A Rejoinder to Hollinger," *Church History* 71 (2002): 848–857; and David A. Hollinger, "Why Is There So Much Christianity in the United States? A Reply to Sommerville," *Church History* 71 (2002): 858–864.

8. Alexandre Koyré, *From the Closed World to the Infinite Universe* (Baltimore: Johns Hopkins University Press, 1957), 1. The American theologian Kenneth Cauthen made the same point, citing Koyré, in *Science, Secularization and God* (Nashville: Abingdon, 1969), 13.

9. Kenneth E. Hendrickson, "Historical Method and the Intelligent Design Movement," *Perspectives on Science and Christian Faith* 57 (2005): 284–300. Some Lutherans, for example, insisted on strictly secular scientific meetings because their beliefs precluded even "joint prayer with those not on the same confessional basis"; see Ronald L. Numbers, *The Creationists* (New York: Knopf, 1992), 112. On the privatization of religion and secularization, see Thomas Luckmann, *The Invisible Religion: The Problem of Religion in Modern Society* (New York: Macmillan 1967).

10. Ernst Mayr, *What Evolution Is* (New York: Basic Books, 2001), 9; Charles Darwin, *On the Origin of Species*, a facsimile of the first edition, with an introduction by Ernst Mayr (Cambridge, MA: Harvard University Press, 1966), 488; Charles Darwin to J. D. Hooker, March 29, 1883, in *The Life and Letters of Charles Darwin*, ed. Francis Darwin, 2 vols. (New York: D. Appleton, 1889), 2: 202–203.

11. Samuel Elliott Coues, *Studies of the Earth: An Essay on the Figure and Surface-Divisions of the Earth, Its Geological and Meteorological Phenomena, and Astronomical Elements* (Washington, DC: Philip & Solomons, 1860), 68–69, 76; [James Read Eckard], "The Logical Relations of Religion and Natural Science," *Biblical Repertory and Princeton Review* 32 (1860): 578.

12. David L. Hull, "Darwinism and Historiography," in *The Comparative Reception of Darwinism*, ed. Thomas F. Glick (Austin: University of Texas Press, 1974), 393; John Fiske, *The Idea of God As Affected by Modern Knowledge* (Boston: Houghton Mifflin, 1885), 119; Enoch Fitch Burr, *Celestial Empires* (New York: American Tract Society, 1885), preface, n.p. Burr left the "eloquent expounder" unnamed, but Judith Ann Schiff has identified him as Silliman in "Old Yale: Learning by Doing," *Yale Alumni Magazine* 64 (November 2000): 80.

13. Peter J. Bowler, *The Eclipse of Darwinism: Anti-Darwinian Evolution Theories in the Decades around 1900* (Baltimore: Johns Hopkins University Press, 1983), 27, 44. Ironically, Bowler went on to write an entire book on post-Darwinian science and

religion: *Reconciling Science and Religion: The Debate in Early-Twentieth-Century Britain* (Chicago: University of Chicago Press, 2001).

14. Edward B. Davis, "Science and Religious Fundamentalism in the 1920s," *American Scientist* 93 (2005): 253–260; "Brief and Argument of the Tennessee Academy of Sciences as Amicus Curiae," *Scopes v. State*, 154 Tenn. 105 (1926), quoted in Edward J. Larson, *Summer for the Gods: The Scopes Trial and America's Continuing Debate over Science and Religion* (New York: Basic Books, 1997), 214. See also Edwin Slosson, "Evolution: The Conference Method of Study," Kirtley F. Mather Papers, Harvard University Archives.

15. Howard J. Van Till, *The Fourth Day: What the Bible and the Heavens Are Telling Us about the Creation* (Grand Rapids, MI: Eerdmans, 1986), 209.

16. Leonard F. Burkart, " 'Only God Can Make a Tree,' " in *Behind the Dim Unknown: Twenty-Six Notable Scientists Face a Host of Unsolved Problems and Unitedly Reach a Conclusion*, ed. John Clover Monsma (New York: G. P. Putnam's Sons, 1966), 44–45.

17. Ronald L. Numbers, *Darwinism Comes to America* (Cambridge, MA: Harvard University Press, 1998), 41. This retrospective survey is based on the eighty biologists, geologists, and anthropologists elected to the National Academy of Sciences after its founding in 1863. I was unable to identify the religious affiliations of twenty-seven of the eighty.

18. James H. Leuba, *The Belief in God and Immortality: A Psychological, Anthropological and Statistical Study* (Boston: Sherman, French, 1916).

19. Edward J. Larson and Larry Witham, "Scientists Are Still Keeping the Faith," *Nature* 386 (1997): 435–436. See also Edward J. Larson and Larry Witham, "Leading Scientists Still Reject God," *Nature* 394 (1998): 313; and Edward J. Larson and Larry Witham, "Scientists and Religion in America," *Scientific American* 281 (September 1999): 89–93. On earlier surveys, see Russell Heddendorf, "Religious Beliefs of Scientists," *Journal of the American Scientific Affiliation* 23 (1971): 10–11; and Rodney Stark, Laurence R. Iannaccone, and Roger Finke, "Religion, Science, and Rationality," *American Economic Review* 86 (1996): 433–437. Stark et al. report that a Carnegie Commission survey of sixty thousand academics in 1969 found that 55 percent of physical and life scientists regarded themselves as religious, with over 40 percent attending church regularly. Social scientists, especially anthropologists and psychologists, were less religious.

20. Larson and Witham, "Scientists Are Still Keeping the Faith," 435–436; Deborah Jordan Brooks, "Substantial Numbers of Americans Continue to Doubt Evolution as Explanation for Origin of Humans," Gallup Poll Release, March 5, 2001, at www.gallup.com; Claudia Wallis, "Faith and Healing," *Time*, June 24, 1996, 63; Martin E. Marty, "Our Religio-Secular World," *Daedalus* 132 (summer 2003): 42–48, quotation on 42.

Index